Freedom of Information.
A practical guidebook

Freedom of Information:
A practical guidebook

Martin Rosenbaum

How to use the Freedom of Information Act
and other 'right to know' laws
to get information from government,
councils and public authorities

Cover design: Adam Rosenbaum

ISBN 978-1-7398005-4-3

Published by Rhododendron Publishing
www.rhododendronpublishing.co.uk

First published in 2023

Martin Rosenbaum is a leading expert on the Freedom of Information Act and a consultant and trainer on how to make use of it effectively. For 16 years he was the main specialist at BBC News in applying FOI for journalism, breaking stories, analysing developments, giving interviews and blogging, as well as advising and training many BBC staff.

From the time that the UK's FOI Act came into force in 2005 he was one of the journalistic pioneers in utilising freedom of information for reporting and investigations. His experience covers all stages of the FOI process, from planning requests through complaining to the Information Commissioner to presenting legal cases at tribunal hearings.

He has also been a frequent speaker on the topic of FOI at UK and international conferences and events, and has given evidence to parliamentary committees.

At the BBC he was an executive producer in the political programmes department, overseeing a range of radio output and podcasts, such as Political Thinking and The Week in Westminster. He edited or produced many radio documentaries and series, across political, social, historical and investigatory subjects. He also worked as a duty editor and producer on Radio 4's Today programme. Prior to joining the BBC he was a freelance journalist, author and campaigner.

His website is at www.rosenbaum.org.uk.

In the words of government officials discussing his FOI applications (in emails disclosed following subject access requests):

'Martin Rosenbaum has considerable expertise in the terms of the FOI Act. It may be helpful to talk this one through.'

'Martin Rosenbaum is a frequent FOI requestor, and is aware of the process and complaints procedure, so we really need to try and pull our socks up with this.'

'Martin Rosenbaum is a clever journalist and has shown some persistence with all of this.'

'I am pretty sure this is not the last we have heard from Rosenbaum …'

Contents

Abbreviations

AHRA	Access to Health Records Act
DP	data protection
DPA	Data Protection Act
EIR	Environmental Information Regulations
EISR	Environmental Information (Scotland) Regulations
FOI	freedom of information
FOIA	Freedom of Information Act
FOISA	Freedom of Information (Scotland) Act
FTT	First-tier Tribunal
GDPR	General Data Protection Regulation
ICO	Information Commissioner's Office
LAAA	Local Audit and Accountability Act
NCND	neither confirm nor deny
PIT	public interest test
QPO	qualified person's opinion
SAR	subject access request
SIC	Scottish Information Commissioner
UT	Upper Tribunal

1. Introduction

According to Tony Blair, this book should probably be called 'How to hit people on the head with a mallet'. But despite the former prime minister's negative view of freedom of information, I certainly haven't included any advice on wielding hefty wooden implements against political leaders and public officials. What the book does do, I hope, is explain how to squeeze information out of them.

One day in January 2019 I was surprised to read a newspaper article about the award of an OBE - to a businessman whose company had been accused of grossly overcharging the NHS for medicines. In the circumstances it wasn't exactly clear why he'd been deemed worthy of an honour and the mark of distinction on behalf of the nation that it represented. As a BBC journalist specialising in using the freedom of information system, I sent an FOI request to the Cabinet Office asking for material relating to this award.

Then one day in February 2021 I was equally surprised to read an email that had just arrived in my inbox. The Cabinet Office had eventually been forced to send me a revealing document. It disclosed that officials who'd carried out background checks on the businessman involved had neglected to do their work properly. They hadn't noticed the complaints about his company, although these had been reported in detail and raised in Parliament. This even included somehow failing to find the prominent article on the front page of The Times which had first exposed the accusations of overcharging. A civil servant in the business department wrote that officials would therefore now be 'undertaking a lessons learned exercise'.

Without the Freedom of Information Act it would have been impossible to obtain this document. It went some way to explaining the failings in this case, and its release punctured the traditional secrecy surrounding the operation of the honours system. It was the first time the government has been compelled under FOI to disclose this kind of detail relating to an individual award where the recipient is still alive. I wrote the story for the BBC.[1]

It's one illustration of how the FOI process sometimes works. It took time (over two years) and persistence. I had to submit an appeal to the Information Commissioner and later put my case at a tribunal hearing. This involved a lot of arguing about whether or not openness would best serve the overall public interest. But eventually it was productive and the outcome helps to make the public better informed, and hopefully it pushes the system to work more thoroughly in future.

This was just one of many FOI-based stories I worked on at the BBC in the 16 years I spent developing and using my expertise in this area. Some also required tenacity, others involved a lot less effort. They ranged from revealing how the then Prince Charles lobbied Tony Blair against genetically modified foods, to discovering which makes of cars had the best and worst records on passing or failing MOT tests; from disclosing that large employers were failing to use hundreds of millions of pounds of government money intended for training apprentices, to showing how university entrance chances can be affected by date of birth.[2] On the other hand, there were numerous other FOI requests that failed to obtain anything of interest, or in some cases anything at all.

Freedom of information is a very good thing. It gives you the legal right - under certain circumstances - to get answers to your questions, whether they concern far-reaching and controversial national policies or the day-to-day activities of public service delivery at a local level. It leads to greater transparency and accountability in government and other public authorities, exposure of wrongdoing, identification of problems to be addressed, and more knowledge and power in the hands of citizens. But it also has gaps and flaws.

Since the UK's freedom of information law came into force in 2005, it has been used extensively, with a mix of success and frustration, not only by journalists like me but by large numbers of campaigners, businesses, charities, academics, researchers and active citizens, and not least by lots of private individuals with their own personal concerns. Despite the widespread problems of delay, lack of cooperation and political interference, FOI has become a popular tool for many people and organisations and an occasional resource for many more.

It seems extremely likely that millions of people in the UK have put in an FOI request at some point since 2005, and quite possibly several million people have done so. An opinion poll in 2021 suggested that 14% of UK adults, one in seven, had submitted at least one.[3]

As for the total number of requests, there's no doubt that several million have been made. Official statistics are only collated centrally for requests to UK government and some other major national authorities (amounting to 52,000 in 2021),[4] and also for many Scottish public bodies under the similar law in Scotland (72,000 in 2021).[5] But these figures are only a small fraction of all the FOI applications submitted annually across the UK as a whole to all the many public authorities covered. Some research implies that local councils in England and Wales receive several times as many as central government does.[6] Similarly, about 900,000 requests have been sent over the years via the whatdotheyknow online portal to the approximately 45,000 bodies listed there,[7] but that again will only be a small sample of the total number.

These statistics mean that FOI has been a very widely utilised piece of legislation. They also mean that it's even more important that the large number of people using the law should be doing so in the most productive way possible.

It's easy to make an FOI request. But making an effective and successful FOI request is harder.

Of these millions of FOI requests, many will have gleaned and helped to disseminate useful information in the public interest, across all sorts of topics and issues, material which could not have been obtained otherwise. When FOI works, it produces documents, records, data, raw facts - rather than the spin and presentation that public authorities would sometimes prefer to communicate.

But on the other hand some requests achieve little or nothing due to obstruction and delay from recalcitrant or inefficient public authorities. Many others fail because they are badly phrased, poorly targeted, inadequately considered, or do not take into account the nature of FOI law and how it operates.

This book is a practical guide to how to use the freedom of information system in the most effective way. I try to distil and pass on what I learnt during my 16 years as BBC News's leading specialist in using FOI for journalism.

I'm very grateful to my BBC colleagues with whom over the years

I discussed requests and responses, options and tactics. My gratitude also goes to those in the FOI community (public officials, ICO staff, campaigners, journalists, bloggers, lawyers and others) who have valuably added to my knowledge and broadened my perspective. And not least, my thanks too to the FOI officers from many public authorities who have devoted time and effort to answering my requests, even if I wasn't always entirely happy about the answers.

This book provides a detailed account of law and practice relating to FOI and other rights to request information held by public authorities which is not already released proactively. It guides you clearly through all stages of the process, from the basics of making a simple request to the legal complexities you may encounter. There are full legal references to legislation and cases so that you can look them up and quote them if necessary when in contact with a public authority, the Information Commissioner's Office or a tribunal.

The book is structured as follows. In Part A I briefly summarise the law and set out some basic principles to employ throughout the process to be effective in exercising your information rights. Part B looks at requesting, explaining the implications of the law in detail and providing thorough guidance on how to draft productive requests. Part C considers the sort of replies you might get, outlining the various obstacles to obtaining the information you want and how to counter them. Part D provides a full practical account of all the stages in how to appeal against refusals and redactions, through internal reviews, the ICO and tribunals. Part E describes other information rights, including environmental information, subject access requests under data protection, and the situation in Scotland. Part F covers some issues that often arise on how best to use the information you have succeeded in getting. The appendices include template letters for making requests and a guide to useful sources of further information.

The advice here is solidly based on my extensive experience. It's not about how FOI should work in ideal circumstances, it's about how the process with all its current defects and difficulties actually functions in reality. In my view the FOI law should be extended and strengthened, its implementation requires a great deal of improvement, and enforcement needs to be tougher. However the purpose of this book is to provide helpful and realistic guidance in the world as it is.

Since the law was introduced there has been a persistent backlash from many politicians and officials, although its fundamentals have survived. Tony Blair was the prime minister who introduced FOI, but he later decided that it was a thoroughly bad idea. In his memoirs he wrote 'I quake at the imbecility of it', and, presumably while quaking, condemned himself as a 'naive, foolish, irresponsible nincompoop'.[8] He explained: 'For political leaders, it's like saying to someone who is hitting you over the head with a stick, "Hey, try this instead", and handing them a mallet.'

Yet if a country's FOI system is at all effective then it's bound to cause trouble for and annoy political leaders. David Cameron was similarly hostile once he was in Downing Street, describing FOI as one of the 'clutteration' factors that impede the process of governing.[9] Doubtless prime ministers are only informed about the most sensitive and difficult requests, which they are unlikely to regard positively while seeing them as gifting heavier weaponry to their political opponents.

However in terms of tool-based metaphors, I see freedom of information not so much as a mallet as, say, a spudger or a crowbar. If used properly it can enable you to pry open some of the lids covering up the workings of the state and its many branches. The aim of this book is to help you use that tool.

PART A: Overview

2. Summary of FOI law

This brief section provides a very basic initial overview of the freedom of information process. For those who are completely unfamiliar with FOI, this is what you need to get started. Later in the book I explain the workings of the law and its implications in full detail.

The underlying principle of the Freedom of Information Act 2000 is that if you ask a public authority for information it holds, then you should be given it, unless there is a valid justification for not doing so. Naturally, however, there are numerous possible reasons for requests to be refused.

The procedure is simple. You just contact the public authority in writing to ask for what you want; most requests are made by email. Anyone can make an FOI request; you have to give a name and an address but an email address is sufficient. As a general rule there is no charge. Your motive in seeking the information should make no difference to how the request is dealt with.

The authorities covered range from major government departments through key public services such as the police and state schools to tiny parish councils and individual GPs. The larger authorities receive many FOI requests, while those at the other end of the spectrum get very few.

One of the most common reasons for requests to be rejected is that they are too time-consuming and costly to answer. This means it's a good idea to be precise and sparing in the information you ask for.

Requests can also be turned down because of their subject matter. There are some 'absolute exemptions', categories of material which explicitly lie outside the reach of FOI, for example anything relating to the security agencies. There is no point asking for that.

But most exemptions (for example, information relating to formulation of government policy) are what are called 'qualified exemptions', where the material might be released or might be withheld, depending on which option is in line with the overall balance of the public interest. This 'public interest test' is a crucial concept in FOI law and practice, and the focus of much argument between requesters and authorities.

Requests should be answered within 20 working days, but an authority is allowed to take longer if it needs time to assess the public interest under a qualified exemption. In practice, delays are common and a major obstacle.

Scottish public authorities are covered by the Freedom of Information (Scotland) Act, which is similar but not identical to the FOI Act for the rest of the UK. Generally in this book my remarks refer to the latter law, except where it's explicitly clear I'm discussing the Scottish one.

Information about the environment is not covered by FOI law as such but by a separate set of rules, the Environmental Information Regulations (EIR), which feature some differences and are marginally more favourable to requesters. In practice the FOI and EIR regimes are operated closely together, and when I refer to the FOI system in general terms, I'm including the EIR process within that.

If you are not happy with the response to your request for information, you can ask the public authority for an internal review. If you are still unhappy, you can complain to the Information Commissioner's Office (ICO). You can appeal against an unwelcome ICO decision to a tribunal.

3. First principles

Using freedom of information is straightforward in theory and can sometimes be straightforward in practice. A simple request, expressed in the obvious way, may get you what you want. However experience shows that very often success relies on care, effort, shrewdness or tenacity.

To get the best results from FOI, avoid the pitfalls and exploit the opportunities, you have to adopt the most productive strategies. Before working through the law in detail, it's worth noting some fundamental underlying principles that should guide the approach you take.

1. Be realistic

Your use of FOI will be more efficient if it's informed by understanding the chances of success or failure. Naturally it's much easier to get some forms of information rather than others.

A good grasp of law and practice (not least through reading this book!), plus the practical experience of making requests, will help you predict what you should get easily, what you probably won't get at all, and what is the stuff in the middle which you may get but will need determination and persistence.

Often you can find useful pointers in previous FOI disclosures by that authority or by other comparable ones (eg other police forces). You might locate these in a 'disclosure log' listing past FOI responses which some authorities maintain on their website, or at the whatdotheyknow.com site which contains large numbers of requests and replies and is easily searchable. The advice issued by the Information Commissioner's Office[10] and its database of past decision notices[11] shows what it expects and how it has ruled on cases.

At the more straightforward end, requests may involve numerical data on some aspect of the public authority's operations, performance measures or spending. This kind of information is often the subject of routine requests that can be answered simply and reasonably quickly. In very crude terms, it's often easier to get numbers rather than words.

On the other hand, it will probably be harder to obtain, say, records of internal government discussions or documentation that touches on the various possible exemptions, such as law enforcement or commercial interests. That can require argument over what is in the overall public interest in order to obtain significant material. It may well be worth doing, but you should be aware of the time and effort likely to be involved.

To borrow a metaphor employed by the journalists Brendan Montague and Lucas Amin, they talk of two different but valid approaches to exploiting FOI - 'grazing' and 'mining'.[12] The first involves fields where garnering the produce is comparatively easy if not always that exciting, the second involves the tougher and uncertain challenge of digging for more valuable finds which lie well below the surface.

And don't ask for more information than you are able to process. There's no point in gathering vast quantities of material which exceeds your capacity to do anything productive with. If you're flooded with information from lots of authorities, it's harder to spot items which are actually of use. Focus on what you really want.

2. Phrase requests carefully

Think clearly about what you want to find out. Then take care to make sure your request accurately and precisely describes the actual information you are trying to obtain, without internal inconsistencies, ambiguity or scope for misinterpretation. Composing FOI requests is a task where you will be rewarded for effort and punished for laziness.

Over the years I have become accustomed to seeing so many cases where requesters did not get what they wanted (possibly getting some useless information instead), because they just didn't think rigorously enough about how to state their request.

So, as the saying goes, be careful what you ask for, you might get it. While Aesop, the likely originator of this maxim, chiefly wrote his didactic fables to illustrate useful lessons for life in general, in this case it may be that he specifically had in mind FOI.

See chapter 5 for detailed advice on how best to formulate a request.

3. Cultivate a 'recorded information' frame of mind

FOI requesting is essentially about finding out what you wish to know by accessing material that a public authority has actually recorded somewhere.

To frame and target requests properly you should be considering which documents or other records are likely to contain what you want and which authority is likely to hold them (and often - this can be crucial - what records might be located within the cost limit, of which more later). You need to approach this from the public authority's perspective, understanding why and how it would keep and process recorded information.

So think documents: correspondence, emails, messages, texts, reports, drafts, minutes, transcripts, agendas, presentation slides, handouts, memos, briefings, policy statements, guidelines, contracts, surveys, lists, spreadsheets, graphs, diagrams, datasets, database entries, completed forms, call logs, intranet pages, invoices, receipts, expenses declarations, itineraries, maps, photographs, CCTV recordings, audio recordings, recordings of phone calls or remotely conducted meetings, diary entries, metadata ...

From the outside it can be difficult to assess what sort of material is likely to be held, by whom and with what ease of retrieval, but the more knowledge you acquire about how a public authority operates and stores information, the better placed you will be. There are some sources that can help in certain circumstances.

Under the FOI Act, a public authority has to provide requesters with reasonable 'advice and assistance'.[13] How different authorities act on this requirement varies enormously, but in some situations cooperative FOI officers may provide good explanations of what information is held and how easily it can be obtained.

Disclosure logs and whatdotheyknow.com are again indicators as to what records authorities possess. Old responses can also be excellent guides to the correct terminology to employ in your questions in order to specify relevant information.

Another valuable tool sometimes is the 'blank form'. This can show you what information is potentially being recorded about the subject in question. Suppose for example you're interested in the welfare of zoo animals, the gov.uk website has a copy of the form used for zoo inspections, so you can see from that what sort of material is, or is not, noted by the inspectors.[14]

If you go to a public authority's website and search it for the word 'form', you'll probably come up with a long list of all sorts of different online blank forms. These examples will illustrate the data being collected on a range of topics. Or when necessary you can make an FOI request for the relevant blank form.

When you're interested in the contents of a particular database, before making specific requests it can be a good idea to ask (under FOI) for a list of the field names and any explanations or descriptions of them. This should clarify how the information is categorised and stored, so you can target what you want while avoiding fields likely to contain exempt material (eg personal information).

You can also ask an authority for a list of file titles or the folder structure in a particular records system. That can help to focus requests and is a perfectly legitimate approach. Bear in mind, however, that while some FOI officers see this as sensible, it is unpopular with others who regard it as indicative of requesters who don't know what they want and are engaged in some kind of fishing expedition.

4. Be prepared for delay

The main practical problem which requesters encounter is often delay. FOI can be a slow and cumbersome formal process, where the delays built into the system are sometimes exacerbated by inefficiency and obstruction. Getting an answer will almost certainly take weeks, possibly months, even occasionally years.[15] There have been rare occasions when I've been pleasantly surprised to receive a full response on the same day I made a request. At the other extreme, one case of mine (which resulted in cabinet minutes being disclosed under FOI for the first time) took five years and eight months, mainly because the Information Commissioner's Office extraordinarily took over four years to decide my appeal.[16]

Requests on sensitive, high profile topics or ones made by journalists or campaigners may particularly take longer. They are often passed through more internal hoops for consultation and checking.

Generally it's only worth making an FOI request when the information involved would still be useful and relevant some weeks later. If you're aiming to hit a deadline, plan well in advance if you can. The more time you give yourself, the more chance you will have to submit supplementary questions and chase up any failures to respond.

If you have another possible route to the information, think about trying that first (for example, if you're a journalist, by phoning the press office to see if they will send it to you anyway without a formal FOI request). And before you make a request, do check if the information you want - or similar material which is good enough for your purposes - is already publicly available. But when there is no other option, FOI is still the means that may enable you to force the information out into the open.

5. Be persistent

You should know what you're entitled to and why, within what timescale, and pursue it. Sometimes it will need persistence.

For example, if you've sent the same request to multiple public authorities, then one whose staff expect their authority will come out badly compared to others in a 'league table' might not bother to reply the first time around - unless you chase up all the non-repliers. I've talked to FOI staff who confessed to this approach being adopted as a matter of deliberate policy.

Similarly, authorities may sometimes send you a refusal at the initial stage which they realise is unsound in the hope that you won't challenge it. Occasionally documentary evidence of this comes to light, such as when the then Department for Communities and Local Government dismissed a request about ministerial visits, despite internal advice that 'there is a strong likelihood of a decision to withhold the requested information being overturned' - advice which proved to be entirely correct.[17]

Or, if the decision on whether to release or not is genuinely finely balanced, then an initial rejection can easily be reversed later via an internal review or complaint to the Information Commissioner's Office.

To get the story revealing how the then Prince Charles had secretly lobbied the then prime minister Tony Blair against the use of genetically modified foods, I had to make four separate successful complaints to the ICO about the Cabinet Office: first, when it didn't respond within time; second, when it refused to confirm or deny if it held any relevant material; third, when it failed to comply on time with the ICO's decision overturning this refusal; fourth, when it maintained it held no relevant environmental information.[18] This is a particularly extreme case - the Cabinet Office has an especially bad track record of obstructiveness and delay on FOI.[19] But it shows how perseverance can be necessary and rewarded.

If you use FOI extensively, it's helpful to acquire a reputation in the eyes of public authorities as an annoyingly persistent person who knows their rights and will pursue the appropriate cases with determination. Theoretically all requesters should be treated identically, regardless of whether they are known for their good understanding of the law and a willingness to complain, but that's not the way the world works. Show that you've noticed when deadlines have been missed and you care about it, you haven't forgotten your requests, you will keep chasing, and you won't accept poorly justified rejections. However you do need to understand the legal position, so that you're on firm ground. It's a waste of your time - and that of perfectly reasonable FOI officers - if you repeatedly challenge public authorities who are responding properly and in full compliance with the law.

6. Keep good records

Anyone who employs FOI seriously will inevitably have to chase up requests, ask for and follow up internal reviews, and so on. To make the process efficient, you'll need some system that suits your way of working to keep track of all this. Make sure you keep copies of everything. If you have a phone conversation with an FOI officer, make a note of it. You will want to know when replies are due or late, so you can follow up promptly. You'll also want to be able to easily locate the full history of a request if you're appealing to the Information Commissioner.

If you dispatch a 'round robin' request to many authorities, then a spreadsheet is almost certainly the best way to monitor who's replied and who hasn't.

If you send several different requests to the same authority, you might want to create your own system of reference numbers for them, so that you can readily identify which one is being referred to by acknowledgements and other administrative responses such as extensions of the time limit. Although the final substantive reply will probably quote your question(s), messages about postponements are less likely to.

7. Keep FOI separate

Keep FOI requests separate from other communications. If you're involved in some complaint, dispute or campaign about a public authority, don't place your FOI request in the middle of a broader message about your concerns. It could easily get missed or treated as just part of general dissatisfaction and delayed while the authority attends to the other issues. And the same point applies if you're in existing contact with the authority about any other matter. Put an FOI request in a separate email specifically for the purpose of asking for information, clearly indicating that it's an information request. This also makes it simpler to follow up later, including if necessary taking the case to the ICO.

Similarly, don't add extraneous expressions of opinion, complaints, remarks about different topics or other material to an FOI request.

8. Build relationships with FOI officers

Try to build good relationships with FOI officers if you get the chance, especially if you regularly deal with the same public bodies. Be polite and friendly in your contact with them. Their level of accessibility and helpfulness ranges greatly, but sometimes discussion with them can be very constructive. They know how their record systems are organised, what information is kept for how long, what is the appropriate jargon or terminology, what kind of request is practical, and what they've answered already.

Requesters are entitled to receive reasonable advice and assistance from an authority. Often this comes into use when a request has been rejected, particularly due to the cost limit, but in fact you can also seek advice before submitting a request on the best way to go about it.

In this book I use 'FOI officers' to mean staff in public authorities who are responsible for overseeing and implementing the process of handling FOI requests. This is generally how the term is used, even though many of them aren't called 'FOI officer' in their job title. Some may be dedicated to this role on a full-time basis, for others FOI will be just one element - sometimes a small one - within their responsibilities.

Over the years I've received plenty of useful guidance on what to ask for and how to ask for it from FOI officers - some of it consisting of straightforward explanations of record systems and retention policies, but even including things they're not really meant to do, such as tipping me off about a request they'd received so that I could put in the same, and hinting that I ought to appeal against a particular rejection which, I assume, they had been forced to issue against their own wishes.

It can be difficult to speak to FOI officers directly. Some staff are reluctant to talk to requesters, particularly journalists, and prefer all communication to be by email. Often authorities do not publish a phone number for their FOI team, even though that is a breach of the ICO's guidance.[20] However, it's worth trying when you can. There's no harm in including your phone number in a request and asking the authority to call you if clarification is needed.

Don't shoot the messenger when you get an unwelcome answer which you think is unjustified. It's easy to regard the FOI staff who send you the refusals as the obstacle. And they might be. On the other hand, sometimes they are your advocates. Some are keen on openness, that's why they took on the role. Others will simply adopt a straightforward process-driven or legalistic approach, in line with the law, guidance, relevant precedents and seeking to avoid an adverse ruling from the ICO. The FOI team may be arguing your case within the public body against reluctant senior staff who don't want to release embarrassing information.

In the view of experienced FOI officer Paul Gibbons, an authority's FOI staff 'can find themselves caught between determined FOI applicants, who see them as blocking their access to information, and angry colleagues, often in positions of power, who view them as the enemy within'. He adds that the most difficult part of their job is not applying the technicalities of the law correctly or handling impatient requesters, but 'dealing with colleagues who refuse to cooperate, or may even be actively hostile to the aims of the FOI officer'.[21]

Think of an organisation's FOI unit not as impeding your route to knowledge but as a potential pathfinder. If you can give them background information and useful precedents which might strengthen the internal argument to disclose, do so. Sometimes they will be most helpful if they fully understand the motive behind your request. FOI officers tend to be hesitant about asking requesters for this, in case they get criticised for doing so. But in some cases you might be entirely willing to explain, and it can make things easier for everyone. However they can't require you to disclose your underlying purpose if you don't want to.

And don't be rude or hostile. I sometimes come across people referring to making an FOI request 'against' a public authority. In my opinion that phraseology is to be avoided. You would like the respondent authority to be cooperative. It doesn't help to adopt language and a frame of mind which treats an FOI application as an act of aggression on your part.

PART B: Requests

4. Requesting information: The law

The law on freedom of information is laid down in the Freedom of Information Act 2000 (FOIA), covering England, Wales and Northern Ireland. It has remained broadly, but not entirely, unchanged since being passed in 2000 and coming into force in 2005. This chapter sets out the legal detail and the key implications for requesting information.

What is an FOI request?

An FOI request has to be in writing, state your name and an address, and describe the information you are asking for. That's all, in terms of legal criteria.[22] There is no set form of words you have to use. You don't have to do or be aware of anything else, and it's up to the public authority to respond in line with the full requirements of the law. Obviously there's a lot more to making an effective and worthwhile FOI request, but nevertheless some points do follow from this simple definition.

You don't have to say why you want the information or provide any justification for releasing it. You also don't need to make any reference to the FOI Act. However I usually do include a statement along the lines of 'This is a request under the Freedom of Information Act'. I can't see any harm in doing so (apart from cases where a very easy request to answer would instead be treated more quickly on a routine 'business-as-usual' basis, rather than possibly nudging it into the formalities of FOI). It could help to ensure that the request reaches the right staff and is dealt with properly. It might also suggest that you know your legal rights and will pursue them.

An FOI request can be sent to anyone in the public authority concerned. It will still be legally enforceable and require a proper answer. But it's obviously sensible and quickest to direct one to the team specifically charged with processing them.

Public authorities do answer all sorts of routine requests for information - such as immediate practical questions about services, standard responses to general queries, sending out copies of leaflets and publications, etc - without going through the legalistic and cumbersome FOI process. These are often called 'business-as-usual' enquiries and aren't described as FOI requests or included in FOI statistics.

As long as the public authority is going to provide the material sought, this is clearly pragmatic and in everyone's interests. Theoretically however they would be FOI requests in legal terms, as long as they meet the basic criteria laid down (in writing, with name and address, and describing the information wanted). And importantly, whenever the authority wants to refuse to supply any information requested, then legally that has to be under one of the possible reasons specified in the FOI Act, and so that should go through the FOI formal procedure.

Names

I've often been asked if you actually need to give your real name, even though it is a legal requirement for a valid FOI request.[23] Despite the obligations on public authorities, some people suspect their request will be treated more obstructively or slowly because of who they are. Others fear that use of FOI could damage their relationship with the authority.

In some cases these worries are understandable. Requests from journalists and campaigners undoubtedly sometimes go through extra administrative hoops (such as internal referrals to the press office) and can end up being dealt with more slowly and cautiously. This is often true even if occasionally the fear of bad publicity from a requester who knows their rights can push an authority in the opposite direction, to reduce delay. Or to take an extraordinary recent instance from Scotland, the chief education officer of Aberdeenshire Council reacted to one set of FOI requests by angrily contacting the requester's employer and threatening to take the council's business elsewhere.[24]

Doubtless some requesters don't give real names, and it's clear from cases on whatdotheyknow.com, for example, that even obvious pseudonyms sometimes get substantive replies. The ICO advises authorities that in most cases they should 'accept the name that has been provided at face value' and not take steps to check the requester's identity.[25]

However, as a general principle my view is that you should approach public authorities in an honest and straightforward manner, which means using your real name. This is particularly true if you are a journalist or a campaigner. Furthermore, if the authority surmises a pseudonym has been used, it is legally entitled to reject the request and may well do so. Even if this doesn't happen, a false name would cause difficulty at a later stage if you take the case to the ICO (which may be suspicious and despite its advice to other authorities will reject any pseudonymous complaint[26]) or if you subsequently want to appeal to the First-tier Tribunal.

In any case, if it concerns a clearly sensitive or high-profile topic, an authority's staff may well be just as cautious and slow about a request from a name they don't know as for one from a journalist or campaigner they do, and still insist on sign-off on the response at a high level.

If a request is made by an agent acting on your behalf (eg by a solicitor), then the ICO's position is that the name of the client behind the request and not just the agent has to be provided.[27] So (in theory, anyway, if not always in practice) that would not be a method to disguise the identity of the requester.

However, a valid request can be made in the name of a registered company without providing the details of any individual. The ICO also recommends that authorities should accept requests made in the name of an unincorporated association.[28]

Addresses

While you need to supply an address, that is an 'address for correspondence'.[29] This means any address via which you can be contacted, so it does not have to be your residential or work address, and an email address is entirely sufficient.

'In writing'

The criterion of 'in writing' includes requests sent by electronic means such as email.[30]

A valid FOI request could indeed be submitted via social media to an authority's account on a particular platform (provided that it includes the requester's actual name and address for correspondence). But for people genuinely wanting information it's not a good way to proceed, as such a request could easily be missed. It may also be tricky to express it fully within a limited number of characters.

Those seeking information in a hurry may sometimes want to avoid getting caught in the slow procedures of FOI, say if you are a journalist putting questions to a press office. Obstructive press officers may state that they want to handle particular queries under the formalities of FOI. Your enquiry should only be treated as an FOI request if it's been put in writing. In some circumstances you might prefer to avoid doing that, but on the other hand, unless you do so you have no legal right to receive a response.

Email addresses for public authorities

Public authorities should state their email address for FOI requests clearly on their website. Alternatively you can visit the FOI-requesting portal whatdotheyknow.com and find the email address used there for an authority via the page for that organisation. The FOI Directory website has lists of email addresses for numerous categories of public authorities but, while many will be correct, they're not reliably up to date.[31]

Some public bodies prefer you to submit requests by filling out an online form on their website, as it is more convenient for their case-management system. A few may even give the impression that they insist on this, but in fact they are not allowed to do so. If you choose to ask for information by email it can't be ignored, they still have to respond properly. In my experience they will back down if you insist on your rights. Legally they have no alternative. If you receive a reply or auto-reply to your request which appears to state you must re-submit it via an online form, I suggest that you email again asking the authority to confirm it will process your request as already submitted.

If you are completely unable to find an email address which is designated for FOI requests, under the law you can send the request to anyone in that authority and it must still be dealt with (and the

20-working-day period for replying begins as soon as anyone in the authority has received it). If it does come to this, I would recommend sending the request to some other information access role that might be publicised such as the data protection officer, or someone with responsibility for the topic your request covers, or alternatively the head of legal affairs, or (probably the last resort) the chief executive of the organisation - explaining that you are doing so as you can't find any public indication of the FOI email address.

If you want, you can send a request via whatdotheyknow.com, where it and the reply will be publicly available for all to see. This has the benefit of immediately making the information you obtain accessible to anyone else interested.

Some authorities were uneasy about this portal, which was established by mySociety, a group that promotes active citizenship, and initially tried to resist its use, but it is now clearly accepted as a legally allowed and popular method. The site also offers a paid 'Pro' option, which journalists, campaigners, researchers and others can use to keep requests and responses private until they are ready to go public with their work.[32]

Who can submit an FOI request?

The answer is simple - anyone can. You don't need to have any direct connection with the public authority involved. If the request is aimed at a local council or police force, say, there's no need to be based in that area. In fact, there's no requirement to be a UK citizen or resident at all.[33]

Furthermore, as a general rule, the identity and motives of the person making the request should not affect the response provided. The term often used in FOI circles to describe this position is that the process should be 'applicant-blind'.[34] There are a few exceptions to this when the identity of the requester does matter, for example if someone submits a series of very similar requests or if the material at issue contains the requester's personal information.[35] Nevertheless it does hold as an important broad principle governing how FOI should function. The disclosure of material has to be assessed as if it is disclosure to the world at large, not to the particular individual asking.

Which public authorities are covered?

The FOI Act stretches all the way across the wide range of the UK's public sector, from the heart of government at 10 Downing Street to local providers of public services. This is an extensive spread compared to FOI systems in many other countries. Bodies which come under the law include the following:

- UK government departments and executive agencies
- The administration of the House of Commons and the House of Lords
- Welsh Government and Senedd
- Northern Ireland Executive and Assembly
- All levels of local government, from large county councils, London boroughs, mayoral authorities, through to very small parish councils, including various joint authorities, passenger transport executives and Transport for London
- The National Health Service, including hospitals, the ambulance service and pharmacies, down to GPs, dentists and opticians providing NHS services
- Police forces, Police and Crime Commissioners, the National Police Chiefs' Council and the Police Federation
- Fire service
- Armed forces (except the special forces)
- State-funded schools including academies and free schools, and universities and colleges receiving direct public funds
- Network Rail (but not private train operating companies)
- Publicly-owned companies, including those owned by local councils or universities
- A large number of quangos, advisory bodies, regulators, national museums and galleries - these range from Ofcom and the Charity Commission to the General Medical Council and the British Museum, as well as many much smaller and less well-known organisations, from the Administration of Radioactive Substances Advisory Committee to the Welsh Pharmaceutical Committee
- The Information Commissioner's Office (which as a result has to rule on complaints about itself and sometimes

embarrassingly ends up rebuking itself)

If you want to check if a particular organisation is covered, you can consult the current lengthy list published as schedule 1 of the FOI Act.[36] However the online version is not always completely up to date. Also, a few other organisations have been added separately via a different legal procedure and so are not included there (Network Rail, the Universities and Colleges Admissions Service, the National Police Chiefs' Council and the Financial Ombudsman Service).[37]

A small number of institutions are only partially covered. For example, the BBC and Channel 4 are subject to FOI but not for information held for the purposes of 'journalism, art or literature', while the Bank of England is included except for information relating to monetary policy, its financial operations and its banking services.[38]

The major authorities are used to dealing with very large numbers of FOI applications. On the other hand, some less important and local bodies get very few and may find it disconcerting to receive one.

On the whole private organisations and companies lie outside the reach of FOI, but there are some exceptions. For example, in legal terms GPs are private businesses and universities are private institutions, although broadly perceived and experienced as part of the state's activities. Private companies which run pharmacy stores, such as Boots, LloydsPharmacy and leading supermarkets, are covered by FOI in relation to their NHS work.[39] But in general the mere fact that a private organisation is employed to do something by a public body does not bring it within FOI.

Although all the authorities listed fall under the same law, there is a great deal of variation in how they implement it in practice. Their performance ranges enormously in terms of how prompt, efficient and cooperative or obstructive they are. It also changes over time. In my experience over the years various government departments, quangos and councils have moved from good to bad or bad to good, and perhaps back again, in line with the changing commitment and expertise of their FOI staff, the level of resources dedicated to FOI, and the attitudes of their senior management.

Who isn't covered?

While the list of organisations covered is very wide, there are elements of the public sector which are not subject to FOI for a variety of reasons, some of which seem more anomalous than others. This is not just limited to the most traditionally secretive parts of the British state, the security services and the royal family. Those not covered by the FOI Act include the following (although note that some still come under the Environmental Information Regulations):

- MI5, MI6, GCHQ
- Special forces (within the military)
- National Crime Agency
- Advanced Research and Invention Agency
- Electoral Registration and Returning Officers
- The Royal Household
- Individual elected representatives such as MPs and councillors
- Individual courts and tribunals (although HM Courts and Tribunals Service is covered)

There are various other organisations which play an important role in our national life and are often asked about in this context, such as political parties, sports governing bodies (eg the Football Association or Swim England), the Church of England and other major religious institutions, trades unions and professional membership associations, some voluntary industry regulators like the Advertising Standards Authority, and well-known large private charities - these are not public bodies (even in the case of the Church of England, despite its officially established status) and they are all outside the remit of FOI.

Many public services are delivered not directly by public authorities but by private contractors on their behalf. Although there has been a long-running campaign for FOI to be extended to private companies contracted to deliver such services, this has not happened. This is a major gap in the way the law functions, undermining transparency at the everyday level of public services. However, it may still be possible to obtain some limited information about the provision of these services through asking the public authority issuing the contract, although financial figures are often held back to protect commercial interests.

If you're seeking material about a private company you should also consider what might be held by any public body which in some way regulates, inspects or oversees its activities, and then make a suitable FOI request to that body.

Generally it's very clear legally whether an organisation is subject to FOI or not, but the boundary does lead to some anomalous and surprising situations, which may work either for or against requesters. For example, of the three main school examination boards in England, AQA and Edexcel are outside FOI because they are entirely private institutions, but OCR is covered as it is owned by Cambridge University.

If you are not sure whether an organisation is covered, you can still send your request to it and see what happens. Sometimes you might be given the information anyway, if the organisation is cooperative. Some institutions (such as the Bar Council and the Law Society) state they will try to reply to information requests in the spirit of FOI, even if they're not formally subject to it. The whatdotheyknow website also lists some bodies which do not fall under FOI (where this is the case, it is made clear), and you can then use the site to ask for information.[40] But of course if any of these organisations doesn't give you what you want, you don't have the legal right to pursue further action in the way that FOI provides.

What kind of 'information'?

An FOI request is a request for information. It doesn't have to be a request for copies of documents, although it could take that form. So if you want you can simply ask a straightforward factual question, such as 'how many ...?'. This is more helpful than some other FOI systems internationally which only provide a right of access to documents. Alternatively, you can phrase your request as asking for documents if you prefer, since it is clear that effectively encompasses all the information contained in those documents.

In one of the numerous legal cases involving MPs' expenses, the Court of Appeal ruled that retyped transcripts of the wording of invoices and receipts were not a sufficient response to an FOI request for copies of the 'original' documents. These transcripts omitted features like logos and letterheads, and did not convey aspects like layout and design or the style of handwriting, all of which the court said constituted 'information' in the circumstances of this case, and so were subject to FOI.[41] This point, that the full information in a document includes layout, headers, annotations, underlining, images etc as well as wording, is confirmed in the ICO's guidance.[42] If these details matter to you, make sure you phrase your request to ask for copies of documents.

Similarly, when an authority redacts some material from a disclosure, the ICO advises that it should provide a copy of the original document with the redactions made to that. This is because 'how the extracts fitted into the original document' constitutes recorded information to which a requester is entitled.[43]

Metadata

You can also ask for the metadata of electronic documents, such as author and editing history, since that is information held by the authority. But the ICO's stance is that to get this you have to specifically request the original metadata, not just ask for a copy of the document concerned.[44]

Keyword searches

It is possible to make a request based on proposing certain electronic keyword searches, asking for copies of the documents returned when specific searches within the authority's records are conducted.[45] This can have advantages - the request is clear, should be simple to carry out, and there is less scope for misinterpretation. When I've done this myself it's usually because I've been particularly worried that a normal request would be interpreted in a very unhelpful way.

But this approach also has significant disadvantages. If you pick the wrong keywords, perhaps because you're not familiar with the authority's own terminology, you could miss out on a lot of material. Furthermore, the keywords may well not be used in email chains, say, that take for granted what the subject of discussion is. You will also not catch paper records. And if you choose keywords that are too common, you could receive a large quantity of entirely irrelevant information, or find that the request is rejected on cost grounds.

Recorded information

Any request has to be for 'recorded' information, but it can be 'information recorded in any form'.[46] Nevertheless the scope of recorded information is wide-ranging: as well as written documents, whether printed or electronic, it could include spreadsheets, draft documents, notes, video/CCTV recordings, audio recordings, photographs, maps, drawings, diary entries, metadata, and so on. And it doesn't matter how old the information is - it can be historical, as long as the authority still possesses it.

Note that FOI does not give you the right of access to other people's minds. You can't demand to know the thoughts, motives, recollections, beliefs, intentions and other mental processes of officials and politicians, or how they'd respond to hypothetical situations - unless it's been written down or otherwise recorded, in which case you can.

Someone in the public authority might know the answer to a specific question which you pose; but if the authority doesn't want to tell you, nothing in the FOI law compels them to, unless that answer is also recorded somewhere.

This means that requests for an authority's opinion, or an 'explanation' or 'clarification' of an authority's policy or decisions, are often ineffective.

To take one recent tribunal case, which arose from a somewhat convoluted and bitter dispute within a Cornish parish council about the funding of local public toilets, the First-tier Tribunal ruled that the following 'why' questions did not count as requests for information: 'Why do the agendas not have the details of income and expenditure included? Why have the minutes not been kept up to date with income and expenditure? Why have members of the public been refused access to the end of year accounts? Why was a business case for the toilets not approved by the council?'[47]

32

New information

You can't use FOI to force an authority to create new information which isn't already in existence, or to collect information which it doesn't already possess, or to update outdated records. Nor can you use it to make an authority transfer information that it holds into a different, possibly more convenient, format, say one which is more easily searchable. If you're convinced that a public authority ought to be collecting and analysing some kind of information which it's failing to do, you may be right or wrong about that - but it's entirely irrelevant to FOI processes, which are only concerned with what the authority does have and the way that it actually holds it.

A tricky grey area in this context can arise when the requested information could be derived from raw data or other material held by the authority but it has not so far been explicitly compiled. In the metaphor adopted in one tribunal case addressing this issue, this is where the authority possesses the 'building blocks' necessary to produce the information involved.[48] The ICO guidance states that the authority does then hold this information, 'unless it requires particular skills or expertise to put the building blocks together'.[49] That will depend on the particular facts of the case, and particularly on how much subjective judgment would be required.

However in the common situation of information kept in a database, the ICO usefully and importantly makes clear: 'When you hold information in electronic files and can retrieve and manipulate it using query tools or language within the software, that information is held for the purposes of FOIA. The use of query tools or languages does not involve the creation of new information.'

Inaccurate information

Another potential difficulty is where the information held relating to your request is incomplete or actually inaccurate. However, if that's what the authority holds, that's what it should disclose (subject to the exemptions and any public interest test). You don't have the legal right to insist on full or accurate information. The focus of the FOI process is always on the information that is actually held, not on any information that should be held.

Public authorities themselves sometimes try to use flaws in information as an argument for not releasing it, on the basis that it would be misleading. But in the words of a tribunal decision, 'if the records are faulty or inadequate and the information turns out therefore to be inaccurate that is irrelevant: the right under the Act is to information which is held'.[50] And the ICO tells authorities: 'You cannot refuse a request for information simply because you know the information is out of date, incomplete or inaccurate. To avoid misleading the requester, you should normally be able to explain to them the nature of the information, or provide extra information to help put the information into context.'[51]

Meta-requests

It's useful to note that you can make an FOI request for information related to the handling of a previous request. This is often called a 'meta-request'. It can be very revealing about how the initial request was discussed and dealt with. It is different to asking for an internal review to challenge the outcome of a request, since it is only seeking information. Some authorities have occasionally tried to dismiss meta-requests as vexatious, but the ICO states clearly that they are valid and should be treated 'in the same way as any other information request'.[52] This has been confirmed by a decision of the High Court.[53]

The ICO guidance notes that the following factors can strengthen the public interest in disclosure in response to a meta-request: increasing the transparency and accountability of the request handling process; helping the public better understand the reasoning behind decisions; and fostering public confidence in the request handling process.[54]

In legal terms any meta-request is also likely to be in part a subject access request under data protection law for the requester's own personal data.

When is information 'held' by an authority?

This can be a much trickier issue than it initially appears to be.

It's important to understand that whether material is 'held' for FOI purposes depends on whether it is held 'on behalf of the authority'.[55] This cuts both ways.

So if an authority has information in its systems or on its premises, but only on behalf of someone else and not in any way for its own purposes, that is not covered by FOI.

Thus if employees have been using their work email accounts for genuinely personal matters unconnected with the authority, the content of those emails is outside FOI (and that's the case whether or not they ought to be behaving like this, which is a separate issue). This would also apply to trade union activity by members of staff.

A more contentious issue that sometimes arises is where a government department or council states that information connected to a politician (a minister or council portfolio holder, say) is purely party political or only related to the politician's constituency or ward work, and so not held on behalf of the authority. This typically may include emails and records of meetings. There may be legitimate instances of this, but authorities do sometimes assert that material is 'party political' and not for official business in doubtful circumstances.[56]

I've also seen instances where government departments have responded with a simple and apparently implausible 'information not held' reply, without explaining (until challenged) that this is the legal ground for their statement - namely, while they do actually hold information, they consider it to be party political and not linked to government responsibilities. If you've received a response like that, bear this possibility in mind. It could be that it's an unjustified basis which the department is hoping not to draw attention to, and it ought to be disputed.

There are also more complex aspects to this question of when information is or is not held for an authority's own purposes, such as when staff have been seconded to another public sector body but keep using their previous email account, or when an authority like a university asserts it is storing material simply to help preserve it.[57]

On the other hand, when someone else physically holds the information, but it is kept for the authority's purposes, then that is covered by FOI. You still send your request directly to the public authority, and it is the authority's responsibility to retrieve and provide the information.

These circumstances can include the use of commercial storage facilities, partnership arrangements, and also certain situations where the authority employs contractors to provide a service who may then hold information on the authority's behalf. Sometimes there will be objections from contractors who maintain they hold the material only for themselves, not on behalf of the authority. The contract itself could contain provisions that directly or indirectly relate to this. One relevant factor may be what information the authority has a contractual right to access.[58]

Personal devices and accounts

There is another increasingly important point: FOI extends to information held on private devices, such as personal mobiles, or in personal email accounts, where that information is for being used for work purposes.

The ICO's guidance for public authorities states: 'Information held in non-corporate communications channels may be subject to FOIA if it relates to the public authority's official business. Regardless of whether you hold it in an official or non-corporate communications channel, all such information held by someone who has a direct, formal connection with the public authority is potentially subject to FOIA. If the information held in a non-corporate communications channel amounts to public authority business, it is very likely to be held on your behalf.'[59]

'Non-corporate communications channels' covers personal email accounts, text messages on phones, or chat apps such as WhatsApp, and so on.

That is clearly the legal position. It is also accepted by the government, as the Cabinet Office has acknowledged: 'Modern messaging services (such as WhatsApp) are useful tools for speedy and informal communication across organisational boundaries. They have a role in government, as in many other areas of the economy ... All government information, irrespective of format or communication channel, is subject to the Freedom of Information Act.'[60]

However in practice, whatever the legalities of the situation, in many circumstances personal mobiles, WhatsApp exchanges and private email accounts, etc, will not be searched by an authority responding to an FOI request.[61] This is despite the then Information Commissioner Elizabeth Denham telling authorities in 2021: 'When handling FOI requests make sure you consider whether communications held on private correspondence channels, such as WhatsApp, may be relevant to the request.'[62] And, as the ICO's guidance states: 'You should always consider all locations where staff may hold relevant information. This may include non-corporate communications channels.'[63]

This problem is well illustrated by the ICO's issuing of a practice recommendation to the Department of Health and Social Care (DHSC) in July 2022. It followed an investigation into the department's poorly managed use of non-corporate communication channels. The ICO concluded that it was 'likely' that ministers' records of private messaging services had not been searched in response to FOI requests on a number of occasions when this should have been done. The ICO said: 'The Commissioner has genuine concerns that information which should form part of DHSC's official record may not have been retained or accessible for the purposes of properly responding to legitimate FOI requests.'[64]

Therefore requesters might want to request specifically that such accounts and devices are searched, where you have reason to believe they could hold relevant information not copied to official channels. But even then the public authority, if it complies with that, is very likely to rely on the individual involved to hand over material (rather than say an FOI officer seeking direct access to an individual staff member's complete personal email history to look for anything relevant, which would be considered a breach of privacy). This inevitably increases the chance that some information might not be located and considered for disclosure, whether inadvertently or deliberately.

Communications via non-corporate channels are also more likely to be auto-deleted or proactively deleted after a fairly short period of time than for many official records. Another difficulty is that they may become practically impossible to retrieve if the person who had personal copies has left the organisation. Instances of this have happened, for example with the former Downing Street adviser

Dominic Cummings.[65] The ICO does advise that messages sent on authority business via non-official channels should be copied or exported to official systems, but obviously this often doesn't happen.[66]

In the words of a report from the Institute for Government about the use of WhatsApp messages within government: 'Existing legislation is clear that all government business, regardless of how or where it is discussed, is subject to the same transparency requirements. This includes WhatsApp conversations that relate to the work of government. But a lack of formal processes for storing and recording WhatsApp messages means that, practically, they are all too often inaccessible to those wanting to hold government to account … People we spoke to in government said they were not aware of any process for checking whether information held solely in WhatsApp fell within the scope of an FoI request.'[67]

Despite the clear requirements of the law, this represents a definite practical problem for the effectiveness of FOI in some situations.

Backup records

Another category of record you may specifically want to request to be searched, if relevant, is backup files.

Tribunals have ruled that information which has been deleted from active files but is kept within a backup is still 'held' by the public authority and therefore subject to FOI. For example, in a case involving a long-running neighbour dispute and old correspondence from the planning department of Thanet Council, the First-tier Tribunal ruled: 'If requested information is in (or on) back-up tapes which are themselves held by the public authority or is in some way still stored on the public authority's server, we consider that it is clearly "held" by the public authority.'[68]

The ICO guidance for authorities on this topic is more ambiguous. It notes this case but states that 'if there is no indication that you deleted significant information, searches of your 'live' systems and any records held in relevant archives that you maintain are likely to be sufficient'. However if the authority's initial searches suggest that relevant information has been deleted, then 'you need to consider this matter as part of your overall response to the request'.[69]

The Cabinet Office's code of practice on FOI asserts that 'information which has been deleted from a public authority's records before a request is received, and is only held in electronic back up files, should generally be regarded as not being held'.[70] However, its own policy on retention and destruction of records partly contradicts this, pointing out that 'any information that is readily recoverable from a recycle bin continues to be subject to the department's legal obligations in respect of FOI, Environmental Information Regulations (EIR) or data protection information requests'.[71]

In practice, public authorities will not routinely search backup systems holding deleted records in response to FOI requests. If you believe that is where your target information is located and so you want that to be done, you should specifically request this. You can also refer to the Thanet decision to show the position adopted by the First-tier Tribunal. However you should also bear in mind that in some cases the complexities of extracting material from old backup systems (which despite their purpose are often badly disorganised) could exceed the cost limit. On the other hand it is not difficult to retrieve items from desktop recycle bins or trash folders for emails.

What form can the information be sent in?

Requesters can express a preference for how they want to receive the material they are seeking, including whether they want electronic documents or hard copies. If a requester asks for a copy of the information 'in permanent form or in another form acceptable to the applicant', or for a digest or summary of it, or for the chance to inspect the records in person, then as long as it is 'reasonably practicable' the authority has to comply with this choice.[72]

Note that what matters is what you say in the request initially. If you later state an alternative preference when the authority is part way through processing your case or has finished, then legally it could be treated as a different and new request.[73] So it's best to make clear from the start how you want to obtain the material.

The ICO takes the view that where a request is submitted by email, the authority should assume that the requester wants the information also to be sent electronically in reply (unless the request states an outright preference for hard copy). Most authorities will do this anyway, as generally it's easier for them. However, just to make matters completely clear, I still include in my requests a statement that I do want the material to be emailed to me.

Usually people want full copies of the information, in whatever format they prefer. It's unlikely that a digest or summary will be more useful than the raw material itself.

Spreadsheets

The issue that probably arises most often in this context is where requesters want a spreadsheet which they can analyse and manipulate, and authorities want to send them a much less useful pdf file instead (and this can happen even when the pdf document has clearly been created directly from an actual spreadsheet). In one recent example the ICO rejected the BBC's insistence that it had to release data in a pdf to stop it being 'manipulated or otherwise misused'.[74] I have also come across some bizarre files supplied by public authorities and described ridiculously as 'spreadsheets'. On one occasion I received an Excel document where the apparent tables of data had simply been inserted as copied-and-pasted images of the original data tables - and so could not be used for calculations.

Nevertheless, requesters are indeed entitled to receive spreadsheets (and genuine ones). This was confirmed when the Court of Appeal ruled that someone seeking examination data from Buckinghamshire Council had the legal right to be sent the information in spreadsheet as opposed to pdf format.[75]

Furthermore, the law now states explicitly that where the information constitutes all or part of a dataset, then if you ask for it to be in electronic form, as long as it is 'reasonably practicable' the authority has to send the information in 'an electronic form which is capable of re-use'.[76] A pdf file clearly does not satisfy this criterion.

A 'dataset' is defined as an electronic collection of factual information which is not the product of analysis or interpretation and whose mode of presentation has not been materially altered since the data was recorded.[77] In other words, it's likely to be what is usually thought of as 'raw data'. This provision was added to the original FOI Act as an amendment coming into force in 2013, as part of the government's enthusiasm at the time for making greater use of open data in the public sector.[78]

The government's FOI code of practice adds a useful rider that the release of a dataset should be 'accompanied by sufficient metadata and contextual information about how and why the dataset was compiled or created'.[79]

So if you want to receive data in a proper spreadsheet format (presumably because that is the means by which you are going to analyse it), then you should definitely ask for that in your request and you should be sent one (generally as a csv file). If that does not happen, then you should go back to the authority and restate your requested format.

There are limits, however, to insisting on the structure of information supplied. Requesters sometimes ask for figures to be laid out in a particular pattern of columns and rows. There is no harm in seeking this where it would help you process the data, but the ICO's position is that any spreadsheet sent by the authority does not have to comply with such a specific pattern, as long as it contains the information.[80]

Inspection in person

Another context where the means of communication can matter is where the information sought is contained in a large collection of old, badly organised paper files. I have found occasionally, with a cooperative authority, that offering to inspect records in person can then ease things. Ideally this would be on the basis that you are then sent copies of the select subset of documents that you indicate you actually want, or you are allowed to photograph them there and then. It can also sometimes be useful to have the opportunity while visiting to chat informally to the FOI officer (in fact, this can be an advantage to inspecting records in person even if it's not needed due to the state of the documents).

How quickly should your request be answered?

The law says FOI requests must be answered 'promptly' and also 'in any event' within 20 working days.[81] While the ICO clearly states that the 20-day limit should be regarded as a 'long stop',[82] in practice the 'promptly' requirement generally gets ignored and the period of 20 working days is treated as the legal deadline. Most simple requests will be answered within this timeframe, although there is no guarantee this will happen.

On occasions I have received a full response with all the information on the same day I submitted a request. It's not impossible when the authority is efficient and the request is straightforward. However it's much more likely that you will have to wait about four weeks or so, and longer in some cases. You have to take such likely delays - and worse - into account when thinking about your use of FOI. Whatever the law says, you have to be realistic and plan accordingly.

This relates to getting the substantive answers to your questions. You will receive a simple acknowledgment of your request quite quickly from most authorities, but that does not count as a legal response. It will probably confirm the date by when you ought to get a full reply, and should also include the authority's reference number for the request, which you'll need if following up later.

Sometimes you get an initial acknowledgment but nothing else within the 20 working days. That is not allowed within the law. You should receive one of the following (or a combination of them, if relevant to different parts of the material requested): either the information you have asked for, or a refusal to give it to you, or a refusal to confirm or deny whether it is held, or a statement that extra time is needed to assess the public interest.

However, if your request is not clear enough, then the authority may ask you for clarification before it is processed. It should do this rather than make assumptions about what it thinks you mean. The authority can and probably will treat a clarified or revised version as a new request, so that the 20 working days start again. Similarly if your original request is turned down as over the cost limit, and you submit a refined narrower request, you go back to day one.

Exceptions

There are a few minor exceptions to this deadline where more time is permitted for certain authorities. Requests for closed records at the National Archives may take 30 working days, to allow longer for consultation with the department that the records came from. For schools (where staff might be on holiday outside term time) the limit is 20 school days, or 60 working days if this is shorter. And 60 working days can be allowed for information held outside the UK (eg in embassies abroad) or by armed forces on operations.[83]

Extension for the public interest test

There is also one very major and far-reaching exception: any public authority can exceed the 20-day limit if the information comes under one of the qualified exemptions and it needs longer to assess whether the balance of the public interest favours release or not.[84] In this situation the public authority can delay answering 'until such time as is reasonable in the circumstances', a loose criterion that is often abused.

Communications postponing the deadline in this way sometimes describe themselves as 'refusal notices' and state that the information is 'exempt'. The authorities who use this language are legally correct in their terminology but often confuse requesters as to whether their request has been declined when it has just been deferred. Always read an authority's entire message thoroughly to see what it really says, and don't jump to conclusions based on the presence of certain words.

Many FOI requesters are familiar with receiving a series of repetitive messages arriving every 20 working days to say that another similar period of time is required in order to determine the public interest. But the ICO's guidance states: 'Our view is that an authority should normally take no more than an additional 20 working days to consider the public interest, meaning that the total time spent dealing with the request should not exceed 40 working days. An extension beyond this should be exceptional.[85] This is well worth knowing about and quoting, although it is only guidance and does not have the force of law.

43

Requests often concern a mix of some information that is covered by a qualified exemption and subject to a public interest test, and other items of information that are not caught by any exemption and should be disclosed straightforwardly. Importantly the latter material should not be delayed beyond 20 working days because of the public interest test for the potentially exempt information. As the ICO guidance tells authorities, 'You should release any information that is not covered by an exemption within the standard time'.[86] Yet authorities do not always comply with this.

If an authority's response states that just some of the material needs a public interest test but it also holds back the remaining information for the moment, then you should ask for that other information to be sent to you immediately.

Note that an extension beyond 20 days should only be for the purpose of assessing the balance of the public interest. The authority should have established within the initial 20 working days which qualified exemptions are involved and told you, as well as providing an estimate of when the eventual decision will be reached.[87] This doesn't always happen, and if you are simply informed that an extension is necessary but without any of these other details being supplied, then you should ask for them. However it is possible for an authority to later decide that a different exemption is relevant.

Authorities are not allowed to postpone replying past the 20 days for other reasons, although occasionally they do try to do this. For example, I have come across delay being blamed on the fact the records were stored in a distant location (within the UK), but this is not a valid legal justification.

Working days

If you want to be very prompt on chasing up any delay, you should note that the first working day after the date of receipt of the request is counted as day one (not day two), and also that a bank holiday in any part of the UK is not treated as a 'working day'. In other words, a bank holiday just for Scotland (such as 2 January) is not considered a working day in England, Wales and Northern Ireland when it comes to calculating FOI deadlines.[88]

If I haven't received a substantive response from the authority within 20 working days, I'll give them maybe a short grace period and if that is still the case, complain to the ICO that the authority has failed to send a proper response. Alternatively there can be an argument for sending the authority one chasing email first, just in case for example there has been a genuine administrative error about dispatching the reply. But I wouldn't go through that step for any authority with a history of delay.

When it gets complaints of this kind, the ICO will generally contact the authority and instruct it to reply properly to the requester within another 10 working days. The ICO will tell you this is the action it is taking. In my experience this often produces a reply, but if there is still no substantive answer within that period, you should immediately inform the ICO, which is then likely to issue a decision notice formally requiring the authority to respond. The need for ICO intervention in such cases is shown by the fact it had to issue over 800 decisions for this reason in a five-year period, according to analysis by openDemocracy.[89]

In a situation where the authority has extended the time limit for a public interest test, then when this has been done three times, so it is going over 60 working days, I would complain to the ICO that this is not 'reasonable' and there are no 'exceptional' circumstances.

For these complaints specifically about delay you don't have to go through the internal review process before raising them with the ICO.

In both cases I will usually cc the authority's FOI team on my email of complaint to the ICO. In my experience this occasionally appears to prompt them into rapid action, if only so that when the ICO then contacts them, they can say 'We've already replied to him'.

Is it free?

Almost always, yes. Don't be put off by the automatic acknowledgments from some authorities which contain ominous references to possible charges. A fee is only relevant in very unusual situations, and if it is applicable you will be asked in advance to confirm whether you are willing to pay. If the authority has to send you hard copies of documents, you can be asked to cover the cost of photocopying and postage expenses (though importantly you can't be charged for staff time),[90] but even that is unlikely, as for most authorities it's probably not worth the effort of processing the payment.

On the other hand, requests which are particularly expensive for an authority to deal with and so exceed the cost limit can be (and generally will be) turned down.

However, note that FOI does not entitle you to get all forms of information produced by a public authority for nothing. You can still be charged for priced publications, standard reports, extracts or output from datasets normally sold as a service, and other specific items which the authority stipulates in its publication scheme are available at a particular cost or which it supplies commercially in line with another piece of legislation. You would be refused these in response to an FOI request on the basis that the information is accessible by other means, despite the cost involved which in some cases could be substantial.

What help are you entitled to?

Public authorities have to provide FOI requesters with 'reasonable' advice and assistance. If when doing this they comply with the government's code of practice,[91] they are considered to have met their legal obligations.[92]

This includes giving advice to help applicants to reframe a far-reaching request to bring it under the cost limit.[93] And when the authority contacted does not hold the information but it believes that another authority does, it should tell the requester who to ask instead.[94] The ICO recommends that authorities should treat the code as a 'minimum standard'.[95]

Most advice and assistance is supplied in response to requests after they have been submitted, especially those which exceed the cost threshold. But the duty to provide it also extends to helping 'persons who propose to make' FOI requests.[96] You can try approaching an authority for guidance before drawing up your request. Some will be cooperative, some won't be. An FOI officer can explain what might be feasible, and helpful ones may get involved in open-ended discussion of what information is kept on the relevant topic and how easily it can be retrieved, so that you can properly assess your options. But you can't expect anyone in the authority to decide what you ought to be asking for or write the request for you.

Ideally you would discuss these issues on the phone. You would then have to put your request in writing.

5. Requesting information: Tactics and advice

Some FOI requests may be straightforward - say, asking for a copy of one specific document which you know exists and how to describe unambiguously, or posing one clear factual question which can only really be expressed in that way. However even in some of these apparently simple cases, nuances of phraseology can make quite a difference. And they certainly matter a lot when to comes to trickier, more complex or multi-faceted requests.

Take the following example which ended up being resolved by the Information Commissioner's Office.[97] The requester asked for 'a copy of all messages to and from members of the departmental press team, of rank senior media relations officers and above, and ministers of the department concerning … [followed by a list of various things]'. So, does that include messages from one member of the departmental press team to another? And does it also include messages from one minister to another? Or does it only cover messages between the departmental press team and a minister? The Cabinet Office maintained only the latter category was covered, the requester said everything was. The ICO eventually backed the requester's interpretation, but this dispute caused a delay of several months.

Whatever else you do, you must make sure that your request presents a clear and precise description of the information you want. But there can be a lot more than that to constructing a good request and avoiding the pitfalls of a bad one.

Some of the advice in this chapter may not be so necessary when you're dealing with a helpful and cooperative FOI team. But for authorities which are defensive or outright obstructive it will make a big difference, as it will for those who, while not hostile, are just determinedly literal-minded and legalistic in their approach (just as the ICO and tribunals will be if the case happens to reach them).

How not to write an FOI request

Let's start by looking at what would be a badly constructed

request. Here's a thoroughly flawed text for a kind of data survey that is often sent to multiple authorities. While I've written it just now, I have seen real examples of the kind of problems it raises in various draft or actual FOI requests (although I've put them into a different context here). How many defects can you spot?

Dear council,

I am researching how councils reply to Freedom of Information and Environmental Information Regulations requests from their own local residents. Therefore please answer the following questions:

How many FOI/EIR requests did you receive in the last five years?

Please provide a breakdown into how many were FOI requests and how many were EIR requests. Please additionally give a breakdown by whether received by post/email/online form on your website/other.

What were they about?

What has been the cost?

How many staff were employed in the council's FOI team in 2022?

In how many cases did the requester ask the council for an internal review in 2022? In how many cases following an internal review did the council release more information in 2022?

Please send me all emails since 2021 between the head of the FOI unit and the authority's chief executive about FOI cases or EIR cases.

What is the maximum number of requests you could process in a year based on current funding?

Many thanks,
FOI requester

One difficulty is that this list of questions could go over the cost limit, and another is that some of this information may already be publicly available, but putting those familiar points to one side, I'm going to focus on the phraseology. Here are some potential issues with how this is phrased:

a) *'their own local residents'*: So that's what is being researched, apparently. But what are the questions about? Are they meant to be read in the light of the introductory statement here and limited to the requests from local residents (which the councils couldn't separate out, so they'd reject it as 'information not held')? Or are the questions simply meant to stand for themselves as expressed?

I have often seen draft requests containing precursory remarks that don't exactly fit with the questions that follow and so complicate the interpretation of the request. Usually it's better to drop the initial explanation and just make sure the questions are right.

b) *'last five years'*: Ambiguous. Does this mean each of the last five years separately? If so, calendar years or financial years? Or is it just asking for one total figure across all the last five years (calendar? financial?) together? Or perhaps the total for the exact five-year period ending on the date of the request?

c) *'breakdown'*: Not comprehensive. What about ones which come under both FOI and EIR? A separate category, or include in the figures for each?

d) *'additionally give a breakdown'*: Unclear. Does this mean take the separate FOI and EIR figures from the previous question and break them down further in this way? Or could it mean go back to the first answer and give a breakdown, without cross-cutting the data by the FOI/EIR division?

This kind of failure to make clear whether breakdowns of figures should be 'serial' or 'parallel' is a common phenomenon.

e) *'about'*: No reliable or comparable basis for answering. There is no well-defined set of subject-matter options.

f) *'cost'*: Far too vague. Cost of what, exactly?

g) *'how many staff'*: Confused and ambiguous. Does this mean the number of stuff who flowed through the team in that year, in other words the total number of individuals who worked there for any length of time during the year? Or does it mean the number working there at a particular point in time? (This is analogous to the distinction economists make between 'flow' and 'stock'). In which case, on what exact date during the year in question? And then does it mean headcount or full-time equivalent? And does it include temporarily unfilled vacancies?

h) *'release more information'*: Not properly considered. The point here is that the answer to this question can't be directly compared to the answer to the previous one, if you want to assess what proportion of reviews result in more information being released. It takes time for reviews to be processed, and so of the number resolved in this period, some would have been requested last year; and of the number requested in this period, some won't be resolved until the next year. Instead, it would need to say, 'Of the internal reviews requested in 2022, how many resulted in the release of more information?'

Neglecting like this to think through in advance how figures can be correctly compared is a frequent occurrence, and many requesters only spot the problems with the data they've collected when they start trying to analyse it.

i) *'about FOI cases or EIR cases'*: Not precise enough. This could be read as suggesting the authority can either reply with the emails about FOI cases, or with the ones about EIR cases. And since when in 2021 - the start of the year, the end of the year?

j) *'maximum number of requests you could process'*: Not recorded information, almost certainly.

How to write a better request

This example illustrates the need for care and rigour in thinking through and phrasing anything but the simplest request. Time spent doing this at the request stage is a good investment. The following principles are useful.

1. Number all your questions.
Be methodical. Don't run multiple questions together under one number. Split the request out into separate components. Every question and sub-question should be given a separate number. It reduces the risk that anything is missed. And it also means you can cross-refer between questions with clarity (eg if asking for

breakdowns of some previous answers).

2. Be clear.

Try to avoid any possible ambiguity or scope for misinterpretation. Think through all the ways your request could be misinterpreted, whether deliberately or inadvertently, and rephrase if necessary to make it clearer. That means you might have to write a longer request, carefully spelling out all the elements of it separately. Do not be lazy about doing this.

Authorities should check or clarify with you anything which is not clear in your request, but some are reluctant to engage in direct dialogue with requesters and so may just assume an interpretation of what you mean which is convenient for them.

3. Be specific.

Try to define the information you are seeking as specifically as you can, so that the material you would obtain is exactly what you want, and it can probably be located and retrieved within the cost limit.

4. Be rigorous.

Think it through carefully. Take care especially when you're trying to obtain some data to compare to other data. Make sure what you are asking for gives you a fair comparison. You can't compare a flow throughout a time period to a stock which is a snapshot at a particular point of time. Make it clear exactly what data you want broken down into sub-totals and in what order you want the breakdowns done (say, first by gender, then by nationality). 'Serial' breakdowns provide more information than 'parallel' ones, but can run into problems of cost and also personal information when the numbers are small.

I've seen so many instances of requests which get confused between different things and treat them as if they are the same, switching terms as if it makes no difference. One classic example is 'complaints' and 'people who complain', which can crop up in a request which might follow the question 'How many people have complained about ...' with 'How many of these complaints were ...' But complaints and complainants are not the same and do not have identical counts. And neither is equal to the number of incidents complained about. One person can submit multiple complaints; one complaint can be made in the name of many people; there may be lots of complaints about one incident, or one complaint covering many incidents, etc.

This also often arises in the context of requests concerning crime statistics to the police. Numbers of crimes, reports of crimes, victims and perpetrators are all different - four crimes involving three victims and two perpetrators could be reported just once. You have to decide in advance which figures you are interested in, ask for those, and ensure that comparisons are like with like.

5. Be accurate.

Think pedantically. Take care to express things correctly. Your request may be interpreted in a very literal manner. In one case the Scottish Government was asked by the BBC for information relating to special advisors 'clearing freedom of information requests made by journalists to the Scottish Government'. They initially replied that nothing was held. It later transpired this was because, as they put it, special advisors may clear FOI 'responses', they don't clear FOI 'requests'.

6. Use the appropriate terminology or jargon.

Across many public authorities words or phrases are given distinctive, tightly defined meanings which may differ from everyday usage, and your request will suffer if you get this wrong. To give one example, in Home Office language 'deportation' and 'removal' from the UK are not the same thing. In these circumstances you have to understand the vocabulary to ensure your request does what you want it to do. Try to use the technical terms that the authority itself employs to describe the relevant information. This particularly applies to bodies which have a lot of their own specialist jargon, such as the police. You might find useful terminology in previous FOI disclosures by the authority, located on a disclosure log or at whatdotheyknow.com.

7. Avoid judgmental or aggressive language.

Use neutral terms, not ones which the public authority won't like.

Once at the BBC we asked the Nursing and Midwifery Council, which regulates nursing and at the time was in the grip of administrative chaos, for data on its 'backlog' of complaints. We got nothing as the NMC insisted there was no 'backlog'. Some time later, when a highly critical official report into the NMC's management was published, the organisation admitted to having what it called a ... historic caseload.[98] We should just have requested the actual figures, without using terminology that was not welcome.

8. Remember the 'recorded information frame of mind'.

Think about what kinds of records are likely to contain information you want, and which parts of which organisation are likely to hold those records, and express your request in line with that.

Suppose you're interested in how a large authority manages its FOI requests and you ask 'how do you process FOI requests?' This is a vague question that could get all sorts of answers, which would vary in how helpful they are. Instead it's better to ask for 'a copy of the policies, instructions and guidance to be followed by staff on how to process FOI requests'. That specifies an identifiable, retrievable set of documentation which should contain what you want.

Similarly, rather than ask an authority 'why' it did something, which is unlikely to be productive, you should try to think of internal reports, emails, papers for and minutes of meetings etc, which can be requested and might help to provide an answer.

9. Beware the cost limit.

A request which is too extensive - either the questions are too broad or there are too many - is likely to go over the cost threshold and be rejected. This is one of the main practical challenges for FOI requesters.

You need to bear in mind how easy or difficult it would be to locate the material you want, and you may have to compromise on what you request. Focus on selected time periods, sections or roles within an organisation, kinds of records, methods for conducting searches, and other constraints that can both obtain useful material and be realistic criteria for the authority to comply with.

What time period is covered by your request? If you don't specify one where it's needed, then it could be that you're effectively asking for information back to the beginning of time, and well, that's probably going to cost too much. So give a time range.

What part of the authority is covered by the request? Again if you're asking for a search of the records of everyone who works there, that's usually another good way to bust the cost limit.

There can be a tricky balance here, as on the outside it's very difficult to assess what can be done within the limit. A narrower request might be more feasible but it might miss some useful material that a broader request would get.

See chapter 7 for detailed advice on the workings of the cost limit and options for adapting your request in response.

10. Beware of exemptions.

There are lots of reasons why information can be withheld, with many depending on what is in the overall public interest. If you haven't considered the possible exemptions, it could be that your request is a waste of time and effort.

In chapter 8 I explain each of the subject-matter exemptions, and how requesters should take them into account and also approach the issue of the public interest test.

11. Beware delay.

Responses to FOI requests are often badly delayed, and sometimes there is little you can do to prevent this. However, if serious delay would be a particularly bad problem for you, you can try to minimise the likelihood of this. Narrower requests should be answered more speedily. This would probably mean paring back your request to just its simplest elements which are easiest to answer, and omitting any broader questions which would involve more complex searches. You also particularly want to avoid asking for any information which would fall under a qualified exemption and lead to extensions to the deadline for a public interest test to be assessed. You should also make sure you're not asking for something on which an external body is likely to be consulted (for example, as the original supplier of the information), since that is another cause of significant delay.

12. Cover different angles.

Bear in mind that some of your questions might be answered but not others, and it can be difficult to predict which in advance. It could be because some information is not held, the structure of the authority's records system makes locating it unfeasible within the limit, the request hits an unexpected problem with an exemption, or for some other reason.

You may therefore want to approach the topic from a number of angles, while of course trying not to exceed the cost limit.

So in terms of numerical data, this could include asking for a range of figures: totals; mean, median and mode; numbers of instances within certain specified bands; details of the several best or worst instances; etc. As for numerical breakdowns, it's very difficult to know at what level of detail your request will be rejected as involving personal information. So it's worth asking for the high-level breakdowns first, and then the increasingly detailed ones, until this obstacle arises, as opposed to just asking for the very detailed figures.

Often you will want at least three years' figures, to provide some historical context. Two years' data doesn't tell you whether this year is unusual or last year's was.

13. Ask everyone relevant.

If the information is held by multiple authorities, don't just ask one of them. So if you want copies of communications between two public authorities, ask them both. Experience shows that you often receive different material, which can be due to variations in attitudes to openness, views on the sensitivity of the information, administrative efficiency, records retention practices, or ability to locate stuff.

Similarly if you want communications between the UK government and a foreign one, and the other country also has an FOI system, ask both.

And think about whether other public authorities might also have been passed the information you want. Could the authority involved have been required to report it to a regulatory body or central government?

14. Take care over timing the request.

Sometimes a little patience is a good idea. Your request will probably be answered on the basis of the information held by the authority at the time it is received.[99] Certain kinds of requesters often respond to a controversial action or event by immediately submitting an FOI request connected to it. But public authorities frequently create more information in the wake of a contentious event - emails are sent, discussions are held, reports are written. Requests can be more productive if you wait to allow some time for a period of internal reaction to whatever has happened, and then ensure your request covers that material too.

On the other hand, don't wait too long. You might find documents are deleted, not least because of common policies of auto-deletion for emails after say three or six months.

15. Be concise.

There is no point padding a request out with extra verbiage about your motives and intentions, or the requirements of the law, and so on, unless it is for some useful purpose. What an FOI officer dealing with a flow of incoming requests wants to read is not a lot of waffle of little interest, but simply a clear and concise statement of the information being sought.

Remember you don't have to provide any explanation for why you want the information, any justification for releasing it or any statement about what you are going to do with it. And normally I don't. The important thing is to describe clearly what you want, without detracting from that. Sometimes public authorities will focus on particular aspects of any explanation or justification and then misinterpret or even ignore part of the request.

However I do occasionally make exceptions to this.

Firstly, if there is an argument in favour of disclosure which I think the authority might not be aware of for some reason. One possibility is a recent or obscure decision from the ICO or a tribunal which is helpful for me and which the authority's FOI team might not have noticed. Another example would be where I know other authorities have already released equivalent information and pointing this out. Theoretically this shouldn't make any difference, as each authority has to decide for itself, but in practice authorities are frequently influenced by whether comparable bodies are releasing similar material.

Otherwise I don't usually spend time and effort on providing arguments in advance about why certain exemptions don't apply or the balance of the public interest.

Secondly, some less important and local bodies get very few FOI requests and may find it disconcerting to receive one. In this case, depending on what your motivation is, in practice it may be useful and reassuring to explain why you are asking, whether it is part of a broader survey, etc (although legally it should make no difference to how the request is handled).

Some requesters like to include statements about the deadline for replying and other legal requirements. I prefer not to. The FOI officer at the other end knows all that already, and sometimes clearly finds it irritating to be lectured about it. At best it's just a waste of space.

However I do usually include a reference to the authority's duty to advise and assist requesters, as the extent to which this is done is very variable, and I want to stress both that I'm aware of this obligation and that I'm willing to engage in discussion where a request hits practical difficulties such as the cost limit.

I also include a sentence expressing my preference on how I want to receive the information.

16. Keep a standard template.

See the appendix for my standard template for FOI requests. You may want to change it, but it saves time to keep a standard template which you can then adapt as necessary for each use.

Round robins

'Round robins' or batch requests - sending the same request to many public authorities, say to all police forces or to all universities - can be a very valuable use of FOI. If done well, they reveal an overall pattern combined with lots of detail, give a broader context for the information from individual authorities, and enable the contrasting of performance or attributes from different but comparable organisations. However they involve considerable administrative effort during the requesting phase, and then a lot of work to do the analysis.

Before going to these lengths, make sure you need to. For example, check if the authorities involved all have to routinely report the information you want to a central government department or another national public body, and then you might only have to make one request, to that department or body.

Think through in advance how much material you are likely to obtain and what you can do with it. You should only embark on such an exercise if you are confident that you will have enough time and capacity to collate and analyse the substantial amount of data that round robins typically produce.

It is particularly important to get the phraseology correct and precise when you are sending round robins. Firstly, because if you don't, it's a very big waste of time and effort, your own and that of the many FOI officers on the receiving end. Secondly, because you have to take care to ensure that the information really is comparable across the different authorities. If you are only contacting one authority, you might not be bothered whether the information is, say, provided on a financial year basis or a calendar year basis, when you've not specified which you prefer. But send that unspecified request out as a round robin, and some respondents will send you one form of data, others the other form, and the result will be that you've got lots of data which you can't compare and use properly.

With round robins it's also important to ensure that they are composed in a way which fits all the recipient authorities. Sometimes requesters use phrasing which is only correct for a subset of those approached. This is particularly likely when a request is sent to a range of authorities of different kinds. Even authorities in the same sector may use varying vocabulary or abbreviations for the same thing. Try to use a standardised terminology which is universally applicable and clear. But beware of being too generic - you still have to ensure that the request is expressed sufficiently precisely in order to obtain the actual information you want.

Similarly you should check that you are just sending your request to appropriate recipients, as authorities often receive mass-mailed round robins on topics that are not connected to their responsibilities. For example, for parts of the country which have two-tier local government, make sure you know whether the topic of your request comes under county councils or district councils, and only contact the relevant ones.

I strongly recommend that before you send out a large round robin, you do a 'pilot'. Send your request to a very small sample of authorities, between three and six probably (but varied according to what is relevant, eg include large and small, or rural and urban). The replies to this should establish whether they actually hold the information, you have used the right terminology, they can answer within the cost limit, etc, or whether you need to modify the request to make it function properly. It will cause delay on the project by perhaps a month or so, but in my experience in most cases it is well worth doing. Then you can avoid the depressing feeling of having sent all the councils in the country a request that makes no sense and finding your inbox clogged with hundreds of useless replies.

Look out for those authorities which try to push requesters to use online forms rather than submit emails. You may have to go back to them after the initial round robin email to check they are actually processing the request

Authorities of a particular kind may coordinate on responding to round robins, whether formally or informally. In the case of government departments this process has been organised until recently via a unit in the Cabinet Office, the FOI clearing house, but this is to be superseded by another arrangement. Replies from police forces may be coordinated via the National Police Chiefs' Council. Or sometimes FOI officers in similar institutions discuss tricky requests in their informal networks. You should expect this to happen. On the other hand, you may well also experience instances of comparable authorities responding to a round robin request in a widely disparate manner. This could be due to a range of attitudes towards openness, the varying quality of their information storage systems, or different interpretations of the request.

Spreadsheet entries

If you're collecting lots of data via a round robin, you are probably going to put it into a spreadsheet to analyse it. You should try to phrase your request in such a way that it makes the data entry process as simple as possible, minimising the number of keystrokes, not least because any step involves the chance of introducing error.

You will be compiling data received from a variety of sources, and inevitably therefore it will be presented in inconsistent formats if it possibly can be. For example, a question asking 'how long is the average waiting time' for something could produce a series of replies like 'three and a half hours', '3 hrs 30 mins', '3.5 hours', '210 minutes', 'between 3 and 4 hours', and so on. It will help your data entry if you pose your question more precisely and specify the units in which you want the answer - in this case you could state that you would like the time to be expressed in minutes.

One useful option for trying to facilitate the data entry is to send out a blank grid in your request and ask authorities to copy it and fill it out appropriately. If you do this, make sure the grid is laid out in the way which is most convenient for directly copying the cells into your spreadsheet. As a general rule, this would mean just one row of cells (as long as the resulting row is not excessively long) in the order of the columns as you expect to have in the spreadsheet. This is because each authority's data will probably be one row of the spreadsheet, and the data entry task is then the simplest copy-and-paste. But also make sure that the order of your columns is intuitive, to reduce the risk of authorities completing the grid wrongly.

However not all authorities will comply with a request to fill out a grid, and you can't insist that they do so. Some may just give you the data in their own preferred manner of presentation.

PART C: Replies

6. Refusals and redactions

Sending a request is the first stage of the FOI procedure. If all goes well, it could turn out to be the only stage - you find you are rewarded with all the information you wanted. On the other hand, your request might be rejected, either partly or entirely. Then you have to understand the reasons for why this can happen.

If you receive what looks like a refusal, do read it carefully. The legal terminology can be deceptive. For a start, don't get confused between an actual refusal and something which calls itself a 'refusal notice' or refers to information being 'exempt', but is really just a postponement stating the authority needs longer to assess the public interest. When you do get a definite rejection, partial or complete, the options open to you depend very specifically on the justifications given. For example, there's a big difference between the authority saying that retrieving the material would cost too much or saying that disclosing the material would be against the public interest.

Public authorities can't legally dismiss FOI requests simply at their discretion or for some arbitrary reason. Nor can they place material outside the reach of FOI by simply labelling it as 'not subject to FOI' or similar, despite the occasional futile and ill-informed attempt to do so.[100] Requests can only be turned down on the basis of the specific grounds stated in the legislation.

If the authority decides not to supply some or all of the information requested, then its response is called a 'refusal notice' and has to meet some minimum legal requirements. In nearly all cases this includes explaining why the request has been declined and indicating the legal exemption(s) invoked, if applicable. It also has to provide details of the internal review procedure and the right to complain to the ICO.[101]

When valid justifications for non-disclosure cover some but not all of the information requested, authorities should just withhold or redact that material. They are not allowed to keep back everything in a blanket manner, although some have a tendency to do this. If you suspect this is happening because the authority's arguments seem unlikely to apply to everything, it makes sense to ask for an internal review. As the ICO's guidance for authorities states, 'you cannot withhold the entire contents of a document because it contains some information that is exempt. You still have a duty to communicate all the disclosable information in the document to the requester.'[102] Public authorities should not redact a sentence when only a word has to go, or redact a paragraph when only a sentence has to go.

Where information has been redacted, the ICO advises authorities to 'provide as much meaningful information as possible. For example, when redacting names you may still be able to give an indication of the person's role, or which pieces of correspondence came from the same person.' However, this is not always followed by authorities.

The ICO also says that authorities should state 'if possible' which exemption has been relied on for which item or segment withheld.[103] Many authorities will do this, linking exemptions to titles of entire documents withheld or particular passages. If this hasn't been done, you can ask for it. But providing such a list as part of a refusal is not a legal requirement.[104]

Thus in a redacted response to your request you might have received virtually everything apart from a few minor deletions, covering say the identity of some junior officials. Or you might have been sent a reply with a small amount of material en clair but containing pages entirely blacked out,[105] in a manner rather reminiscent of the iconic Kazimir Malevich painting, Black Square.

I once saw Black Square in an exhibition at the Tate Gallery. It may have shocked audiences when first displayed in St Petersburg in 1915, but any frequent FOI requester of today will find its entirely black canvas sadly familiar. The academic Professor Philip Shaw has described the painting as a 'grand refusal' inspiring in viewers 'a feeling of pain brought about by the breakdown of representation'. I can concur with this verdict, while not finding myself fully in agreement with the professor's subsequent remark that this experience will be followed by 'a powerful sense of relief, even elation, at the thought that the formless or massive can nevertheless be grasped as a mode of reason'.[106]

Whether or not the formless can truly be grasped as a mode of reason, in the more prosaic world of FOI law there are some important points to bear in mind in deciding how to respond to a partial or complete rejection. Your decision must be based on a careful reading of what the refusal notice says. They vary greatly in their level of detail and plausibility, not to mention the validity of their mode of reason.

There are two broad categories of refusals. The first are 'procedural refusals', which stem from the requirements of the process. Those in the second set depend on the nature of the information itself, involving particular exemptions laid down in the FOI Act.

Most of the time as a requester you won't need specific knowledge of these exemptions. Don't think you need to know all about them before making a request. You ask for the information you want, and it's up to the authority to apply them correctly. But if your request is rejected and you want to challenge that, then you will need to understand the relevant exemptions.

7. Procedural refusals

The most common form of procedural refusal is on the basis of cost. Other rejections that fall within this category are when the authority says the information is not held, or the request is dismissed as repeated or vexatious.

Cost limit

One of the most frequent reasons for a request to be turned down is that the process of retrieving the information would be too expensive. The operation of the cost limit is one of the trickiest and most frustrating aspects of the FOI system for requesters.

In some cases it should be obvious that to get all the information you want would go beyond the limit as it stands. Asking an authority for 'all the information you hold' on a particular topic is very likely to cost too much. And I have to admit that in the first few months of FOI being in force in 2005, before the workings of the system had become clear, I put in some requests that today seem absurd to me because of the wide range of material they demanded. I now realise you would only need to read a request like one of those to see it's not going to be feasible within the cost constraint.

On the other hand, when you are outside an authority and you don't know how its record systems are organised or how easily certain material can be located, then in many cases it is very difficult indeed to predict what can or can't be done within the threshold. For requesters this may result in further delays. It also leads to difficult and uncertain trade-offs when phrasing requests, between maximising the information obtained while trying to ensure the request is under the limit and actually answered. Nevertheless, the more you understand how the system works, the better placed you are to do this effectively.

The limits

For cost limit purposes there are two categories of authorities.

UK government departments, the House of Commons, the House of Lords, the Welsh Government, the Senedd, the Northern Ireland Assembly and the armed forces have a limit of £600; for other authorities it is £450.[107] FOI requests that require relevant work in excess of this figure do not have to be answered by public authorities.

However, the regulations on costings also state that the time of anyone involved in the process has to be calculated at a flat rate of £25 per person per hour (completely irrespective of whatever they are actually paid).[108] Since the cost of retrieving records normally consists entirely of staff time, this implies that effectively the law lays down not so much a cost limit as a time limit on the work involved - 24 hours for those authorities with the £600 cap, and 18 hours for the others.

If another organisation such as an external contractor holds the information on behalf of the authority, their personnel time can also only be valued at £25 per hour. Again, it doesn't make any difference how much the authority would actually have to pay the other organisation for the time spent by those employees in retrieving records. In my experience authorities don't always get this correct and instead may refer to the payment they would have to make, so look out for this where relevant. But also note that in some circumstances authorities might have to pay other charges to outside contractors for information retrieval which aren't tied to staff time, and this can be included when estimating costs.

Activities to be counted

It's important to grasp which activities can actually be reflected in the cost calculation, since this has significant implications. Authorities can only take account of the following administrative tasks: establishing whether the information is held and then locating, retrieving and extracting it.[109] So crucially the calculation cannot include any time spent on considering or discussing or consulting with others on whether the material should be released. However much time would be spent on this, it doesn't affect whether the request would go over the cost limit. Nor, equally crucially, can it involve time devoted to redacting information from a document.

This has been confirmed by a High Court case.[110]

The point about redaction has one slightly anomalous minor consequence. If you ask for some material and very reasonably state in your request that, for example, personal details of junior officials can be redacted before disclosure, you have converted that task of redaction into part of the job of extracting the information as you have specified it. Thus the redaction work could then be counted towards the cost limit. For this reason I do not add such a rider to a request, even though I fully expect and don't mind that personal information of this sort would be redacted anyway.

These days most authorities will get it right on which activities they can count towards the cost and only include the ones they are legally allowed to. But even so this can't be guaranteed, and it is well worth being vigilant on this, in case any inappropriate activities have been added which push the request above the limit.

Estimating and challenging

Authorities only have to make an estimate of likely costs, not an exact calculation (which probably couldn't be provided in any case unless they had actually done the full retrieval work involved). According to the government code of practice on FOI, estimates should be 'sensible and realistic'. Public authorities should focus 'on the locations most likely to hold the relevant information'.[111]

The ICO will require an authority to provide 'cogent evidence' that an estimate is realistic if a complaint is received. It must be based on the 'specific circumstances of the case', not on 'general assumptions'. The guidance indicates what the ICO would expect to be told about the authority's planned location and retrieval strategy. This includes whether the estimate is founded on a random or representative sampling exercise covering part of the information requested; the search terms to be used for querying electronic records; how the information is stored; and how many files, boxes, documents, records or emails need to be reviewed.[112]

There is no legal requirement for authorities to tell requesters how an estimated cost has been determined, but some kind of justification will usually be supplied. Given the obligation to provide requesters with 'advice and assistance', explaining an estimate is likely to be part of indicating how a request might be narrowed to come under the limit. This is in line with the recommendations in ICO guidance.[113]

If you receive a refusal based on a cost estimate it's worth checking the reasoning to see if it seems plausible and realistic. This is particularly true when it only exceeds £600/£450 by a smallish amount, so that the use of slightly different assumptions could easily have brought the request under the threshold.

On the other hand, if the estimate reaches well into thousands of pounds, it's much less likely that an alternative view on what needs to be searched or how long certain searches will take would make the request viable.

You can challenge estimates if they seem poorly evidenced or unreasonable. Ask yourself the following questions: Is the arithmetic correct? (This might seem mundane, but you should always check.) Has the authority explained how it would search for the material, and does that make sense? Does it involve unnecessary steps? Has it made unjustified claims about how long a particular task will take? Has it released or proactively published comparable information in the past, and if so, has it explained what is different with this request? And have other similar authorities provided the information within the cost limit? This last point is not a key factor, since possibly the state of this authority's record-keeping system entails that it couldn't do so, but it could be a supporting point that is worth quoting.

However, even when you think you do have good grounds to challenge an estimate, that process can take a long time, especially if you have to complain to the ICO. Compromising on a narrower request which is clearly under the limit may well get you some information more quickly, although it may be only a selection of what you originally wanted. Generally when you are told a request is too expensive, your next step will be to think about how best to reduce its scope.

Note that even once a request is under the cost limit, this can just be the initial stage of getting it answered. It could still be entirely or partially rejected due to the subject-matter exemptions. Where the cost issue arises, an authority will go through the cost estimation procedure first. If satisfied on this, it would then move on to actually retrieving all the material and considering whether the content allows for or prohibits disclosure.

Requests over the limit

When a request exceeds the limit, the authority can still choose to answer it on the condition that the relevant amount is paid by the requester.[114] In this situation the charge would include staff time (which will almost certainly be the main cost), as well as any direct expenses on photocopying etc.[115] However this option is rarely offered. Nearly always the request will be rejected outright. Even if you say you are willing to cover the estimated cost, the authority can still insist on a complete refusal. Unless it has some other motive for wanting the information to be public, an authority will generally be reluctant to process the request. It will probably want to avoid any unnecessary administrative effort, and the sum it can seek from the requester is unlikely to meet the real full expense involved.

Also, if it wanted to do so, an authority could give you the information without making any attempt to charge you anything, despite the cost threshold being exceeded. The limit can be ignored at the authority's discretion. This is extremely rare, but very occasionally an authority does decide to do this, possibly because it's in line with its overall policy stance for the information involved to be made available, it accepts it would serve the public interest, or perhaps it just thinks it would be good for its reputation and avoid bad publicity.

Records management systems

The speed and cost of information retrieval will depend on the often mysterious complexities (even sometimes to those who work there) of how a public authority's record-keeping is managed.

This can range from the comparatively orderly and systematic to the hopelessly chaotic. Authorities will have a range of information systems for different categories of data. Some may be disorganised, dispersed, badly catalogued and possess inadequate search functionality. Often the process of locating material needs the experience and expertise of FOI officers as to what is usually kept where or by whom, and relies on the knowledge, recollections or personal record-keeping practices of individual staff members.

If you want an illustration of all this, here's one of my favourites - a request to the Foreign Office for various items of information to do with the former US national security operative, Edward Snowden. Lengthy email exchanges among officials handling the request included the following. One asks colleagues to 'search your P drives and Outlook (including PST files)', adding 'I'll cover the S drive, iRecords, high classification and paper files separately'. Another official responds: 'In terms of the paper files, all of IPD central policy files from 2011 are stored in a cupboard which I can open up for you ... there appears to be nothing titled Snowden. We do have some more vague titles e.g. "FOI" which you may want to have a look at.' During subsequent discussions one official asks another to search a shared drive that the first one doesn't have access to; a different official states 'Nil return from me – that might sound hard to believe but I shifted all my emails to the Snowden file which was then transferred to your team'; and another official who may have found some potentially relevant documents invites the coordinator of the response to call 'so I can take you to the one and only machine' on which they are apparently stored.[116]

This request was actually answered, but no one without a very good understanding of Foreign Office file keeping could possibly have a clue as to whether all this record retrieval activity could be completed within a total of 24 hours.

Or to take another example, in a recent case at the ICO, the Cabinet Office listed ten different substantial categories with voluminous content within its record systems that would require separate searching to comply with a wide-ranging request (whose initiator apparently intended it to prove simply that no relevant information was actually held).[117] While this may not be impressive in terms of the quality of records management and convenient information retrieval, it is nevertheless indicative of the reality of the process.

So everything depends on the authority's record-keeping policies and how they are implemented. One frustrating result is that authorities with badly organised records may reject requests that can be answered easily by their better administered counterparts who can locate material quickly and simply. As an FOI requester you soon learn not to be surprised by how some police forces, for example, insist it would be a complex and prohibitive task costing thousands to retrieve information which other police forces manage to find speedily without any difficulty at all.

Implications for requesting

The fact that it is so hard to assess what can be done within the cost limit when you are outside an organisation and not familiar with its record systems is a major practical problem for FOI requesters. It may take a lot of careful thought and judgment, plus sometimes some lucky guesswork, to craft a request which covers a good chunk of what you want but can also be answered within the cost constraints.

If you have enough time, you can start by putting in a broad and ambitious request, on the basis that if it's over the limit, you can narrow it down.

The authority should provide 'advice and assistance' on the best practical ways for doing this - whether that it is curtailing the time frame, the sections of the organisation involved, the range of subject-matter, the sort of documents, etc. In line with the government code of practice, authorities should help requesters to 'reframe or refocus their request'.[118] It is not sufficient for an authority to simply tell the requester to have another go without offering any advice on options.[119] However, it's not up to the authority to solve the problem for you. In the words of the First-tier Tribunal, an authority is not obliged to go so far as to provide 'a menu, or a price list, for retrieval of the various types of information it may hold'.[120]

Authorities generally make an effort to suggest something, but the quality and specificity of any advice you may receive varies considerably, from extremely helpful to minimal and more or less worthless. While it can be a good idea to be ambitious initially and compromise if necessary, either with the benefit of useful guidance from the authority or without, it might not advance matters much and it does introduce delay. A narrowed-down formulation constitutes a new request which starts another 20-working-day period from the beginning.

Requests can in some cases be pushed over the cost limit by the proposed use of excessive and disproportionate search methods. Authorities often take the view that once you have stated what you want in your request, the search strategy is up to them. Nevertheless, it can be worth asking what keywords they were planning to use and which systems or files they were planning to search - so that you can say you would be happy with only part of this being done.

If you have a phone conversation about the interpretation or variation of a request, which may well be a good idea, then afterwards either you or the authority should confirm the conclusion in writing, so that there is a clearly agreed written outcome.

Otherwise there are some approaches you can adopt with the hope of getting it right first time. The goal to have in mind is to maximise the chance of getting a good proportion of what you want, while minimising the effort and time involved for the authority locating stuff. This is a very tricky trade-off. Tackling this well is part of having that 'recorded information' frame of mind, and involves considering which documents are both likely to contain useful material and are also more easily locatable.

Generally the points to focus on are the choice of (a) which unit, team or individuals within the organisation to target; (b) the kind of records to seek; (c) the time period to select.

For example, one technique I have used successfully on more than one occasion is to ask the Foreign Office for copies of communications between the Foreign Office in London and the British embassy or high commission in another country, which relate to a particular topic and are within a particular time frame. The advantage of this is that it selects documents which are both easily identifiable and retrievable, and also informative - they should contain significant and genuine reporting and discussion of important developments. It's a way to define and obtain a fruitful slice of the mass of records held by a public authority.

The same desirable criteria can also apply to asking for briefings provided to government ministers, although they would tend to be more formal in tone and content. You should think creatively about other ways to achieve the same end.

Keep in mind how searches for the information you're seeking would realistically be conducted. You might have to adapt your request to fit with practical considerations.

Say you ask an authority for emails received from people who are linked to a particular external organisation. The authority might reject this on the basis it can't check if every email correspondent with a gmail address etc is connected to that organisation. Instead you could ask for emails received from people with that organisation's domain name in their email address. You'll miss those who correspond via gmail accounts and so on, but at least you may feasibly get something.

Further useful tactics can include stating that you only want electronic records searched and not the much more time consuming business of going through any paper ones. And, rather than describing your request via its subject matter which could then require all sorts of complex searches, you could just specify simple searches you want conducted - eg, ask for the full text of all records created between one date and another which contain specific terms or keywords, although you would probably also have to specify the record system(s) you want searched.

Ironically it can even be the case occasionally that a wider request is more likely to get under the cost limit than a narrower one. For example, this can happen where the wider request is simply and obviously demarcated as a collection of material, but the narrower alternative requires the authority to work through the contents of individual records to check if they are relevant. In other words, if you ask for all emails between X and Y within a time period, that should be easy to locate and retrieve. If you ask just for those emails between X and Y which are about topic Z - and there are no simple keywords which will pick out the topic Z stuff - then someone would have to read all the emails to see which are about Z, and that could go over the limit. If you put in the wider request and it succeeds, it leaves you to read them all to find the ones about Z - but that's taking up your time, not theirs. It's all a matter of thinking through how records might be organised and retrieved.

In general, often there will be a significant element of chance involved in what is the best strategy, given that requesters are operating under uncertainty as to what is a feasible request that fits with how records are managed. It is sometimes just a matter of luck whether a broader request, which is potentially more productive but is more likely to go over the cost limit, is better or worse than a narrower one, which might miss something valuable but is more likely to get an answer of some kind.

One tactic that requesters sometimes try is to ask authorities to work through a request in a specified order of priority, or chronologically through a time period, and keep searching until they hit the cost limit, then stop and respond with whatever information has been retrieved so far. Some authorities will take a pragmatic approach and may agree to do this. This is most likely when the searching priority and process is clear, the authority is reasonably happy for the material involved to be made public, and/or it thinks that if it doesn't do the searches now, it will just have to do them in future in response to another, narrower request from you. And if you have firmly decided on how you want to frame your request but you fear it might go over the limit, there's no harm including this suggestion in case it does come in useful. If you do this for a request containing several questions, then for clarity you should list and number your questions in your order of priority for answering.

However there is no legal basis for requesters to insist on this process, and authorities are fully entitled to refuse to comply.[121] The legal position is that a request for information sets out the information being sought, and if answering that would go over the cost limit, then answering it would go over the cost limit, and it can therefore be completely rejected.

Similarly, if dealing with any one part of a request would exceed the limit, the public authority can refuse to answer the entire request. Again, depending on the circumstances and the incentives they face, some authorities may well be pragmatic and provide responses to the parts which are answerable within the limit. But they are under no legal obligation to do so.

Aggregation

You can't evade the cost limit by splitting a request into several part requests and sending them in separately. For cost purposes, authorities can aggregate requests received within 60 working days from the same person which 'relate, to any extent, to the same or similar information'.[122] Nor can you escape the limit by dividing a request between a number of requesters who each send in a component of it. Authorities can also aggregate requests received within 60 working days which 'relate, to any extent, to the same or similar information', where the requests are made 'by different persons who appear to the public authority to be acting in concert or in pursuance of a campaign'.[123]

The use of the phrase 'to any extent' in determining whether requests cover 'similar information' means that this provision is far-reaching and will probably catch almost any questions which are linked in subject-matter.

Nevertheless, authorities can't aggregate requests from the same person (or a group of people acting together) where they are about entirely different topics. If you do want to make a number of unconnected requests to an authority, you should make sure to put them in different emails, to reduce the risk that the authority tries to aggregate them for its cost calculations.

Authorities also can't aggregate a request that has to be considered under the Environmental Information Regulations with one that falls under FOI, even if there is some subject-matter connection.

Information 'not held'

One sometimes puzzling response to an FOI request is to be told that the public authority does not have the information you have asked for. The more helpful authorities may provide some kind of explanation or justification, such as indicating how this kind of information is not actually relevant to their functions, or stating when and why material was deleted, or at least outlining what searches they conducted to look for it. The less helpful ones may simply state the information is not held and leave it at that. However, ICO guidance does tell authorities that 'it is good practice to explain, if you can, why you consider that you do not hold the requested information'.[124]

According to the government's code of practice, an authority only has to conduct 'reasonable' searches, concentrating its 'efforts on areas most likely to hold the requested information'.[125] If that process does not find anything relevant then it can reply that the information is not held.

If you receive an 'information not held' reply without any plausible reason given, the first thing to do is re-read your request very carefully and utterly literally to see if you phrased it badly. It's possible that on a narrow interpretation of its wording you did not in fact correctly describe the information you were trying to get.

If this does not apply, and you want to pursue the matter, there are a series of questions you can then put as further requests, including:

- Was the information deleted?
- If so, when?
- Who authorised the deletion of the information?
- What reasons, if any, were recorded for the deletion?
- Was the deletion made in pursuance of the authority's records management policy at the time?
- Please send a copy of the authority's policy (as in force at the time the deletion occurred) on the retention and deletion of records of this kind.

Under the government's code of practice on records management, authorities ought to have a written policy and schedule for the retention and deletion of various categories of records. They should also be able to explain why any information is no longer held, by referring to either a record of its destruction or to a provision in the authority's overall records policy.[126]

Occasionally the situation arises when an authority deletes information after it has been requested under FOI. If the deletion was done 'regardless of the receipt of the request' (possibly say in line with a routine disposal schedule) and within the standard 20-working-day deadline for replying, the authority can then respond saying the information is not held.[127] This doesn't happen very often, but when it does, it naturally tends to make requesters both angry and suspicious. The ICO guidance says it is not 'good practice' for authorities to do this, but it is nevertheless legal.[128]

However if anyone in the authority destroys, conceals or alters any information with the intention of blocking its disclosure under FOI, then that is a criminal offence.[129] Prosecutions have been very rare.

Repeated requests

Authorities are also entitled to reject any request which is 'substantially similar' to a previous one from the same person 'unless a reasonable interval has elapsed'.[130] The question of what is 'substantially similar' depends not on the wording of the request, but on the scope of the information requested - in other words, whether there is a substantial overlap. And what is a 'reasonable interval' will reflect all the circumstances of the case, including the nature of the information involved and how often it changes.[131] Therefore you should try to make sure that a request does not cover much of the same ground as an earlier one, unless there is now likely to be new or different information.

'Vexatious' requests

An FOI request can be dismissed entirely if it is deemed 'vexatious'.[132] It's the request itself which has to be 'vexatious', rather than the requester as a person, although in practice the requester's history of FOI applications and other contact with the authority may well be taken into account.

The FOI Act does not define the meaning of the word, which can be a problematic matter. Many requests are bound to be at least a bit vexing to their recipients. The way that this term is interpreted in the FOI context largely derives from what is usually called the 'Dransfield case'.[133] The eponymous figure is Alan Dransfield, regarded by himself as a 'tireless health and safety campaigner',[134] and by Devon County Council as the sender of correspondence which was 'voluminous', 'continual', 'disproportionate and obsessive', 'an unjustified distraction from the council's core functions', and constituted 'an unreasonable level of harassment'.[135] The particular request in the case related to the topic of lightning protection, one of Dransfield's main concerns, for a pedestrian bridge at the Exeter Chiefs rugby ground.

The Upper Tribunal (UT) said that determining whether a request is vexatious is 'a multi-faceted balancing exercise'. Its ruling accepted that the ICO's criterion of 'whether the request is likely to cause distress, disruption or irritation, without any proper or justified cause' provided a useful starting point; and then identified four factors to be considered in deciding that this request indeed was vexatious (while also stating they were not exhaustive nor a 'formulaic check-list'): the burden on the authority in answering the request, with 'the number, breadth, pattern and duration of previous requests' being part of the context; the motive of the requester; the extent of the request's 'value or serious purpose'; and whether there was evidence of 'obsessive conduct that harasses or distresses staff'.[136]

The Court of Appeal later upheld this decision, its judgment stating: 'The UT was right not to attempt to provide any comprehensive or exhaustive definition. It would be better to allow the meaning of the phrase to be winnowed out in cases that arise … The starting point is that vexatiousness primarily involves making a request which has no reasonable foundation, that is, no reasonable foundation for thinking that the information sought would be of value to the requester, or to the public or any section of the public. Parliament has chosen a strong word which therefore means that the hurdle of satisfying it is a high one'.[137]

In summary, a request is most likely to be refused as vexatious on the basis it has no serious point, it would impose a major and disproportionate burden, it harasses staff, and/or it is intended to cause disruption. However, although this case lays down certain criteria, it still leaves plenty of room for interpretation, meaning there is no specific and rigid test for what is vexatious.

An authority does not have to explain to the requester why it believes a request is vexatious, but it does need to have a justification that it could later provide to the ICO if necessary. In the first few years after the FOI Act came into force, public authorities were often reluctant to deploy 'vexatiousness' as a reason for rejection. One reason was that it's an unfortunate and emotive term which seems insulting and tends to make requesters more vexatious than they were in the first place, prompting time-consuming complaints and appeals. However the ICO has encouraged its usage, which has become more common. This can now impact on reasonable FOI applications, reaching well beyond those requests which are clearly trivial time-wasting or purely one more futile stage in an individual's lengthy and tangled feud with a public authority.

Assuming that you do not have a belligerent history of insulting the staff of an authority, and that your FOI request does actually have a serious purpose to it, you may still find that it can be dismissed as vexatious. In particular, given that time spent on redacting material can't be counted towards costs, public authorities occasionally find themselves in the following position. The requested information can be retrieved within the cost threshold (maybe because it has already been collated for some other reason); but there is a great deal of it, and interspersed within is a substantial quantity of material exempt from disclosure; and it would genuinely take a long time (well over what is otherwise the normal limit) to identify and make the necessary redactions before release. Under these conditions the ICO now tends to be sympathetic to authorities who maintain the request is vexatious because it imposes a 'grossly oppressive burden'.[138]

However such special circumstances are actually rare. Some authorities have taken to asserting compliance with a request would be 'grossly oppressive' along these lines without providing much in the way of supporting justification. This claim does need to be substantiated and should be challenged if evidence is lacking. Furthermore, however onerous responding to a request would be for whatever reason, the public interest in disclosure of the information has to be considered before it can be rejected as vexatious. And vexatiousness should be treated as a 'high bar' to reach.

Nevertheless, if it does seem plausible that your request would entail a very great amount of administrative work while not breaching the cost limit, then it could be pragmatic to accept that and put in a less burdensome request instead. The authority should give you advice and assistance on what would be a narrower and less problematic alternative.

Another kind of request which some authorities like to reject as a speculative 'fishing expedition' and vexatious is one which is not tied to a particular subject but identifies information in a different manner. However there may still be a substantial public interest in such requests, shedding light on the workings and arrangements of an organisation, which has to be taken into account.

For example, one case decided by the First-tier Tribunal involved a request to the energy market regulator Ofgem that was simply for copies of all emails received by the chief executive and another senior member of staff within a specified three-day period. Ofgem refused to answer, dismissing it as a random 'scattergun' approach and a vexatious 'fishing expedition'. However, the FTT upheld the requester's argument that there was a serious purpose and significant public interest in providing 'insight into the operations of Ofgem', and that the burden of answering was not excessive.[139]

If you reasonably think that a public authority is unjustified in dismissing a request on the grounds of vexatiousness, then you should challenge it, asking for an internal review and if necessary complaining to the ICO. But of course please don't pursue authorities with FOI requests which truly are trivial or intentionally disruptive. It's a waste of staff time and public money, and it's bad for the reputation of FOI, which is always under attack from its enemies in officialdom and positions of power.

8. Exemptions

The major obstacles to getting the information you want are usually the numerous exemptions which relate to the nature or subject-matter of the material requested. Assuming your request is within cost, not vexatious or repeated, and involves information that is actually held, these exemptions represent the next hurdle. Some are wide-ranging and crop up frequently, while others are much more specific and only rarely encountered. There is a lot of variation between authorities in terms of which exemptions are most relevant to their work and so are deployed most often.

In this chapter I describe the exemptions and set out some arguments for challenging their use, focusing on points specific to the most important ones. See the next chapter for a general approach to the public interest test.

Qualified and absolute exemptions

In dealing with exemptions it is essential to grasp an important division between two categories - 'qualified' and 'absolute'.[140] Most of the exemptions listed in the FOI Act are qualified ones. For these, the fact that the material comes within the scope of the exemption does not necessarily stop disclosure, and the decision on whether it should be released depends on a further consideration - whether the overall balance of the public interest favours disclosure or secrecy. This is usually called the 'public interest test' or PIT, and is a central and crucial feature of the FOI process.

In the case of the absolute exemptions, which are fewer in number, information is excluded from release just because it falls within the scope of the exemption, and there is no requirement for a public interest test. However some have their own internal criteria which mean that they do not operate in quite the 'absolute' manner often presented.

The term 'absolute' is given in the FOI Act;[141] the term 'qualified' does not actually appear in the Act in this context, but it has become the standard terminology in generally accepted use with this meaning throughout the community of those involved with FOI.

If you are disputing the use of a qualified exemption, arguments usually focus around the outcome of the public interest test. In the more difficult situation of objecting to an absolute exemption, you normally have to challenge the claim that the exemption genuinely applies to your request.

Class-based and prejudice-based exemptions

It is also common in FOI circles to draw another distinction within the qualified exemptions, between those which are 'class-based' and those which are 'prejudice-based'. The former are those which apply when the information simply fits within a defined class (eg it relates to the formulation of government policy); the latter only apply when some particular harm or prejudice is likely to be caused (eg disclosure would prejudice relations between the UK and another state). All the absolute exemptions are class-based. These terms are not in the wording of the FOI Act but again are broadly accepted usage.

This distinction is more important for authorities than it is for requesters. In the case of prejudice-based exemptions, the authority has to go through the additional process of determining that harm is likely before the exemption can be used. The ICO will also do this when considering a complaint.

Sometimes as a requester challenging a prejudice-based refusal you might want to argue that there is no likely prospect of any significant negative consequences, and so the exemption is not applicable at all. There is no downside to putting forward this argument. The ICO does sometimes reach this conclusion when an authority's case is especially weak. But in this situation an authority trying to withhold material would surely also lose on the public interest test anyway. If there is no likely resulting harm, then it is virtually certain that a PI test would favour disclosure (unless, on the other side of the scales, the benefit is minimal and even less likely to be significant, in which case there's not much point seeking the information). So the practical impact of this extra condition is very limited. It doesn't affect what kind of FOI requests you should be making.

QUALIFIED EXEMPTIONS

Information intended for future publication (section 22)

This covers information which is held with a view to its publication 'at some future date'. The date does not have to be specified, but withholding the information for however long would be involved, whether fixed or not, has to be 'reasonable'. The authority must have the settled intention of future publication before the FOI request is made. It can't just decide it will publish the material at some later stage in response to getting the request.

Clearly there is room for dispute over what is 'reasonable'. There's a big difference between, say, briefly holding back statistics which are going to be issued in the following week in line with a regular and well-advertised schedule, and hoping to avoid publicity for awkward information for months until a more convenient time arises. In one case I was involved in at the BBC, Arts Council England initially refused to release some figures to us on the grounds that they would be published later - in 18 months' time! We appealed against this in an internal review, and it then backed down and disclosed the data, which (as we suspected) revealed the lack of success of a special ticketing scheme.

The practical difficulty, however, in challenging the use of this exemption is that the process of internal review and then complaint to the ICO, if necessary, will take considerable time (several months, for the ICO) - by which point the material should have been published anyway, except in particularly extreme cases. But it may still make sense to start going down this route, as you probably don't know in advance whether your case would end up as one of the extreme ones where ICO intervention will actually be needed.

There is one particular point which you should always check carefully if section 22 is used. This exemption should only lead to full rejection of your request if all of the exact same information you've asked for has been earmarked for future publication. Authorities sometimes wrongly resort to this exemption to dismiss requests, when really what is already planned is publication of just some of the material or perhaps a summary, or information which is similar or connected or overlapping but not actually the same.

Section 22 is also sometimes deployed incorrectly when the authority expects to publish something along the lines of the requested material but has not yet identified exactly what, perhaps because it intends to consider keeping some of it secret under other exemptions. This exemption can only be used to withhold information which has already been determined as intended for publication.

Research (section 22A)

This exemption was added to the FOI Act in 2014, following a lobbying campaign by universities.[142] It covers information derived from a continuing programme of research which will lead to a report being published and where early publication would be prejudicial to the interests of those involved. In this special case of a research programme, the information to be published eventually does not have to be the exact same material that was requested for the exemption to be valid. Once the research programme has been completed and the final reports have been published, then the exemption is no longer applicable.

National security (section 24)

While information relating to specific security bodies comes under the absolute exemption laid down in section 23 of the law (see below), section 24 is a qualified exemption for material not related to any of those organisations but which must be made exempt for the purpose of 'safeguarding national security'. The term 'national security' is not defined in the FOI Act. According to caselaw it includes the security of the UK's people and the protection of democracy and the legal and constitutional systems of the state, as well as military defence.[143] (Defence also has its own specific exemption, section 26).

Section 24 can sometimes be deployed in conjunction with section 23, to leave it ambiguous whether the information requested actually relates to a listed security body or has some other implication for national security. This is an exception to the rule that a public authority must make clear which exemption(s) it is relying on, and is a form of response allowed by the ICO.[144]

Defence (section 26)

This covers information which could harm national defence or the effectiveness of the UK armed forces or other forces they are cooperating with (although note that UK special forces are separately treated as absolutely exempt from FOI under section 23). It is not limited to material actually held by the Ministry of Defence or the armed forces themselves, although not surprisingly they are frequent users of this exemption.

International relations (section 27)

This section refers to information that could prejudice the UK's interests abroad, or relations between the UK and another state, an international court or an organisation which has states as members. It also extends to 'confidential information' obtained from another state or international court or organisation. Note that the interests of the UK as a whole would have to be undermined by disclosure, not just the international links of the public authority involved.

Decisions on this exemption by the ICO and tribunals have reflected the fact that public opinion and politicians in some other countries may react in a hostile way to disclosures that would not be so sensitive within the culture of the UK.[145]

Relations within the UK (section 28)

This covers information where disclosure may damage relations between any of the UK Government, the Scottish Government, the Welsh Government and the Northern Ireland Executive.

There is a parallel provision in the Scottish FOI Act which would apply to information of this kind held by a Scottish public authority.

The economy (section 29)

This relates to information which could undermine the economic interests of the UK or any part of it, or the financial interests of the UK Government or the devolved administrations. The threat would have to be to the economy of the UK or a geographical area, not just to the private interests of a particular company.

Investigations and proceedings (section 30)

This exemption has two parts. Firstly, it broadly covers information which has been held at any time by an authority for a criminal investigation or proceedings which that authority has the power to conduct. This is most often used by the police but can apply to some other bodies such as regulators. Secondly it covers material held for a wider range of investigations where it 'relates to the obtaining of information from confidential sources'. As well as criminal matters this could include for example investigations into other forms of misconduct, the need for regulatory action, or the causes of accidents.

The use of this exemption by authorities depends on their specific legal functions. If an authority (other than a police force) quotes the section 30 exemption, it is worth checking carefully on which subsection(s) it is referring to and whether its argument is truly relevant, given the particular circumstances of the case and the authority's powers and responsibilities.

Law enforcement (section 31)

This exemption stipulates a long list of topics related to law enforcement. They include the prevention of crime, the apprehension of offenders, the administration of justice, the collection of taxes, the operation of immigration controls, and security in prisons. It also covers material which could undermine an authority exercising its functions for any of the following: investigating non-compliance with the law, investigating improper conduct, establishing the need for regulatory action, ascertaining competence in the management of companies or authorised professions, establishing the cause of an accident, protecting charities against misconduct or loss, and securing the health and welfare of people at work.

While many of these are very wide-ranging, a public authority using this exemption should make clear which particular part of this section it is invoking, and you should check that it does genuinely apply.

Information can only come under this section if it does not fall within section 30. However the two exemptions are closely connected and are often deployed in tandem, to cover different elements of information tied to one request. If you make FOI requests about alleged misconduct or scandals, then you are likely to encounter the use of this pair of exemptions.

Audit functions (section 33)

This is a very specialised exemption. It covers information which would damage the work of a public authority in auditing other authorities or assessing their efficiency in the use of resources. It only applies to authorities with appropriate audit or inspection functions, such as the National Audit Office and some regulatory bodies like Ofsted or the Care Quality Commission. It can't be used by the authorities which are the subject of the audit or assessment, and it does not apply to internal audits.

Formulation of government policy (section 35)

This is a particularly significant and far-reaching exemption which rapidly becomes very familiar to anyone making FOI requests connected to government policy.

It applies to UK government departments, the Welsh Government and the Northern Ireland Executive,[146] and takes in four important categories of material: a) information relating to the formulation or development of government policy; b) ministerial communications; c) the provision of advice by government Law Officers; d) information on the operation of ministerial private offices.[147]

One point that crops up occasionally is that government departments include executive agencies such as HM Courts and Tribunals Service, as well as non-ministerial departments like HM Revenue and Customs. So theoretically they are entitled to deploy this exemption, although in practice they are more likely to be involved in the implementation of policy rather than its formulation. However, the exemption does not extend to non-departmental public bodies, of which the Information Commissioner's Office would be an example. It's often hard to know the legal status of a particular 'arm's-length body', as they are called, without directly checking it.[148]

Policy formulation

The first exempt category - policy formulation and development - is especially consequential. The question of what exactly comes within it has been contentious in many cases.

The ICO very importantly distinguishes 'formulation and development' from policy 'implementation', which is not covered by the exemption.[149] Although the two concepts can be hard to disentangle, policy formulation is more likely to involve devising a 'framework', while detailed arrangements, minor adjustments and case-specific issues would be matters of implementation. Very often once the key decisions are taken policy then moves from the 'formulation and development' phase into an 'implementation' phase.

The ICO guidance also contains some key indicators for determining what counts as making 'policy': the government intends to achieve a particular external outcome, the effect of the decision involved is wide-ranging, and it is made or at least signed off by a minister.[150] It does not include purely presentational matters, the explanation of existing policy, or issues of internal administration.

Government departments are often quick to invoke section 35 in relation to the policy process. When faced with this as a requester, it is worth thinking carefully about whether the exemption really is applicable in the light of these considerations and the ICO's guidance, and challenging this if it isn't. In particular, ask yourself if the material is purely about implementation (and thus outside the exemption) rather than formulation. Departments frequently fail to make this distinction themselves.

In terms of factual information used for policy-making, section 35 also includes a rider that in assessing the public interest, 'regard shall be had to the particular public interest in the disclosure of factual information which has been used, or is intended to be used, to provide an informed background to decision-taking'.[151]

Safe space and chilling effect

Assuming the exemption is genuinely relevant to the request, you will then be involved in arguments about determining the overall balance of the public interest. The points at issue will generally include preserving a 'safe space' for ongoing internal discussion in private and preventing a 'chilling effect' that would deter free and frank debate in future. This means assessing how much the disclosure of the particular information requested will affect these factors, and weighing that up against the benefits to the public interest of the information being available to all.

The ICO and tribunals have considered many such cases over the years. Some have been decided in favour of disclosure, and some against. This is not surprising since the outcome has to be based on the individual circumstances of each case. This can make it hard to predict how the ICO or First-tier Tribunal will rule on a particular request - especially for requesters, who obviously haven't seen what the requested information actually contains.

It is clearly accepted that there is a public interest in maintaining a safe space and avoiding a chilling effect. It is equally well accepted that these considerations are not overwhelming and they can be overridden when the benefits of disclosure are sufficiently great. Given this, the extent of these benefits can be a very important consideration. That will be influenced by factors like the significance of the policy, the numbers affected and how they are impacted, the level of any public concern, the advantages of greater public understanding of why the decisions were made, and the opportunity for public debate, as well as the general contribution of accountability and scrutiny.

Since the specific details of any individual case are vital to the outcome, there is limited value to quoting precedents. However there are some general principles enunciated by the ICO which can be useful to requesters:[152]

(i) Authorities can't have a blanket policy of non-disclosure for certain types of information.

(ii) Arguments for secrecy must focus on the effect of disclosing the particular information in question, not on the effect of routine disclosure of that type of information.

(iii) The ICO is also not keen on 'generic chilling effect arguments about unspecified future policy debates' (and nor are tribunals).

(iv) Civil servants are expected to be impartial and robust when giving advice, and not easily deterred from expressing their views by the possibility of future disclosure. This particular point is frequently stated in ICO decisions. To quote just two recent examples: 'As the Commissioner has commented previously he considers ministers and advisors to be robust in their positions and not easily influenced by disclosures to inform the public.'[153] And: 'The Commissioner expects civil servants – particularly senior ones – to be individuals of robust character. They should not easily be dissuaded from providing frank and candid assessments to ministers, in the best traditions of the civil service.'[154]

It is also worth noting that civil servants in any case have to abide by the Civil Service Code, which requires that they 'provide information and advice, including advice to ministers, on the basis of the evidence, and accurately present the options and facts'.[155]

(v) It is possible that the threat of disclosure can in fact lead to better quality advice and more robust, well-considered decision-making in future.

(vi) Once policy has been finalised (or a short time afterwards), a safe space for deliberation will no longer be required and this consideration will carry little weight. This means the timing of the request and the stage of policy-making at that point can be crucial (rather than the situation at the later point when the ICO might consider the case). The chilling effect may still be relevant, but it will become more speculative and less convincing as time passes.

(vii) There is likely to be significant public interest in allowing public scrutiny of details of policy (including risks and alternatives) while the policy is still in the public consciousness.

(viii) Arguments that disclosure would lead to less detailed record-keeping for future discussions will carry little weight, since departments are expected to maintain adequate records.

(ix) In cases where the information would not actually add much to public understanding, disclosure can still carry some benefit as it may remove suspicions of 'spin'.

(x) If only certain interest groups have had access to influence government policy, then this will increase the public interest in transparency, especially when policy is still being formulated and there is still opportunity for others to present views.

(xi) One further point can be added to this list. Officials and ministers are well aware of the FOI law already and therefore the possibility that their discussions will be publicly disclosed where this is in the public interest. This factor is acknowledged in some other ICO guidance.[156]

Ministerial communications

The safe space and chilling effect arguments can also apply for the part of this exemption to do with ministerial communications, which means communications between ministers (including their private secretaries) and takes in the proceedings of cabinet meetings and cabinet committees.[157] Here there is an additional factor which tends to go against disclosure - maintaining the convention of collective ministerial responsibility, which requires that ministers present a united front in public and their differences of view are hidden. But this point won't apply when the information does not actually reveal the opinions of individual ministers.

The ICO generally attaches a lot of weight to this principle.[158] However it is not completely decisive. For example, ministers can themselves undermine it by revealing their divergent opinions. After a process lasting over five years and a tribunal decision in my favour,[159] I succeeded in obtaining the minutes of the 1986 cabinet meeting where Michael Heseltine dramatically resigned as defence secretary, the first time cabinet minutes were disclosed under FOI.[160] This was partly because several ministers had presented their own personal accounts of the cabinet discussion in their memoirs.

Statistical information

The section 35 exemption is significantly weaker in its application to statistical information. Statistical material 'used to provide an informed background' relating to policy formulation or ministerial communications is no longer covered once the relevant policy decisions have been taken.[161] But sometimes statistics are still withheld on the basis that they remain relevant to other policy issues which are yet to be decided.

Legal advice

The content of legal advice from government Law Officers will fall under both section 35 and the section 42 exemption for legal professional privilege. However the phrasing of section 35 also allows departments to exempt whether or not a Law Officer has been asked to advise on a particular topic. The ICO and tribunals normally give substantial importance to protecting legal confidentiality within a public interest test.

Effective conduct of public affairs (section 36)

This sometimes functions as a kind of catch-all exemption which can trap stuff that falls outside the others. In part it is extremely broad. It also involves a special procedure for determining whether the exemption is relevant to the material requested.

Firstly, it covers information which could damage the convention of collective responsibility for the UK Government, or the work of the Welsh cabinet or Northern Ireland Executive. In most cases however this would usually concern UK or Welsh government policy and fall under section 35 instead.

Secondly, and much more significantly, it covers material whose disclosure would inhibit the 'free and frank' provision of advice or exchange of views. However, note that exchanges which consist of factual information do not constitute 'advice' or 'views' and so are not caught by this.[162]

Thirdly, it covers information where disclosure 'would otherwise prejudice, or would be likely otherwise to prejudice, the effective conduct of public affairs'. This is a remarkably general, ill-defined and far-reaching criterion.

The special procedure is that (except for statistical information) the exemption can be deployed whenever it is 'the reasonable opinion of a qualified person' that one of these criteria applies.[163] So the use of this exemption involves the public authority obtaining what is usually called a 'qualified person's opinion' or QPO.

Section 36 itemises who would be a 'qualified person' for certain public authorities. For government departments, for example, this is a minister. However this list is only partial, and for many categories of authorities it is up to government ministers to designate a particular postholder (or alternatively fulfil the function themselves).[164] There doesn't seem to be any available register of qualified persons since the government ceased updating and publishing one several years ago.[165] However you can usually expect it to be the authority's chief executive, chair, governing body or similar. It's not open to the authority to just choose whoever they want.

In most cases in practice less senior officials will draw up briefing material and probably a recommendation to be presented to the qualified person for the opinion to be signed off.

This procedure can make it easier for authorities to argue that this exemption covers the material requested, since it only needs the qualified person's opinion and not any kind of 'objective' test under the law. The Act does state that the opinion has to be 'reasonable', but a QPO would probably have to be clearly flawed and lacking in justification, emptily formulaic or based on irrelevancies for the ICO to deem it unreasonable. The ICO has to accept that an opinion may be reasonable even if its own view would be different.

In the case of 'statistical information', however, the ICO can decide for itself whether the exemption is applicable, as it normally would for other exemptions.

Section 36 is still (largely) a qualified exemption. The QPO procedure is only relevant to determining whether the exemption is engaged. As with the other qualified exemptions, the next stage is the usual assessment of whether disclosure is overall in the public interest. For this evaluation there is no special role for a 'qualified person' or their opinion. (However in the case of the House of

Commons and House of Lords the exemption is absolute, and the ICO cannot overrule an opinion from the Speaker or the Clerk of the Parliaments.[166])

If you make a request which is considered within section 36 and then refused after a public interest test, it can be worth putting in a further request for the date of the QPO, and a copy of the QPO and all the submissions passed to the qualified person for the purpose of determining the opinion, and connected documentation. The ICO expects to be able to see a record of who gave the opinion, their status as qualified person, the date the opinion was provided, the submission made to the qualified person, a description of the information, a record of the factors the qualified person took into account (for and against), the weight attached to them, and the eventual opinion.[167] Some of this may be held back from you, but it might provide you with useful material to help challenge the refusal.

Occasionally this might also reveal that the authority never bothered to actually obtain a QPO. There are instances where some authorities have invoked section 36 without going through the necessary legal process of approval from a qualified person. In one recent case heard by the First tier-Tribunal, the Cabinet Office did not get a QPO until six months after it issued a refusal notice under section 36, which was therefore legally invalid. It also later turned out that the submission which officials eventually made to the minister was 'factually inaccurate' and misleading.[168] However, where an authority fails to obtain a QPO initially it can nevertheless go through the process later, eg at internal review, and then make use of the exemption.[169]

Relationship to section 35

Section 36 cannot be applied by UK government departments and the Welsh Government on matters where section 35 would be relevant, such as information relating to policy formation.[170] Although exemptions sometimes overlap, in this situation they would have to rely on section 35. For other public authorities, section 35 is irrelevant and section 36 can be used on any issue if one of the specified criteria is met.

So the two sections can never apply at the same time, but in some ways they are parallel in effect. While a government department would handle requests for policy deliberations under section 35, the release of comparable internal discussions may be assessed under section 36 by a different public authority as possibly threatening 'free and frank' advice or exchange of views. The use of section 36 then raises equivalent arguments about a 'safe space' for discussion and any future 'chilling effect'. Therefore many of the points I have made above relating to section 35 are similarly relevant here.[171]

The royal family and honours (section 37)

This exemption has two components, one concerning communications with the royal family, and the other concerning the honours system.

The element relating to the royal family is partly qualified and partly absolute. While information on communications with the current monarch, the heir to the throne and the next in line is absolutely exempt, communications with other members of the royal family or staff in the Royal Household are only subject to a qualified exemption and therefore a public interest test. Note that the Royal Household itself is not subject to FOI, so this refers to material held by other public bodies.

The second part of this section, which covers information on the awarding of honours, constitutes a qualified exemption.

Health and safety (section 38)

This covers information whose release would endanger the physical or mental health or safety of any individual. In my experience its use ranges from the justified and important to protect individuals at risk of real and serious threats, to cases where a link between the information and anyone's health or safety is very tenuous and doubtful. Where an authority uses this exemption, you should think through carefully whether there really is a plausible causal connection between releasing the material and the alleged harmful consequences.

Public authorities have been known to invoke this exemption on the basis that disclosure would make someone distressed. But the

ICO guidance makes clear that for mental health to be imperilled, there must be 'a greater impact than causing upset and distress'.[172]

However as a requester it can sometimes be difficult to argue against the use of this exemption, when you lack knowledge of the individual circumstances of those said to be endangered. This means you would be particularly reliant on the independent assessment by the ICO and/or tribunals.

Environmental information (section 39)

This refers to environmental information which comes under the Environmental Information Regulations (EIR). In the case of virtually all public authorities, requests for environmental information are handled in line with the EIR rather than the FOI law. The differences are explained in chapter 15. It's not up to you to choose which system you want - if your request fits within the EIR then it has to be dealt with in that way.

Theoretically you should get a 'refusal' under FOI after a public interest test, while being told that the request is being assessed under the EIR. In the past I have come across authorities which did this. However it has clearly got potential to confuse requesters who do not understand why they are being informed simultaneously that their request is both being rejected and considered. The bulk of authorities now seem to have adopted a pragmatic stance of not following this procedure. But if it does happen in response to a request of yours, then that's why.

Legal professional privilege (section 42)

This exemption involves material covered by 'legal professional privilege', which comprises legal advice and connected documents. The ICO and the courts tend to attach a lot of weight to protecting the confidentiality of legal advice, so it can be difficult to overturn the use of this exemption. Nevertheless this is still a qualified exemption subject to the public interest test, and there are some cases where the ICO or a tribunal has ruled that disclosure is overall in the public interest.

In one case of mine, a tribunal decided that extracts from

discussion of legal advice for the House of Lords Appointments Commission should be released to me in the public interest.[173] In another case a tribunal ruled that a legal opinion obtained by the public transport operator Merseytravel should be disclosed. Its judgment was influenced by 'the amounts of money involved and numbers of people affected, ... and crucially the lack of transparency in the authority's actions and reasons'.[174]

Legal professional privilege attaches to the content of legal advice, and not to the mere fact of asking for it. However if you are interested in whether legal advice was obtained, be careful how you phrase such a request. If you simply ask an authority 'did you get legal advice about your decision to do this?', that would not be blocked by section 42. But if you ask 'did you get legal advice that your decision to do this was lawful?', that implies something about what the advice said, and so would be caught by this section.[175]

Commercial interests (section 43)

This covers trade secrets and information whose disclosure could harm the commercial interests of either the public authority itself or some other organisation.

The exemption often crops up in the context of outsourcing and companies which provide a service on behalf of a public authority. This is a frequent subject for FOI requesting. Large sums of public money may be involved, and accountability and transparency are important, which should be significant factors in assessing the public interest.

Where the commercial interests of an external organisation may be affected, authorities should not just speculate on the probable impact of disclosure but should consult that organisation and obtain evidence of any concerns. This is often the source of delay. However in the end the authority has to take the decision on what is in the public interest, and it does not have to abide by the views of anyone it has consulted.

Confidentiality clauses in contracts can't be used to guarantee information will not be released under FOI. The authority still has to consider any FOI request on its merits in the light of the overall public interest.

ABSOLUTE EXEMPTIONS

Information accessible by other means (section 21)

This exempts information that is 'reasonably accessible to the applicant' by some method other than making an FOI request. Either it is already public, or there is some other way you can get hold of it.

Note that the information has to be 'reasonably' accessible. Thus if an authority insists that its plans for the building of bypasses are already on display to the general public while in a locked filing cabinet in a disused unlit basement lavatory with a sign on the door warning 'Beware of the leopard',[176] that would not be good enough for compliance with the law.

And it has to be reasonably accessible 'to the applicant'. This is one situation where the FOI system is not 'applicant-blind'. Reasonable accessibility depends on the circumstances of the requester. So, for example, it could depend on where the applicant lives. Records which are available on council premises for personal inspection could be reasonably accessible to someone who lives round the corner, but not to someone who is based hundreds of miles away. Similarly, information is unlikely to be reasonably accessible for most people if it requires some specialist knowledge or expertise to locate it.

However it can include material which you would have to pay for, where the authority supplies the information commercially in line with another piece of legislation or the payment is set in accordance with the authority's publication scheme.[177] This lists categories of material that the authority normally publishes as a matter of routine.

The exemption can also be applied when you would have to obtain the material from another source rather than the authority contacted.

This exemption comes up most frequently when the public authority states the material requested is already in the public domain, whether for a fee or at no cost. In this case the authority must be 'able to provide the applicant with precise directions to the information so that it can be found without difficulty', according to the ICO guidance.[178] In one tribunal case it was held that an authority cannot just 'say to the applicant that the information is somewhere to be found on a large website'.[179] However, according to another tribunal case, section 21 can be applied when it not 'difficult' to find the relevant information on a website but merely 'inconvenient', where it is spread across a number of locations.[180]

Authorities also sometimes deploy this exemption when they say the requested information can be inferred, calculated or otherwise derived from material already public. Whether this is valid would depend on whether the information can actually be reliably obtained in this way and the applicant can reasonably be expected to go through this process.[181]

As with section 22 (on information intended for future publication), section 21 can only be used to reject your request entirely where the information already available contains exactly the same material you have requested, and not just a summary or partial selection or something else which is similar. This point is important, as authorities do sometimes try to use section 21 when the previously published information is actually more general or less detailed or just somehow related or partly overlapping. Legally this is not sufficient for the full request to be dismissed.

Security bodies (section 23)

Information is absolutely exempt if it was supplied by or relates to any organisation which is listed as a security body in this section of the FOI Act. This includes not only the obvious agencies such as the Security Service (MI5), the Secret Intelligence Service (MI6) and GCHQ, but also the tribunals that cover their activities, the special forces within the military and the National Crime Agency, which combats serious and organised crime.

The term 'relating to' tends to be interpreted very broadly by the ICO and tribunals, so that more or less any connection to a security body is sufficient. For example, it is now the case that requests for information about the historical work of police Special Branches, as they were known, are routinely rejected on the grounds that they operated so closely together with MI5 that it is assumed the material comes under section 23.

Nevertheless, where just some of the information requested comes under this exemption, the public authority should still disaggregate material for which any connection to a security agency is too remote for the exemption to apply.[182]

Court records (section 32)

Information which is held because it is contained in documents for use in court proceedings is absolutely exempt. This includes tribunals and coroners' courts. It also applies to public inquiries and arbitration tribunals.

Courts themselves are in any case not directly subject to FOI. The main point of this exemption is to exclude court records that are held by other public bodies. The justification given for this is that it should be up to courts and inquiries to control under what circumstances such documents are made public.

The exemption can only be used when the proceedings are underway or definite steps have been taken to instigate them. Furthermore, it does not apply when the information involved has also been obtained for another purpose apart from the legal proceedings and is still held for that reason.

Note that this exemption does not protect all information relating to courts. Although individual courts and tribunals are not public authorities in terms of FOI, HM Courts and Tribunals Service is covered as an agency of the Ministry of Justice, and it holds administrative information about courts and tribunals that can be requested.

Parliamentary privilege (section 34)

This covers information whose publication would infringe 'parliamentary privilege', a loosely defined set of principles intended to safeguard the independence of both Houses of Parliament.[183] If the Speaker of the House of Commons or the Clerk of the Parliaments in the House of Lords states privilege applies to material requested under FOI, then this is treated as conclusive and it cannot be overruled by the Information Commissioner.[184]

Naturally this exemption is predominantly used by the House of Commons and House of Lords. Material likely to fall under it would include information held by formal parliamentary committees, such as draft reports, background briefings and records of discussion. But it can also be used by any public authority if relevant - for example, to cover correspondence with a Commons select committee.

Note that privilege only attaches to protecting 'proceedings in Parliament', which includes the work of the main chambers and official committees. It doesn't extend to the numerous All-Party Parliamentary Groups, which are unofficial, informal groupings. While they are not directly subject to FOI, some administrative information about them may be held by the Parliamentary authorities.

Commons and Lords information under section 36

Although section 36 is largely a qualified exemption (see above), one part of it constitutes an absolute exemption. This applies to information held by the House of Commons or House of Lords. Where the Speaker (for the Commons) or the Clerk of the Parliaments (for the Lords) asserts that the material falls under section 36, then firstly that is considered conclusive (so the ICO cannot query whether this opinion is 'reasonable'), and secondly the exemption is absolute, without the need to assess the balance of the public interest.

The royal family (section 37)

Section 37 is also partly a qualified exemption (see above). However, material relating to communications with the current monarch, the heir to the throne and the next in line is now covered by an absolute exemption. When the FOI law initially came into force in 2005, such information was only subject to a qualified exemption (as is still the case for communications with other members of the royal family). This stronger protection for the monarch and immediate heirs was brought in by legislation in 2010.[185]

It was prompted by fears within government and royal circles about FOI cases working their way through the system which concerned letters sent to ministers by the then Prince Charles. In due course, after a determined and lengthy legal battle by the Guardian, the Supreme Court backed the release of what was called his 'advocacy correspondence'.[186] This revealed examples of Charles's direct lobbying on a range of themes, including armed forces equipment, the situation of farmers, and resources for alternative medicine.[187] Since the information requests involved had been made well before the absolute exemption was introduced, the amended law did not block disclosure in this case. But it prevents any similar revelations in future under FOI (although the legal position under the Environmental Information Regulations is different).

Personal information (section 40)

Section 40 relates to personal information. It is the most commonly deployed exception, certainly for central government but probably elsewhere too.[188] For requesters its use can range from being infuriating to other situations when it is entirely unproblematic, for example to protect the identity of junior officials in which you are probably not at all interested.

Its application can be particularly tricky, because of the way it interacts with data protection (DP) law. It is largely listed as an absolute exemption in the FOI Act, with minor exceptions that are of little practical importance.[189] Nevertheless in reality it is not the absolute bar on disclosure that it is sometimes superficially presented as being.

First, information is absolutely exempt from FOI if what you are asking for is your own personal data.[190] That's because this should instead be treated as a 'subject access request' under the UK General Data Protection Regulation (GDPR) and Data Protection Act (DPA). If you've asked for information about yourself then authorities should automatically handle the request in this way, even if you happen to have called it an FOI request in error. However an authority may also simultaneously issue you with a 'refusal' under section 40, unnecessarily and potentially confusingly. For guidance on how to access your own personal information see chapter 16.

The rest of this passage about section 40 is therefore only concerned with requests that involve other people's personal data.

Data protection principles

Information is also absolutely exempt if it is another individual's personal data and revealing it would contravene the 'data protection principles' which govern DP law.[191] However in my experience authorities sometimes simply assert that the material requested is someone else's personal data and so absolutely exempt from FOI, disregarding that in some circumstances personal information can be disclosed in line with the DP principles. Authorities ought to check whether those circumstances apply.

The legal interface between FOI and DP can be technical and complex, but for a requester the key points in summary are these:

For information to be disclosed, that has to be done 'lawfully', and the DP principles set out several lawful bases for processing personal data. Normally for FOI disclosures the relevant one is that this is allowed where 'processing is necessary for the purposes of the legitimate interests pursued ... by a third party, except where such interests are overridden by the interests or fundamental rights and freedoms of the data subject which require protection of personal data'.[192]

In other words, someone's personal data can be revealed where this is required for the 'legitimate interests' of the FOI requester and/or wider society, and these interests are not outweighed by those of the data subject. This means that the case for disclosure will depend on whether it is necessary for transparency, accountability and whatever other public benefits would result given the specific nature of the information, balanced against the personal privacy of the individual(s) concerned. These are the issues you have to focus on as a requester if you are arguing against a refusal. It is not identical to the public interest test for a qualified exemption, but similar factors can be relevant.

In terms of the balance with the data subject's privacy interests, points that may be considered include whether disclosure will cause harm or distress, whether the individual has objections to disclosure, and what are the reasonable expectations of the individual for privacy. The reasonableness of expectations should reflect the seniority of the person's role, whether this role is public facing, and the authority's existing policies and practice.

For example, it has now become a broadly accepted principle that identities of senior members of staff mentioned in documents will be disclosed but not those of their junior colleagues, and officials should be well aware of this. Further personal information, such as salaries or salary bands, details of expenses, entries on registers of conflicts of interest, and possibly even disciplinary records, will be revealed more readily when the staff involved are more senior, and this again is within reasonable expectations. Other considerations that can be relevant include where normal procedures have not been followed or the topic is a matter of current controversy.[193]

A different ground for the lawfulness of processing would be that the individual involved has given consent.[194] This is an alternative to the 'legitimate interests' test, but is much more rarely of use in the FOI context. Nevertheless it can sometimes be worth asking the authority to check if the individual consents to disclosure.

Under the DP principles, personal information also has to be processed 'fairly' as well as lawfully.[195] You may come across authorities who go through the process of addressing this criterion in some detail, and often before looking at the lawfulness of disclosure. This is in line with the traditional process of consideration that the ICO used to recommend. However the ICO's current guidance states that 'if the disclosure passes the legitimate interest test, it is highly likely that disclosure will be fair for the same reasons'.[196] The 'legitimate interests' test is thus now the crucial issue in practice.

Special category data

However the situation is much more restrictive for more sensitive forms of personal data. This applies to what is called 'special category' data, relating to any of the following: racial or ethnic origin, political opinions, religious or philosophical beliefs, trade union membership, genetic data, biometric data for identification purposes, health, sex life or sexual orientation.[197] Similar protection attaches to data about criminal convictions, although this is not given the formal label of 'special category'.[198]

For any of this information, the lawful grounds for processing it (and therefore releasing it) are much more tightly constrained. According to the ICO guidance, in the context of FOI disclosure they come down to just two very limited options: firstly, that the subject has given consent; or secondly, that the subject has 'manifestly made public' the data concerned (this can be done explicitly or indirectly - for example, if someone stands as a political party candidate in an election, that person is effectively choosing to make their political affiliations public).[199]

However the ICO's internal training materials have been a little more equivocal. For example, one presentation stated instead that these two grounds are the 'only two that are likely to be relevant'. This implies the guidance is too definite in tone and leaves open the possibility that (even if very rarely) there are certain other conditions under which personal data of this sensitive kind could be lawfully released in response to an FOI request.[200] I am not aware of any cases where this point has been addressed since the GDPR came into force in 2018.

Identifiability

An important issue that sometimes arises is whether the material involved actually constitutes personal information in the first place. For this to be the case, it must relate to an identifiable individual.[201] In certain situations it can be tricky to determine whether or not anyone is 'identifiable' - especially when identification would be an indirect process dependent on making inferences from other knowledge or public material. Authorities do have to take the potential for such inferences into account.

Suppression of small numbers

This can particularly come up in cases where authorities release statistical datasets but do not specify the exact numbers of people in a group when it is small. The most common threshold for this is five, when 'under 5' will be stated instead of the actual figure. This is often very frustrating for requesters, not least because it also affects any calculations you would want to do with this data, so frequently making it less informative and productive to analyse the entire dataset.

Authorities do this on the basis that someone in a small grouping could possibly be identifiable, perhaps by those who already know part of the picture. However, for some authorities the use of 'under 5' or similar appears to be simply a kneejerk reaction, without real consideration of whether it is justified.

There is little consistency about this across authorities. In my experience responses to the same request sent by different authorities of the same kind can easily include several who have suppressed numbers under five and several who haven't.

Furthermore, it is often extremely doubtful whether anyone really could be identified by such data, as exemplified by various cases where it has been ruled that this does not apply. In one case which reached the Upper Tribunal, the data journalist Claire Miller succeeded in overturning the suppression of small numbers in some local authority homelessness statistics.[202] In another more recent case, the UT similarly ruled against the use of 'under 5' rather than the actual figures in a release of NHS prescription data.[203] And the ICO has issued similar decisions, for example recently on a request about numbers of vehicles in small census output areas.[204]

Nevertheless some authorities persist in unthinkingly and automatically refusing to disclose figures under five in datasets without proper justification.

It is worth challenging the suppression of small numbers (and quoting these cases) whenever it is unclear or implausible that anyone could actually be identified by the release of the actual figures.

As a qualified exemption

On a more minor point, the FOI Act does set out additionally some ways in which disclosure may be prevented under section 40 in the manner of a qualified rather than absolute exemption - where the data subject has previously tried to object to the processing of the data, and where the material would not be released in response to a subject access request.[205] However these cases are comparatively rare, and often in any case this would only block disclosure when it would also be stopped anyway by the absolute exemption of the data protection principles.

Summary

In summary, in practice the key questions relating to this exemption are:
1. Is anyone really identifiable from the information requested? If not, then the exemption does not apply.
2. If someone is identifiable, does this involve special category or criminal offence data? If so, it can only be disclosed under FOI if the subject of the data consents or has made the information public.
3. Where other kinds of personal data are involved, then (a) is disclosure necessary for the legitimate interests of others?; and (b) do those interests of others match or override the interests of the identifiable individual(s) in privacy? If the answer to both these questions is yes, then the information should be disclosed.

Information provided in confidence (section 41)

This exemption protects information which the public body has obtained from an external source and whose disclosure would constitute an actionable breach of confidence. It can involve commercial, personal or other forms of confidential material. However this is one of the exemptions which is most often misapplied by public authorities.

While legally it is listed as an absolute exemption in the FOI Act,[206] in reality it functions in a similar way to the qualified exemptions. This is because there is a public interest test built into the notion of what would be an 'actionable' breach of confidence. But it is not unusual to come across public authorities which ignore this requirement and state a request can be rejected under section 41 without any consideration of the public interest.

For disclosure of information to count as a breach of confidence, the following criteria must be met: the information must not be trivial, must have a 'quality of confidence' and must have been imparted in circumstances implying confidence, and disclosure must be to the detriment of the confider. But crucially there is a public interest defence against any legal action for breach of confidence. So whether a breach is 'actionable' (in other words, someone can take legal action and is likely to succeed) also depends on whether or not disclosure is in the public interest.[207]

Therefore public authorities have to assess the balance of the public interest from disclosure in order to use section 41. The only difference between this and a public interest test for a qualified exemption is a minor one. In the very unlikely situation that the outcome of the test is precisely balanced - in other words, the extent of the public interest in disclosure is considered exactly the same as the public interest in withholding the information - then under section 41 this counts as against disclosure but under a qualified exemption it would favour disclosure. Despite its legal status as an absolute exemption, section 41 is therefore in effect virtually equivalent to a qualified exemption.

If your request is rejected under section 41 you should check that the refusal notice from the authority includes an assessment of the public interest as part of deciding that this exemption is applicable.

It is also important to note that this exemption is only relevant where the information has originated externally to the authority. It can't be invoked for material which the public authority has itself generated. This is another point which public authorities sometimes get wrong.

In particular the content of a contract between an authority and an external company will not generally be confidential information. This is because it is mutually agreed between both of them rather than consisting of information provided by an external source.[208]

Public authorities sometimes mark documents as 'confidential', 'secret', etc. This is also sometimes done by contractors or others they have dealings with. Such markings do not guarantee that the information involved must be considered as confidential under FOI and therefore an application for it refused. Similarly there is no binding force in any contractual agreements between an authority and a company about treating certain information as confidential. Any FOI request for such material must be assessed on its own legal merits at the time it is made.

Authorities would usually be expected to consult the external source of the information on whether it is truly confidential. As explained above in the similar circumstances of section 43 (on commercial interests), the following points apply: this often causes delay; the authority is not bound by the viewpoint of the external organisation; and while it should take this into account, the public authority has to reach its own independent conclusion based on all the circumstances.

Prohibitions on disclosure (section 44)

Information is absolutely exempt if its disclosure is prohibited by another law (this is often called a 'statutory bar') or would be contempt of court. These statutory bars can crop up more often than might be expected and in surprising circumstances. Some are more reasonable than others. Examples include tax files about individuals held by HMRC, census records within the past 100 years held by the Office for National Statistics, details of trading standards complaints received by local councils, and numerous situations where regulatory bodies have information on organisations they monitor or investigate which they are not allowed to divulge.

9. The public interest test

If you make serious use of FOI, you may well end up spending time arguing about what is in the 'public interest'. This somewhat ambiguous and slippery notion is at the core of the FOI process. Since it determines the application of qualified exemptions, it is the key factor in resolving many requests. Cases that proceed to internal review, ICO and tribunal stages will often depend on it.

The term is not precisely defined and is capable of multiple interpretations. The ICO guidance asserts that 'the public interest here means the public good',[209] while the Scottish Information Commissioner offers that 'it serves the interests of the public'.[210] Neither of these statements adds much clarity. Because the concept is vague and subjective, it gives public authorities a great deal of leeway in how they apply it, it means ICO and tribunal decisions may be difficult to predict, and it can make it harder to decide how best to state your case.

Any argument you put forward about the public interest in relation to a qualified exemption will have to depend on the nature of the information requested. However here are some general points that requesters may find useful when putting the case for disclosure.

Phrasing of the law

The phraseology in the FOI Act is that material can be withheld when 'in all the circumstances of the case, the public interest in maintaining the exemption outweighs the public interest in disclosing the information'.[211] From this, several implications follow.

Firstly, the process is case-specific and contingent on the complete set of circumstances, so there are no simple overall rules, authorities must not adopt blanket principles that information of a particular kind is not to be released, and the full arguments on both sides have to be taken into account. It also entails that due to differing contexts it can be problematic to draw inferences from one case for another.

Secondly, the test involved is a balancing exercise, measuring the impact of the two contrasting viewpoints against each other. When considering requests, public authorities must identify the factors both for and against disclosure before comparing their importance to decide which matter more. As a requester it is likely you will try both to bolster the points in favour of disclosure and also counter those against.

Thirdly, the public interest in disclosure is assessed against the public interest in 'maintaining the exemption'. In other words the overall interest in disclosure is compared to the interest inherent in upholding that particular exemption, one exemption at a time for any that are relevant. (The legal position differs for environmental information under the EIR.) This means that the case for disclosure can be more general, while arguments against would need to be focused on why the release of the particular material involved is harmful in terms directly related to that specific exemption.

Fourthly, in the unlikely event that the public interest is equally balanced, the information should be released, as the interest in maintaining the exemption does not 'outweigh' the interest in disclosure. This will crop up rarely, except possibly for situations where the public interest on both sides is minimal.

Some relevant factors

When arguing a public interest case for disclosure, you have to identify the ways in which releasing the information would bring benefits to the public. You also have to justify why these factors are significant and should be given a great deal of weight in assessing the public interest balance. The benefits will count for more when greater numbers are affected, the consequences are more definite and less uncertain, the issues involved are more serious and far-reaching, and the impact on people's lives is deeper. Similarly you have to undermine the case on the other side, by explaining why any downsides to disclosure are comparatively unlikely or unimportant.

The ICO recognises that 'there is a general public interest in promoting transparency, accountability, public understanding and involvement in the democratic process'.[212] This will always be a component in the public interest test, and sometimes these will constitute the main points in favour of disclosure. They are certainly considerations you should refer to when arguing for information to be released.

However for some requests there will be other more specific issues which could be important, such as information which would enable individuals to take better decisions for their own welfare, or information which would incentivise the provision of high quality services.

Another factor which encourages the ICO and tribunals to back disclosure as being in the public interest is where it would lead to the exposure of misconduct, incompetence or other failings. But if you're the requester and you therefore haven't yet seen the information, you don't know whether it will actually reveal this or alternatively show that everything was done properly. So where this is relevant you probably have to argue that the information should be disclosed whatever is the case - if it exposes misconduct, it's in the public interest to get this out in the open so matters can be rectified and lessons learnt; if it doesn't, disclosure is still in the public interest to correct misconceptions and provide reassurance for the public that all is as it should be, and this requires the public to see the information for itself. In practice, the latter of these two branches of the argument is less likely to persuade the ICO or a tribunal, but it's still worth putting forwards as it sometimes carries weight, particularly when wrongdoing or error has been publicly and plausibly suspected or decisions appear unusual and puzzling. I have used it productively in the past.[213]

Sometimes authorities draw attention to similar information to that requested which is already in the public domain. That may reduce the benefits of disclosure, but it does not necessarily rule out the release of the material held by the public authority. The source and reliability of the publicly available information has to be taken into account. For example, there is clearly a qualitative difference between unofficial information and an authoritative account of events, and in such situations the disclosure of the official material can be valuable.

Timing

It is important to note that the public interest relating to a particular piece of information can change over time, as considerations alter. Usually as time passes the sensitivity of information declines, so that its release becomes less damaging. This is particularly true when policy decisions are finalised or investigations are completed. However the benefit to the public of disclosure can also diminish as the information ages and becomes less useful. The overall position will again depend on all the circumstances, but the key point is that the conclusion of a public interest test at one point in time might be different to that at another point.

The job of the ICO and tribunals is to assess whether a public authority acted in accordance with the law in the way it dealt with an FOI request. That means they have to base their decision on how they see the public interest as balanced at the time of the authority's response. In general they do not take into account how matters have moved on since then, although the ICO and tribunal processes can easily take over a year or more, during which period the public interest considerations could have changed substantially.

The result is that in some situations the ICO or a tribunal could back an authority's refusal as being justified at the time it was issued, when an assessment of the public interest for a current FOI request could now favour disclosure. If the ICO or a tribunal goes against you, but the text of the decision places a lot of stress on the need to determine the public interest historically as it was at time of response, and also the considerations have plausibly altered since that point, then it could be worth submitting a new request for the same material.

Some less relevant factors

It is also possible to identify some factors which should not determine the outcome of a public interest test. If you think the public authority has wrongly relied on any of these, then that is something to challenge.

The ICO guidance makes clear that 'arguments based on the requester's identity or motives are generally irrelevant'.[214] Release of information under FOI should be considered as disclosure to the world in general, not tied to the individual requester.

Similarly, the ICO generally attaches little weight to the possibility that 'the information may be misunderstood if it were released', perhaps because it is wrong, outdated, partial or technically complex. Instead the authority should reduce this risk by adding the necessary extra context to explain it all properly. One exception to this, however, is where material is intended for future release and the publication plans include providing the additional explanation required. Then this can be relevant to assessing the public interest in disclosure prior to then.

Public authorities sometimes argue that disclosing the information is unnecessary because the transparency benefits could be obtained by other means. However, the ICO states that when these other means have not already been implemented, then 'the fact that other methods of scrutiny are available does not weaken the public interest in disclosure'.

Another factor which should not be taken into account is that of potential embarrassment being caused to the authority, its leaders or its staff.

Nor should the public interest be swayed by what promotes the purely private interests of either the public authority or the requester and the requester's close associates, such as tackling an individual grievance which has no relevance or wider ramifications for anyone else. The issue doesn't have to affect the entire population of the country, but it should matter to at least some grouping of the public.

As is frequently stated, being 'of interest to the public' is not the same as being 'in the public interest'. The mere fact that the public are interested in something does not resolve the balance of the public interest. However, the ICO and tribunals may treat the apparent level of public concern and discussion about a topic as one indicator of how much weight to give it.

The public authority must not treat the views of any external body as decisive. While it may (and sometimes indeed should) consult a relevant third party, perhaps say an organisation which originally provided the information involved, and take the opinions received into account, the authority has to take the final decision for itself and not automatically go along with anyone's else conclusion.

Finally and very importantly, as a general rule the ICO tends to take an unsympathetic view of authorities deploying generic, blanket or speculative arguments that do not specifically reflect the actual nature and content of the information involved. You should strongly object to any public interest case against disclosure which is presented in generic or speculative terms, and which does not justify a causal connection between releasing the information requested and whatever harm is alleged.

Some considerations that can favour disclosure

Here is a list of factors which can favour disclosure. If you are preparing an argument about the public interest, you may want to check this list to make sure you have included anything relevant that might strengthen your position. Obviously you should only use those that are appropriate to the situation. There may well also be other more specific points that arise from the particular circumstances of the case.

- Transparency and openness in government and the administration of public authorities
- Scrutiny and accountability of public authorities for how they take decisions and carry out their functions
- The learning of lessons and dissemination of knowledge to improve future decision-making, planning and operational activities of public authorities
- Scrutiny and accountability of public authorities for the spending of public money
- Value for money in public expenditure
- Efficiency in the use of public resources
- Transparent, fair and competitive procurement processes
- Accountability of elected politicians to their electorates
- Improved public understanding of the policies, decisions and processes of public authorities and the reasons for them
- Improved public understanding of the historical reasons for policies and decisions in the past
- Better informed public debate over current issues
- Useful contributions to public discussion on matters of importance
- The correction of inaccurate or misleading information or beliefs already in the public domain

- The addressing of legitimate public concerns
- Providing the public with a full picture of events rather than just a partial one or selective perspectives
- Increased public participation in decision-making
- A more democratic society
- Increased user involvement in the organisation and provision of services
- Enabling the public to make better informed decisions and choices about their own lives
- Public awareness of health and safety or environmental risks and protective measures which may influence appropriate precautions taken by individuals
- Enabling individuals and organisations to understand, influence or challenge decisions that affect them directly
- The exposure of misconduct, unfairness, incompetence or a conflict of interest
- Incentives for failings in public services or administration to be addressed
- Incentives for high standards in the provision of public services and for good public administration
- Public confidence in government and public authorities
- Upholding high standards of integrity in public life
- Reassurance in the public mind that threats to public well-being are being appropriately addressed
- Reassurance in the public mind that public officials are carrying out their duties appropriately and decisions are taken for proper reasons
- Fairness in public administration
- The proper course of justice
- The prevention or deterrence of crime or anti-social behaviour
- Promoting public health and well-being
- Promoting environmental improvements and sustainability

10. Other issues

Historical records

Many of the exemptions do not apply in the same way to certain older or 'historical' records. These are less sensitive due to the passage of time and should therefore be easier to obtain. This is important if you are seeking material from previous decades.

The FOI law now defines a 'historical record' as one which is more than 20 years old, although for records of different dates which are stored together in one file, they do not become 'historical' until the most recent record in the file reaches that point.[215] The age for this definition used to be 30 years, but a change to 20 years was passed in 2010. This reduction was implemented gradually and is now complete.[216]

The following exemptions do not apply to historical records and so cannot be used to stop them being disclosed: the part of section 30 which relates to criminal investigations, section 32 on court records, section 33 on audit functions, section 35 on formulation of government policy, section 36 on effective conduct of public affairs (outside Northern Ireland), and section 42 on legal professional privilege.[217]

Also, in the case of those historical records that have been transferred to the National Archives, section 21 (accessible by other means) and section 22 (intended for future publication) can no longer be used, while section 23 on security bodies becomes a qualified rather than an absolute exemption.[218]

For some other exemptions the 30-year rule is retained, and it is after that period that they cease to have effect: section 28 on relations within the UK, section 43 on commercial interests, and section 36 for within Northern Ireland.

And there are some further exemptions where a different timeframe is stipulated before they become inoperative: a variable period dependent on dates of death for the part of section 37 that involves communications with the royal family, 60 years for the other part of section 37 which concerns honours, and 100 years for section 31 on law enforcement.[219]

The length of the personal data exemption depends on the lifetime of the data subject - it only covers information about the living. With old records where it is unknown whether the individuals mentioned are still alive, it is customary for authorities to work on the assumption that they could live to be 100 and protect personal data until that point is reached. Clearly many of these people will actually have died some time ago. If you want to challenge this you would probably need evidence of death, such as a death certificate or published obituary.

All the other exemptions not mentioned here (such as defence, international relations and health and safety) remain in force indefinitely in principle for records of any age. However, when information is sufficiently old it is obviously harder for its release to cause significant harm. So as time marches on, it becomes gradually less likely (but not impossible) that the exemption would be engaged or the public interest would be against disclosure.

In the case of government departments and some other national public bodies, most historical records still kept will probably have been transferred to the National Archives, which would then hold them for FOI purposes. Many files will be open to the public, but some will be closed and access would depend on the outcome of an FOI request. Note that the National Archives is allowed 30 working days to respond to requests, instead of the standard 20 working days, to permit time to consult with the body that originated the records.

'Neither confirm nor deny'

Refusals to supply information based on an exemption usually occur when an authority acknowledges it holds relevant material but then objects to releasing it. However, under some circumstances public authorities are allowed simply to 'neither confirm nor deny' (NCND) that they hold any information at all within the terms of a request.

This is meant to deal with situations where even a straightforward statement that information exists or it doesn't would in itself reveal a fact that should be protected by an exemption - for example, that a particular company is or is not being investigated by a regulatory body, or an individual is or is not regarded by police as a suspect for a certain incident. So you can't learn anything from asking the police for the information held linking the notorious crime boss Mrs Miggins to last month's mysterious major bank robbery - they won't refuse to divulge their file on this while admitting there is one, they will just neither confirm nor deny the existence of any such material.

NCND replies can be particularly frustrating ones to receive and sometimes difficult to challenge. However they are subject to internal review and the ICO process in the same way as for other refusals.

The response can only be used in relation to a particular exemption, when acknowledgment or denial of the existence of the material would invoke that exemption. The exemption involved must be identified. It can be an absolute exemption or a qualified one. In the latter case, the authority also has to argue that the balance of the public interest justifies the NCND response. Where this is relevant you should check that the authority's refusal notice does indeed include this and object if it doesn't.

In the special case of security matters, if an authority stipulated it was using section 23 covering the security agencies as the basis for an NCND reply, that could be tantamount to suggesting the potential involvement of those agencies in the topic concerned. The ICO therefore allows authorities to use section 23 in combination with section 24 relating to national security in general, without having to make clear which of these two exemptions is actually the relevant one in a particular situation. This approach has been backed in a tribunal case.[220]

The one exemption which does not allow for an NCND response is that under section 21 for information already accessible by other means, since clearly in this circumstance it would make no sense to neither confirm nor deny its existence.

Authorities will have a policy of deploying NCND replies even where they don't actually hold any relevant information, for consistency with the comparable cases when they do hold some but do not want to acknowledge the fact. Otherwise an NCND response would be practically equivalent to confirming that material is held.

How the use of NCND works in practice is illustrated by one case from my time at the BBC, where after a lengthy dispute we eventually discovered that the Metropolitan Police, as it turned out, did not have a Special Branch file on the political activism of John Lennon.[221] The force had issued an NCND reply, on the grounds that it 'wished to avoid setting a precedent for either confirming or denying whether it holds Special Branch related information about any named individual or organisation'. Otherwise, if it stated it kept nothing on Lennon or others, while insisting on NCND for someone else, that would effectively reveal it did have such a file on that latter person.

However in this case the ICO rejected the police arguments. Essentially this was because of the poor presentation of their position by the Met, who failed to demonstrate how the various exemptions they quoted were actually relevant, or to explain what harm might result from answering, or to properly assess the public interest.[222] This was in 2009, when authorities were less experienced at justifying a proclaimed necessity to neither confirm nor deny. A similar instance is less likely today.

Ministerial veto

The FOI Act as passed gave ministers the right to overrule a decision by the ICO or a tribunal.[223] It was presented as a backstop provision and was first used by the government in 2009 against disclosure of Cabinet discussion of legal advice in the run up to the Iraq war. After that occasion the ministerial veto was exercised several times on a range of matters, from an NHS risk register to a review of the HS2 railway. Its use also included an attempt to reverse a tribunal decision in 2012 ordering release of correspondence between the then Prince Charles and government departments. This ruling arose from information requests made by the Guardian journalist Rob Evans. The lengthy legal dispute in this case eventually culminated in an important Supreme Court judgment of 2015, which annulled this deployment of the veto.[224]

This judgment has made it much harder for ministers to use the veto power (and impossible in the case of environmental information, see chapter 15). Given the various reasoning of the different Supreme Court judges, it is difficult to be sure of the ruling's exact implications for when a veto could be legally valid in other cases. But the circumstances are certainly much more limited, especially when it would involve overturning a tribunal outcome. In 2016 the government stated that in future it would only issue a veto in response to an ICO decision,[225] in other words, before a case reaches a tribunal. And since then there have been not been any instances of this happening. It is therefore extremely unlikely that any request you make will be blocked at any point by a ministerial veto.

PART D: Appeals

11. Initial points

So you've had an answer from the public authority.

If you received everything you asked for, great. Alternatively, perhaps the request has been dismissed in its entirety, or you've got some of what you wanted but you're unhappy about a partial refusal or redactions. Read the response carefully, so that you're clear about why - you then have to decide whether and how to pursue the request further.

This section explains the options and the process for appealing, stage by stage: the first is almost always asking the authority for an 'internal review', which is the standard terminology for it reconsidering the case; the second is complaining to the Information Commissioner's Office; the third is taking the case to the First-tier Tribunal, the initial level of the court system.

So when should you challenge a refusal or redactions? While some people may just be hoping to make a campaigning point about openness or its absence on a specific issue, for most requesters it will come down to the practicalities of how strong you think your case is.

A well-evidenced and thoroughly argued negative response from an authority might persuade you against doing so - not necessarily by convincing you that the information ought to be secret in principle, but that in light of what the law says and previous cases, then it's futile to proceed. There is no point wasting your time and public money on disputes over hopeless causes.

On the other hand, many refusals and redactions are flawed and unjustified and should be challenged. But sometimes the less determined requesters don't take things any further. If you have a decent case, then there is a reasonable chance you will obtain more information at any of the appeal stages - internal review, ICO and tribunal. The reasons for this include the following.

Firstly, obstructive authorities may initially dismiss or redact a request just because the information would be embarrassing or inconvenient, and they're chancing their luck. They might be gambling on using a dubious interpretation of the public interest, they might have adopted some contrived argument when it's uncertain whether it will stand up to later scrutiny, or they might be well aware (sometimes because the FOI officer has informed the senior management) that they have a weak case which will probably collapse if challenged - since they're hoping you won't bother to do that.

Secondly, when there are significant arguments on both sides and it's not plain which is stronger, there's a natural and instinctive caution amongst many officials which leads them to hold back information and wait to see if this is appealed. That is almost certainly the more popular and less troublesome decision for them internally, even if it being overturned later might lead to some bad publicity for the authority in the future (by which time the officials involved in the decision may have moved to other roles and this is somebody else's problem). It also probably clears the request from their workload more quickly too. So for them to decide the broadly arguable cases on the side of secrecy rather than openness fits with the pattern of short-term incentives they face, but such cases could very easily go the other way when determined by less cautious internal reviewers, an ICO caseworker or a tribunal judge.

Thirdly, different people will of course assess issues differently, and in particular the public interest is inevitably a vague and subjective concept, which individuals with disparate approaches will take varying views on.

Fourthly, authorities (and especially those which receive fewer requests) do sometimes simply make mistakes or show ignorance about the requirements of the legislation and the implications of previous cases.

And fifthly, as the case moves up the hierarchy of appeal and has to be taken more seriously by the authority, possibly under pressure from their lawyers or the ICO, more thorough searches are often conducted which lead to more information being discovered, some of which may be handed over to you without further argument.

However, even when you do have a strong case which you would end up winning, you have to face the reality that this can take a considerable period of time. In some circumstances frustratingly there will be no practical purpose in going through the appeal stages, because the information would be virtually useless by the time you got it.

Reasons for refusal

Your strategy has to depend on the grounds given for the rejection or redactions.

If a refusal is because the cost limit is exceeded, then it's usually not the best strategy to proceed to an internal review, and even more so afterwards for the generally much lengthier process of complaining to the ICO. When a request costs too much according to the authority's calculations, in my experience it tends to be well over the limit, and even if you can argue persuasively that the expense has been exaggerated to a certain extent, that probably still wouldn't reduce it sufficiently. The main exceptions would be if the authority has plainly made a very large error, or its method of estimation is extremely vague, or in the less likely event it is predicting the cost as not far above the threshold. Otherwise it will probably be more practical to narrow your request down so that it comes under the limit.

If the authority asserts that the information is not held but doesn't clearly explain why, then the first thing to do is to reflect in your own mind on whether your request was poorly phrased. If you still regard the 'not held' response as implausible, then you can ask for an internal review. If you think your request may have been misinterpreted, you should explain what your intention was. You may find this is treated as a new request rather than an internal review.

If your request is rejected as vexatious, that can also be challenged, but then whatever you do, do not dispute this in such a way that it lends support to the charge against you. In other words, be polite and reasonable, not aggressive, rude or sarcastic.

However, most refusals and probably all redactions are based on subject-matter exemptions. In objecting to these, more often than not you will be dealing with a qualified exemption and engaged in a disagreement about the overall balance of the public interest, although sometimes it might concern whether the exemption is engaged at all. Opposing the use of an absolute exemption is harder, but could be successful if you can produce a good argument that the exemption is not actually relevant to your request.

'Late claiming' of exemptions

Bear in mind that as you go through the process the territory of the dispute might change. Once an authority is being challenged and realises it might lose, it may come up with objections to disclosure that it didn't think of initially. In some cases this happens because it gets external legal advice which points out that the authority didn't use the appropriate exemption(s) at the start. This adding or switching of reasons for refusal (usually called 'late claiming of exemptions' or 'late reliance') is often deeply infuriating to requesters, but the courts have clearly ruled that authorities are entitled to do so.[226]

Some public authorities adopt the converse approach. They start off invoking multiple exemptions by deploying every one they can think of which could have any conceivable link to the request. This can create a very misleading initial impression of a strong multi-faceted case against disclosure. But do not be easily deterred by this. Then under pressure of argument they discard the weaker ones until the dispute is focused on the exemption(s) really at issue.

Deletion of records

There is also a small chance that the material you want will get deleted. The ICO advises public authorities that when they have withheld information under a subject-matter exemption, then they should keep the material involved until at least six months after all appeals processes have been exhausted. But when a request has been rejected as vexatious or too costly, then it says that authorities do not have to identify and preserve relevant material, if that information would be deleted in line with the authority's normal schedule for disposal of records.[227]

Precedents

The legal argumentation in appeals often involves quoting previous cases but it's important to grasp their status and significance.

Decisions by the ICO and by the First-tier Tribunal do not have the full force of legal precedent. The principles they lay down do not necessarily have to be implemented or followed. The ICO can change its stance and take a decision which is inconsistent with a previous one. An FTT panel does not have to abide by a ruling issued by another FTT panel in the past.

However in practice previous decisions tend to be very persuasive. Authorities are likely to act in line with them, as they know that if they don't they can expect to be overruled later - unless as occasionally happens they think they can mount a new and strong legal case to persuade the ICO or the FTT otherwise.

Where there are ICO or FTT precedents in line with your arguments, then you should certainly quote them emphatically. If they go the other way, and you nevertheless want to pursue your case despite this, then you will have to state your position from first principles. If the precedents are raised against you, you will have to argue either that those cases are not really relevant to the specific circumstances of the one under discussion and that the apparent similarities are superficial, or that considerations are different due to the passage of time, or (probably as a last resort) that they were wrongly decided.

In contrast, rulings made by courts further up the hierarchy, from the Upper Tribunal and above, do set binding precedents for lower courts and the ICO, who cannot disregard them as wrongly decided. They are therefore extremely important.

Most public authorities also tend to be influenced in practice by how other comparable authorities have handled a similar request, even though they each have to decide things for themselves and may sometimes arrive at different conclusions. It is worth pointing out what other authorities have done if it fits with your case, but the impact may be limited.

Extent of information received

If some material has been sent to you, as well as contemplating whether to challenge any redactions, you may need to consider whether you have really received all the information you expected.

Is it implausibly limited? Is any explanation provided as to why it is surprisingly thin?

You can ask this as part of an internal review, if other material should have been included, or you might need to make another broader request, if your first one now turns out to be too narrow, depending on the circumstances.

Some examples: If you asked for copies of emails, were all the attachments provided? The ICO states clearly that 'emails' includes their attachments.[228] If you asked for a report and the one supplied is strangely brief, it could be worth asking for draft versions - sometimes they are considerably longer and more detailed. If you've received the completely uninformative formal minutes of a meeting, perhaps you should request copies of the notes taken at the time by the people who were present.

12. Internal reviews

As the first stage of challenging a response, an internal review involves asking the public authority itself to reconsider their initial decision. While most of the time it doesn't change the outcome, in a significant minority of cases you will probably obtain some more material. And even if you don't, you might get a more illuminating and detailed explanation of why they won't release the information.

According to the FOI statistics for UK central government, in 2021 internal reviews partly or wholly overturned a decision withholding information in 22% of cases.[229] This feels to me broadly in line with my experience of public authorities in general, that perhaps you might get something more on internal review in one or four or one in five requests. Some research about local authorities by mySociety (who run the whatdotheyknow website) suggests the figure could be higher, estimating that 35-50% of reviews produce something more.[230] In other words, if your case is reasonable, it's worth trying. Sometimes the additional material released may be trivial, but in other situations it will be important and valuable.

Obtaining an internal review is simply a matter of requesting one. The authority's refusal notice sent to you should explain who to contact. If it doesn't, or it only provides a postal address and not an email one, or if there is some other problem, then simply reply directly to the refusal email and ask for your reply to be forwarded on to whoever is responsible for carrying out an internal review.

The government code of practice says that 'it is best practice, wherever possible, for the internal review to be undertaken by someone other than the person who took the original decision'.[231] The ICO adopts the same stance.[232] This does usually happen, but not invariably so, especially in smaller authorities. So you might find that a decision is reviewed by the same person who took it initially, and although that may seem unfair to many requesters, there is no legal obstacle to this occurring.

There is no legal requirement under the FOI Act (unlike the EIR or the Scottish FOISA) for authorities to offer internal reviews. Nevertheless, this is a nearly universal custom. The procedure is recommended in the Cabinet Office code of practice for authorities.[233] The ICO also expects it and then, providing an internal review is available, generally will not consider a complaint about a refusal (as opposed to a failure to reply at all) unless the requester has initiated the internal review process. There are a few rare exceptions - for example, where the BBC has dismissed a request as falling outside the scope of its information covered by FOI, then the BBC and the ICO have agreed that the next step for dissatisfied requesters is a complaint to the ICO rather than an internal review by the BBC.

This also means there is no deadline laid down in law for how quickly you must request an internal review. However the government's code of practice states: 'It is usual practice to accept a request for an internal review made within 40 working days from the date a public authority has issued an initial response to a request and this should be made clear in that response to the applicant. Public authorities are not obliged to accept internal reviews after this date.'[234] The ICO's guidance also tells authorities: 'You are not obliged to provide a review if it is requested after more than 40 working days.'[235]

In line with this, it is common for authorities to stipulate that they will only consider one if it is sought within two months of the refusal. If you miss that deadline you could still ask for a review, but normally you would have to go back to square one and start with the request again.

Stating your case

You are not obliged to provide any counter-arguments when asking for an internal review, you can just say that you are not satisfied with how your request was handled. However, if you want to maximise the chance of a favourable outcome, you should make clear why you are unhappy with the decision and challenge the elements you disagree with.

Reasons could include the following (more than one is possible), and you can add further detail to justify:

- you do not accept that the authority has located and supplied all the information requested (if surprisingly little material has been found, you may want to challenge the authority over how and where it searched for stuff and what search terms were used);

- you do not accept that the requested information falls within the ambit of the exemption(s) quoted;

- in the case of a 'prejudice-based' qualified exemption, you do not accept that the likelihood of any harm being caused is sufficient for the exemption to be invoked;

- in the case of a public interest test for a qualified exemption, you think that the extent of any alleged harm has been significantly exaggerated by the authority and given too much importance, and/or you think that substantial benefits of disclosure have been missed or undervalued by the authority;

- you think the authority has failed to show any reasonable or plausible causal link between releasing the specific information requested and the harm claimed to be likely;

- you think that the authority's arguments are vague, generic, formulaic and/or unsubstantiated, and do not reflect the specific content of the material requested;

- you think that the authority has applied redactions in a blanket manner without considering the precise detail of each item of information involved;

- you may have other objections based on the particular exemptions or reasons given.

The authority's refusal notice should be clear on which exemption(s) it relied on to reject your request and its arguments relating to that exemption. So this should indicate what are the points that it would make sense to challenge. You don't have to object to all aspects of a refusal. For example, if the authority has redacted the identity of junior members of staff as personal information, you probably won't want to dispute that in most circumstances.

It is a common practice among many authorities to put a public interest assessment in an 'annex' to their main letter. This is presumably done in an attempt to make their reply simpler and clearer, so requesters can immediately grasp the overall outcome without having to read through the full reasoning. However I've also come across situations where the result is that requesters just assume an annex must be unimportant and disregard it. Do not do this. If the public interest test is in an annex, then that annex contains the crucial substantive material that you need to consider in order to decide whether and how to take the case further.

Also, authorities sometimes add extra context and presentational points to an FOI response, and often this may be useful, but it can distract from the core legalities. For the moment you should ignore any additional material like this - what you need to understand and object to is the formal legal component of the reply.

Timing

Unfortunately there is no legal limit for how long internal reviews can take. The government code of practice does say that you should be informed of a target date for the response, which 'should normally be within 20 working days'.[236] The ICO states that the time period for a review should be 'no longer than 20 working days in most cases, or 40 in exceptional circumstances'.[237] But this guidance does not have legal force and is often not followed by public authorities. An analysis of the central government FOI statistics for 2010 to 2019 showed that 43% of internal reviews took over 20 working days, which should only be for exceptional cases, and 15% exceeded the 40-day deadline that they should all comply with.[238]

Where an authority delays for a particularly long time, the ICO is increasingly likely to waive its requirement for the internal review to be completed before considering the case. If you have waited for over 40 working days (plus perhaps a grace period) without a final response, it is probably a good idea to complain to the ICO at that point. This is particularly true if you also experienced a long wait at the initial stage too. You should explain that you regard the delay as grossly excessive and this is why you are making the complaint now.

Requesters sometimes find that what they think of as simply an inquiry for clarification of the original response is treated by an authority as a demand for an internal review which then takes several weeks for an answer. If this happens you can try to explain to the authority that all you want is a quick clarification, but this might not succeed when dealing with an unhelpful authority. The ICO guidance says that anything in writing which 'seeks to challenge the outcome' of a request should be handled as an internal review, even if the requester does not ask for one explicitly.[239] If you only want speedy clarification, try to express this in a way which cannot be construed as challenging the outcome.

13. The Information Commissioner's Office

If you're not happy with the outcome of an internal review, then your next option is to complain to the Information Commissioner's Office.

The ICO is the regulator and enforcer of information rights law, including for freedom of information and data protection. In FOI terms it covers UK-wide bodies, England, Wales and Northern Ireland, while there is a separate Scottish Information Commissioner under Scotland's FOI legislation. Despite problems of resource constraints and significant delay (and the fact that I sometimes disagree with its decisions), its existence is one of the strengths of the UK's FOI system - an independent body with the legal right to investigate FOI complaints and overrule public authorities. It can also serve enforcement notices or practice recommendations on authorities with a consistent record of poor performance to get them to improve their FOI processes.

In response to a complaint about an authority's handling of an FOI request, the ICO can issue what is called a 'decision notice' instructing the authority to release all or some of the information concerned. Alternatively it may support the authority's stance. Decision notices can be signed by numerous members of the organisation's senior staff. But whoever has approved the decision it is treated as a ruling made in the name of the Information Commissioner with the full legal status that involves.

Many appeals do not reach the stage of a decision notice, but of those that do, the ICO partly or fully upholds the complaint in about 65% of cases.[240] However not all these would involve ordering the release of material. Some will concern excessive delays by public authorities or other procedural failings. It is difficult to say what proportion of ICO cases actually lead to the disclosure of information, but a reasonable number certainly do.

Complaints process

The ICO has an online form which you can complete in order

to make a complaint. Alternatively you can send an email to icocasework@ico.org.uk if you prefer. This email address has changed in the past (and may of course change in the future), so beware of obsolete alternatives that you might come across online.

It is crucial to attach all the significant items from your correspondence with the authority. At a minimum this will be your initial information request, the substantive response to it, your internal review request, and the reply to that.

You also need to make clear what you are complaining about and what you want done.

This will usually be that your complaint is about the refusal of the authority to supply all the information requested, and you want to the ICO to instruct the authority to send it to you. When relevant you may like to add that you are also complaining about the extent of delay, or the failure of the authority to offer you proper advice and assistance, or any other aspect where you feel the authority has been obstructive or inadequate. If the ICO then rebukes the authority over these procedural matters, it may incentivise the authority to improve in future.

In some cases your complaint will instead be that the authority has failed to respond at all so far. This may be to your initial request, in which case you want the ICO to tell the authority to reply without any further delay; or it may be at internal review stage, in which case you can ask the ICO to move directly to assessing if you should be sent the material you requested (it may or may not agree).

The ICO's task is to check if the authority has complied with the FOI law, and if not, to make it do so. It can't punish authorities for FOI failings, it can't award you any compensation if you win the case, and it won't take any interest in examining any other complaints you have about the authority, even when they form the background to the FOI dispute.

As with internal reviews, you don't have to provide any arguments against the authority, you can just state what you are complaining about and what you wish the ICO to do about it, but this is unlikely to be the best approach. Instead you should provide your reasons (concisely) as to why you think the authority is wrong, for example explaining why you believe the balance of the public interest would favour disclosure. Your arguments should directly engage with the grounds for rejection given by the authority.

You might find it helpful to look back at the points I have made under internal reviews and also in the previous sections on procedural refusals, exemptions and the public interest, for some ways you could structure and justify your arguments. You can also consult relevant sections of the ICO's guidance,[241] to check whether the authority has complied and to quote it if useful.

It may additionally be worth looking at the ICO's past decisions, in case there is a valuable precedent or alternatively the ICO has previously adopted a stance that you need to try to counter. The decision notices are on the ICO's website.[242] The most useful approach to this will almost certainly be to use the option to filter decisions 'by section' (of the law), so that you can locate recent cases that are directly relevant to the specific legal grounds for the refusal you have been given. The latest decisions are also likely to refer to the most significant ICO or tribunal precedents from the past. However you can't rely on the ICO database to tell you if one of its decisions has been overturned at a later stage by a tribunal.

Until 2023 the ICO's policy was that you had to complain within three months of your last 'meaningful contact' with the authority, which will very probably be the internal review reply. At the time of writing (early 2023), it is reducing this period to six weeks. You can check the ICO's website for the latest position, but don't procrastinate over submitting your appeal.

Timing

Bear in mind that ICO cases can take a long time. Unless a complaint can obviously be dealt with quickly and simply (for example, it's rejected as ineligible because the requester hasn't yet asked for an internal review), in many cases it will be months before it is referred for detailed investigation. And then the process can still take more months after that, depending on the complexity of the matter and the promptness of the public authority.

This has been a serious historical problem at the ICO. The current backlog is fortunately not at the utterly extreme level prevalent in the early phase of FOI, when for example it took the ICO over four years to rule that it was indeed in the public interest for me to obtain the minutes of the 1986 cabinet meeting during which Michael Heseltine suddenly resigned as defence secretary. While the present delays are not as bad as that, they are still excessive and give obstructive public authorities the chance to postpone eventual disclosures of information until they are much less likely to be interesting or newsworthy.

The ICO management has adopted a plan to speed up its procedures, and matters have started to improve. The organisation is also introducing a revised process for giving priority to selected cases of greater importance, which should then go through the system more quickly. The criteria for this include whether the case has significant media interest, whether the request raises novel issues, whether a large sum of public money is involved, and whether the requester has the ability and desire to use the information for the wider benefit of the public. See appendix 3 for a full list.

At the time of writing (early 2023) it is not yet clear how much impact this will have in practice. However, if your case would fit within these criteria, then at the same time that you make your appeal to the ICO you should argue that it should be prioritised.

The delays can be exacerbated by the behaviour of public authorities who are very slow to respond to the ICO's questions. The ICO sometimes even has to serve legally binding 'information notices' on recalcitrant authorities to force them to cooperate with its investigations. This formal step seems to be needed about twenty times a year.[243]

Whether or not the ICO successfully reforms its way of working, the reality for the foreseeable future is that many cases which raise substantial issues will take a long time - several months or possibly even over a year - and you need to be realistic about that.

Informal resolutions

The ICO often seeks to resolve a case informally, without it going all the way through detailed consideration to the formal issuing of a decision notice. This can save time and resources. If it's because initial investigations have persuaded the authority that disclosure is inevitable and so the authority is now willing to back down, that's good news. But sometimes the ICO will contact you to

140

say it is minded for some reason to reject your complaint and ask you to withdraw it at that point without a decision notice. Or possibly it will inform you that the authority is now willing to release part of the material but not all of it, and ask if you will withdraw your complaint on the basis of that compromise.

It's up to you whether to agree. Don't feel pushed into it, you have the legal right not to do so, but on the other hand sometimes it might make sense. You have to decide in the light of the strength of the arguments involved. But one point to bear in mind is that if you withdraw your complaint in this way, you won't later be able to take the case further by appealing to the First-tier Tribunal. You can only do that if the ICO has actually issued a decision notice, which you can then appeal against.

Decisions

The issuing of a decision notice is the completion of the ICO's consideration of a case. All decision notices are made public in due course (usually a few days after being emailed to the requester and the authority), although with the requester's details removed. The notices sometimes have a confidential annex, which you won't be sent, in cases where publishing the ICO's full reasoning would reveal details of the information under contention.

If the ICO orders the release of information then the public authority has 28 days to comply (calendar days, not working days). Public authorities do not always obey this deadline. In my experience the Cabinet Office is particularly bad at doing so. If you have not received the information within 28 days, notify the ICO who will instruct the authority to comply. Note however there is a possibility that the authority is not disclosing because it is appealing to the First-tier Tribunal, as for this there is a deadline of 35 calendar days.

14. Tribunals

If your complaint to the ICO is not fully successful, and it decides against the disclosure of information you requested (either all of it or just some), then your next choice is whether to appeal to the First-tier Tribunal (FTT). Equally, if the public authority is overruled by the ICO and ordered to release material, then it also has the option of appealing. In other words any such appeal at the FTT is a case brought against the ICO to challenge a decision notice, whether the requester or the authority is instigating it.

You can take a case to the FTT as long as the ICO has issued a formal decision notice, but not if your complaint was dismissed in some other way (eg, the ICO refused to consider it because you left it too long before complaining).

Whether an appeal is a good idea will depend on the solidity and persuasiveness of the ICO's decision and the importance of the issue. Appealing to the FTT will be time-consuming (for you, the tribunal, and everyone else concerned), so don't just appeal for the sake of it, but on the other hand don't feel intimidated from doing so if you can make a good case that the ICO's ruling is flawed.

The FTT quite often overrules the ICO, including in the favour of requesters, so it can be worth the time and effort involved. In 2021/22, 26% of appeals led to an ICO decision being partly or completely overturned.[244]

The process from appeal to tribunal judgment will probably take between four and six months, but can sometimes be longer.

Tribunal procedure

In terms of legal processes the First-tier Tribunal is comparatively informal and flexible, and it's perfectly feasible for any individual to pursue their own case, both at the initial phase which is in writing and then at any oral hearing which may follow. Many cases are conducted entirely on paper and do not involve a hearing.

Requesters are often concerned by whether they need to be

represented by a lawyer, particularly at an oral hearing. If you can get legal representation that will help, but legal aid is not available for this, and anyway it's far from necessary. I've taken several cases through the tribunal process representing myself or colleagues. The FTT is accustomed to dealing with litigants in person and is sympathetic to their needs and lack of familiarity with the workings of the law. Many FOI requesters represent themselves effectively and indeed successfully.

It can sometimes depend on the case, however, especially at the hearing stage. A lot of FOI cases come down to a fairly straightforward dispute about whether disclosing the information is in the public interest or not. Then it's usually entirely possible for requesters to argue their own cause, informed by their knowledge of the topic and motivation for wanting the material. However there will be others where a key issue turns out to be the application of another area of law (such as the law on confidence), or some general legal principle, or a tricky procedural technicality. It is harder to fight a case of this kind without broader knowledge of the law.

Looking at some previous tribunal judgments will give you an initial appreciation of how the FTT tends to approach a case. These are publicly available, and can be selected by broad subject-matter, which may be useful.[245] It will clearly also help if you have an understanding of how the tribunal operates. Its detailed procedures are published in a set of rules.[246] If you find you are unhappy with how the FTT and its staff are managing your case or the arrangements being made, and you want to contest any aspect of this, then you need to check these rules.

Launching an appeal

If you appeal to the FTT then your action is brought against the ICO, as you are seeking to overturn their decision notice. The public authority will then probably be joined to the case as an additional party against you. However sometimes in cases they regard as less important or perhaps on reflection feel ambivalent about, the ICO more or less drops out of the proceedings and does not take part in any oral hearing. This is usually to save money on legal costs. That would leave the dispute as effectively just between you and the authority. Generally there is a lot of variation in the level of resources and effort that the ICO gives to different cases.

When an authority appeals against an ICO ruling in your favour, then you should be offered the option to participate in the case as an additional party. In some ways you are less well placed to argue for disclosure than the ICO, who will actually have seen the material in question and can fight the case on that better-informed basis, whereas you won't have done and can't. Nevertheless you may still be able to raise further points and put arguments that lie outside the ICO's position. Being involved in a case of this sort is much easier than when you yourself have made the appeal, since the ICO is on your side and should carry the main burden, with you playing a supporting role.

At one time the FTT was reluctant to join a requester to the case as an additional party unless it could be convinced that the requester would play a distinctive role in the arguments, different to that of the ICO. Currently its default policy seems to be to allow the requester to be joined to the case, more or less as a matter of course. If you are asked if you want to be an additional party, I'd recommend as a general rule that you say yes, if only to demonstrate your continuing commitment to obtaining the information.

If the ICO ruled partly in your favour and partly against - backing disclosure for some of the information but not all of it - then it could be that both you and the public authority appeal. Any appeal will have to be made within 28 (calendar) days of the ICO decision notice,[247] whereas the ICO allows the authority 35 days to disclose the information if it is not appealing. Therefore in this situation you have to decide whether to appeal yourself before you know whether the authority is appealing or disclosing. If you have very good reasons to expect the authority to appeal, there is a strong logic for making a cross-appeal yourself. The case will be happening anyway, and this would mean that you can broaden the arguments you put to the tribunal and might also win access to more information.

The FTT can also decide whether or not to accept an appeal submitted outside the 28-day deadline. If you are late in making an appeal you will need to explain to the tribunal why the deadline was missed.

To initiate an appeal you fill out a form and follow the instructions on the FTT's website.[248] As part of this you have to state your grounds of appeal. At this stage you don't need to provide all the full details of your case, but you need to explain clearly which decision you are appealing against and what you disagree with. In other words, if say the ICO has ruled under a particular exemption that disclosure would be against the public interest, you should state that you disagree with this and believe that disclosure would benefit the public interest.

My normal practice when completing the grounds of appeal is to summarise my case and outline its structure. So for example if under one exemption I have three points as to why the public interest favours disclosure, and then I have two points to make under another exemption, I list all these arguments. However at this phase, given the need to hit the time deadline on appealing, I don't supply all the supporting evidence and detail. I have discussed this general approach informally with various FTT members who have largely been happy with it, although I should say their full extent of opinion has ranged from preferring to have all the detail from the start to being entirely content if the initial grounds of appeal simply say 'I appeal this decision' (I do not recommend the latter strategy).

Written arguments

Assuming the FTT accepts your appeal is within the rules and valid, the next stages generally will be that the ICO responds to it (probably within 28 days), then the public authority responds (again, probably within another 28 days), and then you have to respond to their responses (probably within 14 days). In your reply to their comments you should now incorporate all the detailed material that supports your position. The FTT can only decide a case on the basis of the evidence presented to it, so it is important that you don't leave relevant points out. It's also possible that the authority and the ICO make 'closed submissions' referring to the detail of the withheld information which will not be sent to you. All this is done in writing. The FTT will issue the deadlines for each of these stages. The standard deadlines are stated in its rules, but these can be and often are varied in the practical circumstances of particular cases.[249]

Throughout the process you will be sent various case management directions by the FTT's administrative office. If they use legal jargon which you are not familiar with, and you are not clear on the implications for what you have to do and when, do ask for an explanation. The tribunal may also hold a 'directions hearing' to resolve any procedural issues that need deciding. If this happens, you and the other parties will participate, and it will probably be conducted remotely.

As to how you present your case in writing, I recommend that you structure your submissions in the same legalistic manner that the others will adopt.

Put any necessary factual background and chronology first (but there is no need to repeat what all parties accept as common ground), then address each of the legal arguments in turn. Usually they will fall under particular exemptions. State your case on its own merits, but also engage directly with the arguments made by the other side and explain how and why you disagree. Think carefully through the other side's case and what its key strengths are, and include whatever you can say to counter them.

Ensure the overall structure and purpose of what you are putting forward is clear. Use headings and subheadings to assist with the clarity of your documents. Begin with an introduction summarising your stance, and finish with a conclusion stating what you want the tribunal to do. Number all your paragraphs, and when referring to a point the other side has made, quote their paragraph number.

You have the disadvantage that (unlike everyone else involved in the case) you haven't seen the actual information, but don't make things worse for yourself. Although you will be arguing that the withheld material contains useful information, don't include confident but speculative assertions about what you think its specific contents 'must' be. If you're badly wrong (and I've often been surprised by what eventually transpires), it can make your arguments appear beside the point or even ridiculous.

Avoid irrelevancies.

And try to make your submissions easy to read and write notes on if printed out - no smaller than 12 point font, wide margins, 1.5 line spacing.

If the ICO in its decision notice accepted one argument against disclosure, it often won't have bothered to assess the other exemptions put forward by the authority, as it had all that it needed to come to a ruling. However the FTT will consider the case afresh, so you will have to address these other issues in your submissions as well as the one which the ICO actually relied on.

As often in legal cases, it might also be in your interest to state and provide arguments for a fallback position on some points, to be considered as an alternative if your ideal position is rejected. This is normal, and the other side may well be doing it too.

In my experience it is not uncommon during this process for the public authority to release part of the requested material. Once its lawyers start working through their case seriously, they may realise that the arguments for withholding some of the information are very weak, and putting them to a tribunal would be futile or even counter-productive. This can especially happen when the authority brings in external legal advisors who see the case documentation for the first time. If the material is significant you will then be asked if it is sufficient for you to withdraw your appeal. You have to decide that on the basis of how important you suspect the outstanding information is and how strong you think the rest of your case is.

In one of my cases I had asked the Cabinet Office for briefing material that would have been provided to the Labour leader Neil Kinnock had he won the 1992 general election and become prime minister. The ICO largely backed the Cabinet Office's rejection of my request, and I then appealed. The Cabinet Office then disclosed a partial collection of material, and I was asked if I would withdraw my appeal. The information sent to me was bland and boring, and I declined to withdraw, so the case proceeded. Then, three weeks before the oral hearing was due, the Cabinet Office caved in and released nearly everything. This was much more interesting, revealing that civil servants at the heart of government wanted to weaken Kinnock's plans to introduce an FOI system.[250]

The phase of written argument will probably take about three months. Stick to the deadlines you are given. If that is not possible for a genuinely good reason, the FTT will probably expect you to liaise with the lawyers for the ICO and the authority to agree on a possible revised timetable, for the tribunal to approve. Do this in good time, if it's necessary. Similarly, you might be asked to agree to an extension of time for one of the other parties. Insist that any extension for them does not eat into your time - in other words, that your subsequent deadline is moved back by the same amount of time.

Generally the FTT prefers the parties to reach agreement amongst themselves on such administrative matters rather than needing the tribunal to intervene. In my experience I have largely found ICO and public authority lawyers to be pragmatic and reasonable about this (at the same time as exchanging submissions for the case itself which are thoroughly robust in argument), although of course you may come across some who are more difficult and obstructive.

You should be aware that all these written submissions are compiled and exchanged purely for the purpose of the legal proceedings. In due course they may be referred to or quoted publicly at an oral hearing and possibly made available, but they are not to be made public as you go along during the process.[251]

Hearings

The First-tier Tribunal decides many cases on the basis of these paper submissions and all the relevant documents of the case which will be organised into 'bundles'. Members of a tribunal panel will meet in private to consider the documentation, discuss the case and reach a decision; and in due course you will be emailed the judgment.

The alternative is that after the written stage the case will go to an oral hearing. You are asked initially whether you want an oral hearing (and what location you would prefer), and the other parties will also be asked. Even if you don't want an oral hearing, another party might request one, which will probably be granted. Or the FTT itself might decide that the nature of the case requires an oral hearing.

Requesters who are nervous about the idea of taking part in a hearing and disputing with professional lawyers often prefer to have consideration 'on the papers'. This may be sensible, and it is certainly simpler and quicker, but don't be too easily put off. As I've indicated, the FTT is very accustomed to hearing litigants in person and making appropriate allowances for them. Furthermore the tribunal may be impressed by the personal commitment and motivation of a requester who can make a clear, principled and straightforward case about the public interest. There are also some circumstances where you may be disadvantaged without an oral hearing. For example, if the authority has arranged for someone to be a witness and has supplied a written witness statement as evidence, you won't be able to challenge its contents in cross-examination unless there is a hearing.

If you want you can arrange to be represented by someone who is not legally qualified but has the relevant expertise and knowledge to deal with the case well.[252]

Don't fret about the prospect of having to pay the legal bills of the other side if you lose. It's extremely rare for costs to be awarded by the FTT in information rights cases, and it is only possible under very restricted circumstances.[253] Provided that you have behaved reasonably and appropriately during the legal process you shouldn't need to worry about this. The corollary is that if you are legally represented and win the case, you can't expect to get your costs paid by the other side.

If there is a hearing then you and the other parties will probably have to submit 'skeleton arguments' shortly beforehand, with each party presenting its overall case. Skeletons they may be, but they should have quite a lot of flesh on, without being flabby. Make sure your skeleton indicates the overall framework of your argument and brings together in one place all the important points that you definitely want the FTT to grasp. Ensure it does a good job of clearly and persuasively addressing the crucial matters that are really at the heart of the dispute, in a manner likely to appeal to the tribunal. Think of it as your draft of what you would like the tribunal's judgment to be.

If you are representing yourself, either the ICO or the authority will be allocated the task of compiling the 'bundles' for the hearing - the files of all relevant documents (this responsibility will not be given to a self-represented litigant). They will include copies of all the correspondence from the case and argumentation so far, plus the text of legislation, decisions in previous cases ('authorities') and background factual material including any referred to in the written submissions. There will also be a 'closed bundle' probably containing the information at issue and any other material you are not allowed to see. The preparation and content of the open bundles will be discussed between the parties, and you must make sure that all the documents you might want to quote or refer to during the hearing are included. If you leave it until the hearing itself to introduce additional documents, then the other side may well object and you might not be given permission to use them.

Before taking part in an oral hearing you might want to sit in on one in another case, if there is one happening at a convenient time and place, to get an appreciation of how the tribunal operates. You can do this because they are public legal proceedings. The FTT regularly publishes a list of current cases.[254] (Your case will be listed there, including your name as one of the parties).

At the hearing

The FTT will allocate in advance how much time it thinks the hearing will need. This is likely to be between half-a-day and two days, depending on the complexity of the case and whether there are witnesses.

Tribunal panels will generally consist of one judge and two lay members, who will consider the case together. At the hearing any witness evidence and cross-examination will probably come first, followed by the parties making their submissions. The appellant (the side which is contesting the ICO decision) will start, and also at the end will have the chance to reply to the others.

There may be a closed session from which you are excluded, during which the FTT, ICO and public authority, and possibly a witness, discuss the information at issue in detail. If this happens, then when the open session reconvenes you should be told the 'gist' or a summary of what was said in 'closed', without revealing any material that you are not entitled to know. You should also be asked before the closed session if there are specific points or questions you would like to be raised during it.[255] It may be worth thinking about this possibility in advance. Even if you won't find out the full detail of the answers, they could influence the tribunal.

Get ready for the case by familiarising yourself with the bundles, devising lines of questioning for any cross-examination, and preparing what you will say in your submission, both your own argument and counter-arguments against the other side. Make sure you are clear in your mind on what are the key actual issues of dispute that divide you and the other side, and focus on them.

FTT members are addressed as 'Sir' or 'Madam'. Be polite and respectful, but also make sure that you state your case. Don't interrupt the other side, wait for your turn. The tribunal will give you more leeway on procedural matters than they would for a lawyer familiar with the legal process. Do follow any instructions carefully, but don't let any worries about whether you are abiding by the correct procedure at the right time inhibit you from making your points, unless and until you are told that things should be done differently.

Be concise, stick to matters which are relevant to the decisions the FTT now has to take, and don't devote time to making detailed points about irrelevant background. There's no gain, for example, in going over all the earlier flaws in how the authority initially handled your request if events have moved on and that does not affect the issues which the tribunal currently has to resolve.

The FTT is very dependent on the documentation in front of it. In advance you should work through your own copies and tab the pages you intend to cite, so that you can find them easily and quickly during the case. You should know what is in the bundles and where, and in the hearing you should refer to the content of the documents whenever relevant, quoting the bundle page number. Make sure you give the tribunal panel sufficient time to locate the pages and passages involved, particularly for the points that are most central to your argument.

Cross-examination of witnesses can enable you to extract information and establish factual points that will hopefully bolster your case and/or undermine that of the opposition. In other words, it gives you the opportunity, through the use of questions, to contest an opposing witness's assertions and to expose any gaps, weaknesses, lack of conviction, inconsistencies or contrary evidence; and also to elicit facts that support your argument. Again, be polite, but don't hesitate to ask the questions that you need to.

Listen carefully to what the other parties say and take good notes. Ideally you will want to do this in such a way that you can easily incorporate your rejoinders to them into your own oral submission, when you may have little time to prepare additions to it. One technique is to draw a line down the middle of a page, record their points on the left hand side (with their page references to the bundle), and quickly jot any thoughts for a counter-argument opposite each point on the right hand side. You may also find it useful to use different colour sticky notes while listening to the other parties to tab documents they refer to but which you will want to go back to, so that you can easily distinguish these pages from ones you tabbed previously.

Don't just assume that their legal interpretation of any previous case is correct. Check the judgment itself to see if its implications are actually much narrower than they claim.

Whenever there is a break in proceedings, make full use of the time to prepare what you are going to do in the next session.

When it's your turn to address the tribunal, ensure that you respond to the other side's points and make clear your disagreement with them, as well as presenting your own arguments structured in the way that works best for your case. If you can incorporate the extra points you want to make that have arisen from the hearing so far (whether cross-examination or other submissions) into the structure of your submission as you go along, that is best. But if you don't have the time to organise that, towards the end of your submission you can simply say that there are some further points you wish to address and state them. Don't allow the impression to be created by default that you accept part of the argument from the other side, unless it is actually a point that you realise you have to concede.

At the conclusion of the hearing it is possible that the panel will announce a decision there and then, but it is much more likely that they will take time to consider it. It will probably be a few weeks before the judgment is finalised and emailed to you.

Upper Tribunal

Any appeal against a judgment by the FTT would go to the next stage in the legal hierarchy, the Upper Tribunal (UT). It has to be based on a 'point of law', for example that the FTT interpreted the law wrongly or misapplied it or made a procedural error, and not that they simply went wrong on the facts of the case. You first need to seek the FTT's permission to appeal, and this has to be sought within 28 days There is an online form for doing so.[256] As in the case of the FTT, there is no fee, and costs can only be awarded against you if your conduct is unreasonable.

It is possible as well that the authority or the ICO appeals, and you may then find yourself a party to an Upper Tribunal case in this way. If the ICO is on your side then it will again carry the main burden. However if you managed to get the FTT to overturn an ICO decision, and the ICO sticks to its initial stance when the authority appeals, you will find yourself facing both authority and ICO at the UT.

The FTT itself can also seek to transfer a particularly complex case to the Upper Tribunal for a decision.

It is certainly feasible to represent yourself during the Upper Tribunal process, and I have done so. HM Courts and Tribunal Service has published a basic but clear and useful explanatory guide to the workings of the UT in information rights cases.[257] Nevertheless it is considerably more formal and legalistic than the FTT. If at all possible it would be sensible to get legal advice if you are thinking of pursuing your case at that level (although again legal aid is not available).

Any disputes taken beyond the UT would go to the Court of Appeal, which happens to only a handful of FOI cases each year, and finally if necessary the Supreme Court, which in the world of FOI is very rare.

PART E: Other systems

15. Environmental Information Regulations

If you want to access environmental information, from data about emissions to projected impacts of local planning proposals, that is covered not by FOI but by its own separate set of legal rules - the Environmental Information Regulations or EIR.

The term 'environmental information' is defined broadly. It includes not only the state of the environment itself (from air pollution to built structures), but also factors that affect these conditions, as well as relevant policies and legislation. Public authorities sometimes fail to appreciate its full range, and it is not uncommon for authorities to handle requests under the FOI process when they should have been handled under the EIR.

The EIR are similar to the provisions of FOI law but not identical. In many circumstances, but not all, they are somewhat more helpful to requesters than FOI.

When I was at the BBC I revealed how Prince Charles (as he then was) had lobbied prime minister Tony Blair in 1998 against the development of genetically modified foods.[258] It took me nearly three years - and four separate complaints to the ICO - to defeat the persistent obstructiveness of the Cabinet Office and force them to disclose the document. And it was only possible because the then prince's views on GM technology counted as a form of environmental information. While the Freedom of Information Act had been amended to make communications with the heir to the throne absolutely exempt from FOI, this absolute exclusion was not introduced for material covered by the EIR. This is one example of the differences between the two systems.

The special requirements for environmental information stem from the Aarhus Convention, an agreement of the United Nations Economic Commission for Europe that was launched in the Danish city of Aarhus in 1998.[259] The convention sets out measures to be introduced to guarantee three inter-dependent goals: 'rights of access to information, public participation in decision-making, and access to justice in environmental matters'.[260]

In line with this international treaty the European Union

adopted a directive in 2003 (strengthening a previous one) to stipulate how its member states had to provide a legal right of access to environmental information.[261] The specific details imposed by both the Aarhus Convention and the EU directive did not fully coincide with the UK's FOI legislation, which meant that FOI was not sufficient as a means of implementing the convention. So the UK government updated some earlier regulations on accessing environmental data and brought in a new set, the Environmental Information Regulations 2004. They came into force at the same time as the FOI Act, at the start of 2005.

Now that the UK has left the EU, the EIR could be amended or even abolished. However, the UK has ratified the Aarhus Convention, which dictates much of the fundamental content of the EIR, and is still bound by its obligations.

This chapter explains the key ways in which the workings of the EIR differ from those of FOI.

Apart from the aspects outlined below, and a few fairly obscure legal technicalities and nuances which from the perspective of requesters don't crop up much in practice, the EIR and FOI systems effectively operate in much the same way, so the advice in the rest of this book also applies to using the EIR. The points in common include the following: all forms of recorded information (the EIR terminology is any 'material form'[262]) are covered - in the environmental context maps, drawings and datasets can often be important; there exists the important right to receive 'advice and assistance' from the authority,[263] and the government has issued a code of practice to illustrate what this may involve;[264] requesters can specify a preference for the format they want the information to be sent in, which should normally be complied with;[265] and the procedure for appealing to the ICO and to tribunals is the same.[266]

What is 'environmental information'?

The definition of 'environmental information' is extensive and detailed, and it's useful to be aware of it, as a request may be more likely to come inside its terms than you initially thought. From the requester viewpoint this is usually preferable, but public authorities sometimes resist this, claiming that the material at issue does not fit within the definition. It is worth quoting in full to show its breadth:[267]

'any information in written, visual, aural, electronic or any other material form on

(a) the state of the elements of the environment, such as air and atmosphere, water, soil, land, landscape and natural sites including wetlands, coastal and marine areas, biological diversity and its components, including genetically modified organisms, and the interaction among these elements;

(b) factors, such as substances, energy, noise, radiation or waste, including radioactive waste, emissions, discharges and other releases into the environment, affecting or likely to affect the elements of the environment referred to in (a);

(c) measures (including administrative measures), such as policies, legislation, plans, programmes, environmental agreements, and activities affecting or likely to affect the elements and factors referred to in (a) and (b) as well as measures or activities designed to protect those elements;

(d) reports on the implementation of environmental legislation;

(e) cost-benefit and other economic analyses and assumptions used within the framework of the measures and activities referred to in (c); and

(f) the state of human health and safety, including the contamination of the food chain, where relevant, conditions of human life, cultural sites and built structures inasmuch as they are or may be affected by the state of the elements of the environment referred to in (a) or, through those elements, by any of the matters referred to in (b) and (c)'.

As well as this, if you are given material under paragraph (b), you are also entitled to details of the measurement procedures and methods of analysis used to compile that information.[268]

In other words, on top of the list of obvious environmental matters like air quality and water pollution, this definition also reaches into broader notions of 'the state of human health and safety', 'conditions of human life', 'cultural sites' and 'built structures'. This last point refers not just to buildings, but to other structures too, such as roads, railway tracks, electricity pylons etc.

Furthermore, the definition extends to administrative measures, policies, plans, legislation and other matters which could influence environmental factors. This is a very wide range of areas of activity, including political, financial and organisational matters, and it is often this provision that brings numerous requests within the scope of the EIR. One particular consequence is that material related to building developments and planning applications - a common subject of requests to local councils - will normally fall under the EIR.

As the ICO guidance states, 'Information that would inform the public about matters affecting the environment or enable them to participate in decision-making is likely to be environmental information, even if the information does not directly mention the environment'.[269]

The use of the phrase 'any information ... on' at the start of the definition is also important and implies it should be treated broadly.

The extensive range of the definition has been illustrated in court cases. The current leading case laying down a wide interpretation was decided in 2017 by the Court of Appeal, which ruled that the EIR applied to a review of the communications and data component of the government's smart energy meter programme.[270] Significantly the court based its reasoning on reflecting the central purposes of the Aarhus Convention, including 'the requirement that citizens have access to information to enable them to participate in environmental decision-making more effectively, and the contribution of access to a greater awareness of environmental matters, and eventually, to a better environment'.[271]

The definition has also been construed broadly in various tribunal cases, with rulings that environmental information includes an equality impact assessment for the building of a controversial memorial,[272] an appraisal of external alterations to buildings in a conservation area,[273] the identity of companies owning particular mobile phone base stations,[274] and plans to introduce tolls for a proposed bridge.[275]

On the other hand there are of course some limits to this, and it can be difficult to assess exactly how far the definition stretches. The environmental connection has to be sufficiently significant, otherwise almost anything could be held to have some environmental effects. The Upper Tribunal dismissed a claim that the details of a certain car safety test constituted environmental information, on the basis that the link in this case was 'too tenuous'.[276] There is inevitably a grey area and this does mean that it is sometimes uncertain which is the appropriate system.

Since on the whole the EIR provide stronger rights of access to information than FOI does, it is usually better for you if your information request is handled under these regulations rather than the FOI Act. If you believe your request is for environmental information, it's a good idea to state clearly that it is made under the Environmental Information Regulations.

This is particularly important in the case of those authorities which get few EIR requests and might not spot one by themselves, instead defaulting to handling it in line with their standard FOI procedure. Even some local councils with responsibility for various areas of environmental policy can slip surprisingly often into disregarding the EIR. Stating this point will matter less in the case of authorities like environmental agencies who would anyway assume that many of their information requests are EIR ones.

Some requests will cover a mix of environmental and non-environmental topics, and in that case you can state that the request is made under both FOI and EIR. The authority will have to decide where exactly to draw the dividing line, and which portions of the information should be considered under which system.[277] This includes, once it has divided the material up, assessing any issues of the cost limit or charging separately for the two kinds.

If you're not sure whether the material you are seeking counts as 'environmental', that's not a problem. You can just ask for the information you want. It's up to the authority to identify which process is the appropriate one for it to use.

But note that it's not a matter of free choice for you or the authority to select whichever system is preferred - it is meant to be decided by an objective test of whether the material actually comes within the legal definition of environmental information or it doesn't.

If a public authority responds to an information request by releasing all the material asked for, then in practice it's unimportant whether this is done under the correct system or not. It's certainly not worth arguing about. But when an authority intends to withhold some or all of the information, then the differences can matter in a big way. If an authority has insisted on treating your request as an FOI one despite you labelling it an EIR one, you can argue against this in an internal review or appeal to the ICO.

Which authorities are covered by the EIR?

The FOI Act includes a long list of named public authorities and specified categories of authorities which are brought under freedom of information.[278] The EIR also cover those bodies, with just a very small number of exceptions, such as the BBC and Channel 4, who are only partly subject to FOI.[279] And in a few cases the EIR are only partially relevant: they don't apply to any authority 'to the extent that it is acting in a judicial or legislative capacity', or to Parliament 'to the extent required for the purpose of avoiding an infringement of the privileges of either House'.[280]

As a requester you can usually assume that any authority covered by FOI is also covered by the EIR, unless the authority then tells you otherwise, which will be very rare. (This doesn't imply it can ignore a request on an environmental topic, it just means that it would consider the request under the normal FOI process rather than the EIR).

However the EIR reach further than the FOI list and also apply to any other body 'that carries out functions of public administration'. This can include private companies. And the regulations also cover any organisation which has public responsibilities affecting the environment and which is 'under the control' of a body already subject to the EIR.[281]

It is generally evident if an organisation is subject to FOI or not, because it, or a category containing it, is either specified in the law or it isn't. But for EIR, since the regulations also contain these descriptive criteria, there is a lot of scope for interpretation and argument over whether some organisations are covered. This is particularly true given the large variety of ways in which private firms are now involved in public services and national infrastructure.

The leading court case concerns water companies who had rejected information requests from a group called Fish Legal, which initiates legal action to promote angling and combat water pollution.

In 2015, after consulting the Court of Justice of the EU, the Upper Tribunal ruled that the private water companies of England and Wales were indeed subject to the EIR - this was because of their special legal powers, such as compulsory purchase, access to property, and the making of byelaws.[282] This is now explicitly accepted by water companies, although they strongly resisted it prior to the Fish Legal case. It is also confirmed on the gov.uk website.[283]

Whether other organisations with a public role come under the EIR is a difficult issue to be decided on a case by case basis, depending in detail on their specific functions, legal powers, responsibilities and oversight.

In 2020 the ICO ruled that the energy supply company E.ON is subject to the EIR, in a case arising from a request about an offshore wind farm.[284] E.ON stated it did not actually hold the material sought (so in practice there was no substantive issue of information access to dispute) and dropped its initial plan to appeal against this decision. The ruling implies that other electricity and gas companies who supply consumers would also come under the regulations, although they may not all be happy to accept that.

The ICO has also found that electricity and gas distribution companies are bound by the EIR.[285] And National Grid, the private corporation which operates major energy transmission networks, acknowledges that it falls within the remit of the regulations.

With regard to other industries, a tribunal resolved that the Port of London Authority (a self-funding trust not covered by FOI) is subject to the EIR.[286] And the ICO has decided that a somewhat more obscure body - the Verderers of the Forest of Dean, who fulfil an ancient role of forest officials in Gloucestershire - also come under the regulations, and so had to respond to an information request about the local population of feral boar.[287]

In contrast, the Upper Tribunal has determined that a private registered provider of social housing is not subject to the EIR,[288] and the First-tier Tribunal has ruled that nor is Heathrow Airport Limited[289] - both of these judgments involved overturning earlier decisions by the ICO who took the opposite view. It has also been ruled that the sovereign and the Royal Household are not covered by the EIR.[290]

In 2021 the Scottish Information Commissioner decided that

what was then the private rail company Abellio Scotrail was subject to the equivalent Scottish set of regulations for environmental information,[291] but the ICO does not consider the EIR as applicable to England's private train operating companies.

The resulting situation is tricky and confusing. In practical terms for requesters, these various decisions mean that - apart from those bodies for whom a clear legal determination has now been made - it is often unclear whether the EIR will be held to cover some private institution with important public functions. The application of the EIR will doubtless be strongly opposed by many of them, as they would prefer to avoid the obligations involved. Any contested decision is likely to involve lengthy and elaborate legal argument whose outcome is difficult to predict. If you want to make an EIR request to such an organisation, you lose nothing by trying but be realistic and bear this in mind.

What counts as a request?

The EIR are less restrictive than FOI on what is needed for a valid request. There is nothing to stop you using a pseudonym if you want,[292] or asking for information orally rather than in writing (although putting the request in writing and directing it to the relevant team in the authority is still obviously the sensible thing to do).

If your request is too general in the way it is formulated, then the authority has to assist you in how to make it more particular, so that it can be answered.[293]

Exceptions

The EIR use the term 'exceptions' to refer to the possible reasons allowed for withholding information, analogous to what the FOI Act calls 'exemptions'. While many of them have a similar effect to FOI exemptions, there are also some significant differences. There is a great deal of overlap but a fully detailed comparison is intricate and complex.

Unlike FOI, there are no absolute exceptions in the EIR which automatically prevent the release of information. The exceptions referred to in this section are qualified ones - in other words, when I say that one 'covers' or 'protects' material, etc, that is just the first stage in making a rejection possible; the authority then has to conduct a public interest test, and the exception must only be used to actually block disclosure if that is in the overall public interest. There is one situation which diverges from this, the case of personal data, where the process for assessing the decision is somewhat different, as described below.

So one consequence of this, for example, is that the security agencies, which are entirely excluded from the remit of FOI, have from time to time had to release material under the EIR in line with the public interest - such as the occasion I obtained data from MI5 on its recycling rate and energy consumption.[294]

When an authority refuses a request, it has to provide its reasons, including which exception(s) it is relying on and the matters it considered in assessing the public interest.[295]

It is worth noting that the EIR have to be interpreted in keeping with the purposes and content of the Aarhus Convention from which they derive and to which the UK is a signatory. The convention seeks to promote public access to information, and it states that 'grounds for refusal shall be interpreted in a restrictive way, taking into account the public interest served by disclosure'.[296] This means that in cases of doubt, authorities should take a narrow and not expansive view of when they consider an exception to be relevant. Some authorities that rarely deal with EIR requests may not be aware of this point.

Procedural exceptions

Similarly to the position under FOI, the EIR exceptions can be divided into procedural ones and subject-matter ones. The procedural grounds for refusal are: where the information is not held; or, despite the authority having asked the requester for more specifics, the request remains 'formulated in too general a manner' (which means too vague rather than too wide-ranging); or the request is 'manifestly unreasonable'.[297]

This last criterion is usually considered as equivalent to 'vexatious' in FOI terms. Public authorities also often use it to reject very time-consuming requests as excessively burdensome. Since the EIR do not contain a cost limit (unlike the FOI system), it is the only way that authorities can refuse particularly expensive requests, although this would still have to be subject to the public interest test. If an authority wants to invoke this reason for rejection, it also has to provide reasonable advice and assistance on how to submit a less problematic request.[298]

Subject-matter exceptions

As for the subject-matter exceptions, some refer to the same broad themes that also feature as FOI exemptions, although they are phrased differently, generally with less detail. Other EIR exceptions in effect cover similar material to various FOI exemptions, but come at the topics from different angles, based on different kinds of criteria. All this can have subtle consequences for the exact nature of the comparative information that FOI and EIR exclusions each protect.[299]

The EIR have subject-matter exceptions that are roughly parallel to FOI ones for information which would adversely affect international relations, defence, national security, public safety and the course of justice (including criminal and disciplinary investigations).

In the particular case of national security, the EIR make it possible for ministers to issue a 'conclusive' statement that release of the requested information would adversely affect national security and be against the public interest.[300]

There is also an exception (unlike under FOI) to protect intellectual property rights, but this is rarely used. Intellectual property cannot be infringed simply by an authority releasing material in line with the law in response to an EIR request.[301]

In the case of the first four listed above - international relations, defence, national security and public safety - the authority can issue a 'neither confirm nor deny' response if appropriate (although its use would still depend on a public interest test), but not in the case of any other exceptions.[302] This is more tightly constrained than under FOI.

There is another batch of exceptions which are somewhat

narrower in effect. They cannot be used to block release of information which is about 'emissions'[303] (a term that is not further defined), while they can still protect other environmental material. The relevant exceptions are those concerned with safeguarding the following: the confidentiality of an authority's proceedings where this is 'provided by law', commercial confidentiality, the interests of an individual or corporation who provided the information involved, and the protection of the environment.[304]

These EIR exceptions cut across the territory that falls under a range of FOI exemptions, notably those for commercial interests and information provided in confidence. Although not equivalent, they incorporate some of the same elements and protect some comparable classes of material.

The EIR also introduce two other important exceptions which are rather wide and do not precisely correspond to any FOI exemption.

The first of these is for 'material which is still in the course of completion, unfinished documents or incomplete data'.[305] This could refer to a lot of information, although there has been some scope for dispute over exactly what it encompasses. Draft versions of documents remain covered, even after the final version has been published.[306] However data which is already being used can't be considered 'incomplete' simply because it might be modified later.[307] If your request is rejected because of this exception, you should be told 'the estimated time in which the information will be finished'.[308]

The second is for 'internal communications'.[309] This can be very far-reaching in the case of many authorities, but particularly for central government, since the regulations explicitly add that it includes communications between different government departments.[310] It also therefore involves exchanges between departments and executive agencies, which are formally part of their parent department. Nevertheless it doesn't cover government communications with non-departmental public bodies, or with local authorities and the devolved administrations. Nor generally does the term 'internal' include an authority's contact with outside advisers, consultants or contractors.[311]

On the other hand, the EIR do not have an exception directly about 'formulation of government policy' (as in the FOIA exemption of section 35) or a catch-all backstop like avoiding 'prejudice to effective conduct of public affairs' (FOIA section 36).

Instead, it is largely these two exceptions (for unfinished material and internal communications) which function as the provisions within the EIR for authorities wanting to protect a 'safe space' for exchange of views and/or avoid a 'chilling effect'.

But this means there are some subtle yet crucial differences between the policy discussion material that the two systems of EIR exceptions and FOI exemptions can each catch. It's worth thinking this through carefully if you're particularly interested in environmental policy. For example, there is no EIR exception which generally encompasses finalised communications about government policy on emissions exchanged with an external organisation (although of course in relevant situations the material could come within other specific exceptions, eg the international relations one). As a result, the EIR have led to a number of revelations about lobbying on environmental policy which for any other topic would have been resisted by government under section 35 of FOIA.

Furthermore, unlike sections 35 and 36 of FOIA, neither of these EIR exceptions is in the list of those that allow a 'neither confirm nor deny' response. So it may be possible for a carefully phrased request to establish that something was considered, even if the content of the discussion is withheld.

The number of EIR exceptions is smaller than the number of FOI exemptions. Thus there are other categories of material which do not have general explicit protection under the EIR of the kind they do under FOI. This includes communications with the Royal Household and information that could damage relations with the devolved institutions. Note that while legal professional privilege does not have the specific exclusion provided under FOI, it can be protected under EIR by the exception relating to safeguarding 'the course of justice'.

Similarly, there is no exception in the EIR that corresponds to the absolute FOI exemption for information whose disclosure is prohibited by another law. In fact, the EIR state that any such law would not apply.[312] In some cases authorities can instead rely on the EIR exception where confidentiality is provided by law for an authority's 'proceedings' (a term which can be interpreted broadly).

But it is legally possible that some material which another law says should be kept secret could nevertheless be released under EIR.

Personal data

The EIR also contain an exception relating to personal information. Unlike the other exceptions, in most normal circumstances the use of this does not depend on a public interest test. Instead, the position is very similar to that under section 40 of the FOI Act. See chapter 8 for more detail, but in summary:

If the material you have asked for includes your own personal data, then that element is not considered under the EIR but must be dealt with separately as a 'subject access request' under data protection law.[313]

The more frequent situation is when the material requested contains the personal data of someone else - information relating to an identifiable living individual.[314] Release of this is lawful in line with the data protection principles if it is 'necessary' for the 'legitimate interests' of others (such as the requester or wider society), unless this factor is outweighed by the personal privacy of the data subject. Another, less common, ground is that the individual concerned has given consent. But for more sensitive 'special category' personal data, disclosure requires (according to ICO guidance) either consent or that the individual has effectively made the information public already.

As with FOI, there are some much rarer situations where disclosure might be blocked on the basis of a standard public interest test: where the data subject has previously tried to object to the processing of the data, or where the material would not be released in response to a subject access request.[315]

This exception is also one of those where it is possible for an authority to 'neither confirm nor deny' that it holds relevant information.

Historical records

Unlike under FOI, the EIR do not contain any special provisions on historical records with any of the exceptions ceasing to have effect. However the workings of the public interest test are such that old material is less likely to cause harm if disclosed and therefore to be kept secret.

Public interest test

The public interest test is even more important for the EIR than for FOI, given that all the exceptions (except for the personal data one) depend on it and authorities can only refuse a request if the balance of the public interest is evaluated as against disclosure.

The consideration of the public interest operates largely in a similar way under both systems, and the same kinds of factors are relevant, although there are some differences under EIR which could matter in some cases and are worth noting.

On the one hand, the EIR have a default stance which is explicitly in favour of openness, stating that 'a public authority shall apply a presumption in favour of disclosure'.[316] And as I have already indicated, the EIR have to be interpreted in the light of the Aarhus Convention and its overall purposes of promoting the right of access to environmental information, accountability and transparency.[317] This adds something to the weight of argument on the side favouring release of the material. The ICO regards it as a point which sometimes 'tips the balance' in cases where the conclusion of the public interest test is 'not clear cut'.[318]

On the other hand, there is a factor which can work against disclosure compared to the FOI process. If the requested information falls within two or more exceptions, then authorities are allowed to aggregate all the public interest considerations against disclosure under all the relevant exceptions when comparing them to the benefits of disclosure. This is instead of just taking each exception in turn, and only assessing the case against disclosure under these individual exceptions against the general advantages of releasing the information.

This stems from a decision in 2011 by the European Court of Justice in a case involving Ofcom and the locations of mobile phone base stations.[319] The ECJ was ruling on the interpretation of the EU directive which followed the Aarhus Convention and which the EIR were introduced to implement. In practice, however, it is rare to encounter an authority justifying a rejection on the basis of such aggregation rather than any single exception.

The ICO view is that this process of aggregation can only apply to the public interest test on environmental material under the EIR and does not affect the position under the FOI Act for other information.[320]

Time limits

The EIR lay down some tighter legal deadlines compared to the FOI Act.

For the first stage, it's much the same. As with FOI, authorities have 20 working days to respond to an EIR request.[321] If it needs clarification, then the revised version is considered a new request and the time calculation starts again. The regulations do actually also state that the response should be sent 'as soon as possible', and in one case the ICO has ruled that taking 15 days was not 'as soon as possible' in the particular circumstances.[322] Furthermore the Defra code of practice says that authorities 'must not delay responding until the end of the 20-working-day period ... if the information could reasonably have been provided earlier'.[323] Nevertheless almost universally in practice the full 20-day period is treated as the legal limit.

Then if the authority believes that 'the complexity and volume of the information requested' makes it 'impracticable' to respond within that time frame, it can push back the deadline by another 20 working days.[324] However, unlike in the case of FOI, no further extension is allowed for any reason. This is a significant improvement on the position under FOI.

Naturally it doesn't guarantee that authorities never breach the legal limit and exceed 40 working days, but if you've not had a substantive reply to an environmental information request in this period you should complain about the delay to the ICO, who will normally issue the authority with an instruction to respond to you within 10 working days.

Once you have received a response from the authority, if you are not happy with it, then your next action is to ask for an internal review (which is legally required to be available under the EIR, unlike FOI where it is just an advisory norm). You have to do that within 40 working days and in writing. Unlike the FOI Act, the EIR importantly stipulate a time limit for how long authorities can take over internal reviews - this is 40 working days.[325] You can complain to the ICO if it isn't complied with.

Costs and charging

This is one aspect in which the Environmental Information Regulations are less positive for information requesters than the FOI system, although the downside is often more in theory rather than in practice. The EIR allow authorities to make charges for the release of environmental information. This can include the cost of staff time in locating and collating it. Any fee has to be line with a published schedule of charges and must be 'reasonable'.[326]

However the practical impact of this legal position is constrained by the stance adopted by the ICO on what it would accept as 'reasonable'. The ICO's guidance states: 'The Commissioner's position is that routinely charging for supplying information under the EIR is not reasonable, as it does not align with the purpose of the EIR and may act as a deterrent to requesters.'[327]

This guidance also advises public authorities as follows: 'Access to environmental information is an important right and the financial cost of making a request should not prevent the ability to exercise that right. You should ensure that any charge you apply does not mean that only those who can afford it can access the environmental information you hold. It is vital that everyone has access to environmental information and has the same opportunities to contribute to public debate. If an applied charge does deter requesters, this undermines the intended purpose of the EIR and the fundamental objectives that it is seeking to achieve.

'The ICO considers that you should accept the costs associated with the routine administration of complying with requests as part of your obligations under the EIR. Most authorities follow this line and do not charge for complying with requests.'

The ICO does say there are certain circumstances where the context of a request would tend to make charging reasonable, such as land searches for a property transaction where the information is clearly only of use to the requester, who would not be deterred by a fee, and it will not assist the broader public.

In assessing the reasonableness of charges the ICO may also take into account the comparison with the FOI system's threshold for free access of £450 or £600 (depending on the category of the public authority). In 2019 it issued a statement warning public authorities to 'bear in mind that the ICO may consider that a charge under the EIR is unreasonable where the cost of answering the request falls under the appropriate limit provided by FOIA'.[328] (The term 'appropriate limit' refers to the £450/£600 threshold).

For example, the ICO has rejected one council's plan to charge £325 for copies of documentation from planning officer meetings, and another council's attempt to charge £100 for data on fly-tipping.[329] In these cases the ICO found it 'useful' to its consideration to note that the same level of work on an FOI request would not result in a fee. On the other hand it allowed Welsh Water to charge £9 for a map of the local water system.[330] A small fee linked to a property transaction or building development is much more likely to be approved than one for material with wider public benefit such as details of pollution discharges.

So, while there are authorities who stipulate in their schedule of charges that they bill staff time at £25 per hour for answering EIR requests, in practice this would often be overruled by the ICO. Nevertheless there is no hard-and-fast rule, and it will always depend on the full circumstances of the case.

Some authorities adopt an approach of providing environmental information for free where the expected cost would be under the equivalent FOI cap of £450/£600, except for a number of standardised chargeable items like property searches. If the figure exceeds this FOI threshold, they then dismiss the request as 'manifestly unreasonable' (unlike under FOI, the EIR do not explicitly provide for authorities to reject a request because it would cost too much to answer).

But the stance adopted by the ICO in its guidance is that while the FOI comparison may be 'a useful starting point', it is 'not, however, determinative in any way', and 'public authorities may be required to accept a greater burden in providing environmental information than other information'.[331] The ICO will take account of the size and resources of the authority involved, as well as the nature of the request and the information.

In a recent decision the ICO ruled it was not 'manifestly unreasonable' for Lambeth Council to have to provide a substantive response to an EIR request about documentation for a building development, even though the expense would be well over the equivalent FOI limit of £450.[332] Nevertheless a request involving an extremely large cost could be held to be manifestly unreasonable.

Remember that like the other EIR exceptions, the 'manifestly unreasonable' exception is a qualified one and can only be deployed by an authority when it complies with the overall balance of the public interest.

If an authority seeks to charge you for environmental information which has public value and not just individual benefit, then (unless the estimated cost is really very large indeed) you have a very strong case for challenging that, by quoting the ICO guidance and relevant decisions. The strength of your case can be influenced additionally by the importance of the issue involved and the extent of the public interest in disclosure, as well as how the size and resources of the authority affect the burden of replying. You should also check if any proposed fee really is in line with the published listing of charges. And it can be worth asking if the charge would be reduced if you visited the authority to examine the information on site in person.

However, if you are dealing with a recalcitrant and obstructive authority, then in practice you may sometimes face a tricky trade-off between paying now in order to get material more quickly or waiting several months or so for the ICO to rule (assuming it does) that you should get it for free.

Note however that if you try to evade any issue of a fee by seeking to insist that, despite its environmental subject-matter, your request should be handled under FOI and not the EIR, this argument would be rejected by the ICO.[333]

Accuracy

The EIR also state that where a request involves information that authorities compile, then the response to an EIR request should be up-to-date and accurate.[334] There is no comparable statement in the FOI Act. The ICO treats this requirement as applying to factual data which the authority collects anyway on an ongoing basis.[335] Otherwise, as under FOI, factual correctness is not a necessary condition for the release of information. A public authority may have to disclose whatever relevant material it holds, whether thought accurate or not, as in a recent case relating to the disputed height of a pavement kerb at a particular location in Lambeth.[336]

Ministerial veto

When they were introduced, the EIR (like the FOI Act) initially contained a provision for ministerial override, allowing government ministers to overturn a decision notice issued by the ICO or a tribunal. Under the EIR this was deployed in connection with the requests from the Guardian for copies of communications between ministers and the then Prince Charles. Some of the correspondence involved environmental information. In 2015 the Supreme Court ruled that this ministerial veto was invalid. The judgment said that as well as some broader problems with the legality of the veto, it was incompatible with the EU directive underlying the EIR, particularly its requirement that requesters had access to an independent review procedure whose outcome would bind a public authority.[337] The EIR were amended in 2018 to drop the override provision,[338] so it is clearly now not possible for ministers to veto either an ICO or a tribunal decision on releasing environmental information.

16. Other information rights

There is a range of miscellaneous legal rights for citizens to request access to information which lie outside the FOI/EIR systems. This encompasses several which are obscure, specific to particular industries and probably rarely exercised. There are also others which are important and valuable, and these I outline here.

Data protection

The most significant and useful right to access information other than under FOI/EIR is for when you want to discover what personal information has been kept about you. This is not covered by the FOI Act, since that excludes requesting personal information about yourself as an absolute exemption.[339] Instead this right is laid down in the law on data protection - the Data Protection Act (DPA) 2018 and the UK General Data Protection Regulation (GDPR), which combine together to create the relevant legal framework. That framework applies throughout the UK, including Scotland.

Asking to receive personal information of which you are the subject is called a 'subject access request' (SAR). In many respects this is a more powerful right than is the case for FOI requests, although there are still some limits to the material you can obtain.

Along with access to your personal data, you are also entitled to receive some details of how it is processed, such as the recipients to whom it has or will be disclosed.[340]

Data protection law is extensive and detailed, imposing a wide and intricate range of responsibilities on data controllers and processors. This is an explanation just from the perspective of someone wanting to make a subject access request, with advice on the best way to go about doing that, including in conjunction with FOI.

Subject access requests – principles

SARs don't have to be put in writing, but obviously that is still the sensible thing to do, so that you have a record. You should state clearly that you are making a subject access request, to ensure it is processed properly as such and help avoid any misunderstanding. It's probably useful to put 'subject access request' in the header of an email making one.

Usually you should be able to find the email address for sending in a SAR on an organisation's website (often in the section for 'Data protection'). Some organisations have their own standard form on their website for making a SAR, particularly those who receive a lot of them. It's entirely up to you whether you use this or not - a request sent by other means is still legally valid.

As with FOI requests, keep SARs clearly separate from other correspondence. Don't put one in the middle of a message about various other issues where it might be missed or incorporated into a broader response without being properly answered.

Make sure that you clearly identify yourself and provide sufficient details so that the organisation will grasp correctly who you are. I was once in the past sent information about another Martin Rosenbaum in response to a SAR of mine, though fortunately in this case I only received an anodyne list of magazine subscriptions.

Organisations will frequently ask you for proof of identity. Some state on their website what forms of identity they require. If you want to speed up the process as much as possible, you can attach proof of identity to your SAR whether or not it's explicitly made clear this is needed (usually the standard documents of passport copy and utility bill with your address should suffice). Thus you can avoid the delay if asked to supply it later.

Data protection law reaches much further than the public sector which the FOI system covers. You can also send SARs to private institutions and companies which process your personal data, as well as to public authorities.

There is no charge for a SAR. The only exceptions are if you ask for further copies or if the request is 'manifestly unfounded or excessive', although in this latter situation the organisation is more likely to exercise its right to refuse to answer it at all.[341]

Organisations have to respond without undue delay and in any event within one calendar month. This can be extended to three months if your case is sufficiently complex or you make further requests.[342]

You are entitled to receive the information in an 'intelligible' form, so you should ask for an explanation of any terms in the response that you do not understand.[343]

'Personal data' is defined in the UK GDPR as 'any information relating to an identified or identifiable natural person'.[344] In many practical circumstances it is clear and straightforward whether information does or does not fit within this, but there are some difficult issues at the margins about what exactly relates to an identifiable individual. This can depend on context, and organisations vary considerably in how restrictively or loosely they interpret it.

You are entitled to relevant material which is in photographic, audio or video formats (such as CCTV footage featuring you), as well as written information. However you are not entitled to obtain complete documents, emails or recordings, unless they are entirely about you. The law gives you a right of access to your own data, not to surrounding or contextual material, although there are substantial grey areas here which again different organisations will treat differently.

If an organisation's staff are allowed to use their own electronic devices or private email accounts to process data for work purposes about individuals, that information may legally fall within the scope of a subject access request.[345] In practice these are unlikely to be searched. If you have good reason to want any such devices or accounts checked for a SAR, you should state this very clearly and explain why.

There are numerous categories of material which can be withheld or redacted rather than disclosed to you.[346] These are not identical to the exemptions in the FOI Act, but some of them are similar. Potential justifications include familiar reasons such as privacy for the personal data of others, the prevention of crime and the protection of legal advice, as well as some much more specific ones, for example to do with confidential employment references. In the case of certain exemptions you can be sent a rejection which neither confirms nor denies that personal data is held about you.

Each situation has to be assessed on a case-by-case basis, and the legal criteria for when these exemptions apply can be complicated. There is some useful guidance available from the ICO, which you should consult if you want to challenge the use of an exemption.[347]

If you are not happy with how your SAR has been handled, you can complain to the ICO. Bear in mind that the ICO wants potential complainants to first raise their dissatisfaction directly with the organisation involved, although that's not a legal requirement as the law stands at the moment. Further details are on the ICO website.[348]

It should be noted that, at the time of writing (early 2023), the government is introducing legislation to alter aspects of data protection law, in its Data Protection and Digital Information (No. 2) Bill. However, in the form this currently takes it will not introduce substantial changes to the procedure for subject access requests.

Phrasing a subject access request

A valid SAR could just state: 'Please send me the personal information you hold about me'. However, much of the time it will work better if you are more specific and add further details.

Depending on the nature of an organisation and your relationship with it, it might hold all sorts of information about you, only some of which you are bothered about. For example, if you are a journalist who sometimes reports on your local council, in its different departments it could hold material on your use of council services, council tax payments, any complaints about local issues, comments on local planning applications, etc, along with your dealings with the press office, officials and councillors - as well as of course your FOI requests. You might only really want to obtain copies of some of this information. It's also possible that the authority might not realise it holds all of this about you and omit something you do wish to receive.

Therefore, when I send a SAR, I generally draw attention to what I'm interested in, by including something along these lines: 'You are likely to hold personal information about me in relation to … [eg my FOI requests]. Please focus your searches in this area and ensure that all the material connected to this is included in your response'. I may also specify a particular time period. Similarly, if you are only seeking a copy of one particular document about yourself, you can just request that. In many situations this approach is likely to be both quicker and more productive than simply asking for all the personal data held about you.

Sometimes a SAR will result in a collation of brief references to you that have been extracted from various documents. It's often difficult to interpret these and understand their significance without the context of the full documents.

I therefore often submit a combined SAR and FOI request (when dealing with a public authority subject to FOI, not a private organisation), in which I state something like:

'This is a subject access request under the Data Protection Act and UK GDPR, and also a request under the Freedom of Information Act. Please send me the following:

1. A copy of the personal data you hold about me in relation to …

2. Where any of this personal data consists of an extract from a longer document, the full text of that document.'

This should not be a problem. In the normal course of events public authorities will frequently receive information requests that partly relate to the requester's personal data and so are actually part-SAR and part-FOI (and possibly part-EIR too) - often without requesters even realising this, as the less well-informed may think that they have simply put in an FOI request. The ICO's guidance makes it clear that authorities should deal with this one request and split it appropriately for handling under the two systems; they should not ask for a second, separate request.[349]

This approach can also help to get around the tricky issue of exactly what counts as personal information. If something is considered to be personal information, you have asked for it under part 1 of the request, and if it isn't but it occurs in the same document, then you've covered it under part 2 (although the material could still be subject to different exemptions according to whether it is treated as personal information or not).

However, if you are not in a hurry and you prefer, you can also do this as a two-stage process, putting in the SAR first and then the FOI request asking for the full text of documents after you get the SAR response.

Health records of the deceased

Data protection law and the term 'personal data' only apply to living individuals. Dead people have no privacy rights under the GDPR and DPA.[350]

The most contentious issue involving access to the personal information of the dead tends to involve their medical records, often in difficult and sensitive contexts. This is governed by a separate piece of legislation, the Access to Health Records Act (AHRA) 1990.[351] It's in force in England, Wales and Scotland, and there is a similar law in Northern Ireland.[352] It grants a legal right to obtain the health records of a deceased patient to (a) the patient's representative (eg an executor of the patient's estate, but importantly not simply any surviving family member or next of kin), and (b) anyone who may have a claim arising out of the patient's death.[353]

If you fit within these criteria then you should contact the medical service holding the records concerned and ask for copies under the AHRA, not FOI.

If instead you were to try to make an FOI request for the medical records of a dead person, you can expect it to be refused - not as personal information (since that exemption is only applicable to the living), but either as material available by other means if you do have the right to it under the AHRA, or as confidential information if you don't. The First-tier Tribunal has ruled that the ethical obligations of medical confidentiality continue even after someone has died, in line with traditional medical professional norms,[354] and the ICO follows this line.[355] (Of course the records may also contain some material whose disclosure would be refused anyway on other grounds, such as personal information relating to medical staff or surviving relatives).

Nevertheless, even when there is no legal obligation, in my experience there are limited circumstances where medical authorities will comply with a suitable request from an appropriate person and use their discretion to grant access to health records of the dead. In line with government guidance, the wishes of the surviving family and the passage of time since death should be and probably will be important factors in deciding on this.[356] Note incidentally that death certificates stating cause of death are public documents in any case.

The AHRA is limited to medical records created by health professionals, it does not extend to providing access to social care records or other information.[357] If you make an FOI request for a dead person's social care records it will be probably be rejected as involving confidential information.

Local audit records

There is a comparatively little known and underused right to inspect financial and accounting records of many local public bodies, which stems from the auditing process. Historically this preceded FOI by many years, dating back in an earlier manifestation to the Poor Law Amendment Act of 1844. The underlying purpose has been to facilitate the discovery of any concerns or objections before an audit is completed, but you can consult the documentation without then raising any issues with the auditors.

In its current form this right in England is laid down in the Local Audit and Accountability Act (LAAA) 2014.[358] It operates as described below. There are similar laws in Scotland, Wales and Northern Ireland.[359] The time periods involved for inspecting records and some of the rules vary, but most of the broad legal principles and the overall advice to be followed are the same.

Authorities covered by these provisions of the LAAA include local councils, police forces, police and crime commissioners, fire and rescue services and national park authorities, but not any part of the NHS.[360] The act gives the right to access information to 'persons interested', which would include local residents and others with a reasonable connection to the authority's activities, but otherwise not just anyone who wants. Importantly the right has also been extended to all 'journalists and citizen journalists', defined as 'any person who produces for publication journalistic material (whether paid to do so or otherwise)', and this applies whether or not they have any significant link to that authority.[361] Journalists and bloggers are therefore able to exercise this right with regard to any authority covered by the LAAA, irrespective of geographical location.

Under this law you can inspect and get copies of a very wide range of financial records relating to the accounts for the previous financial year, including contracts, invoices and receipts.[362] Crucially the exemptions are much more limited than under FOI, although there are some restrictions for commercial confidentiality (subject to a public interest test) and personal information. Furthermore in 2021 the High Court ruled that a council which was asked for a lot of material could not use the time and cost of compliance as a justification for refusing to provide it.[363]

However the key practical constraint is that the right of access is limited to an 'inspection period' of 30 working days each year. This must include a 'common inspection period' of the first 10 working days in June for larger authorities, or the first 10 working days in July for smaller ones.[364] During inspection periods the records involved have to be available 'on reasonable notice at all reasonable times'.[365] These dates reflect the normal legal position, but recent (financial years 2020/21 and 2021/22) inspection periods were postponed until August due to the covid-19 pandemic.[366]

The exact dates should be announced on the authority's website (probably in May each year), along with the procedure for access. This will be in a formal notice which is unlikely to be prominently promoted and may need some determined searching to locate. Contact the authority's finance department if you can't find it. Access to the material will generally involve visiting the authority's offices to examine the documents there. Inspecting the documents in person is free but you could be charged for obtaining photocopies.

If you are not sure exactly how to specify material you want, the expenditure data that local authorities are required to release regularly can provide useful pointers, as can the draft set of accounts that authorities should publish before the inspection period.

There is now more awareness of this right than there used to be, but in my experience authorities can be badly prepared for people who want to exercise it. It is prudent to make your visit(s) to see records as early as possible during the inspection period. Authorities are sometimes slow to provide some items despite what the law says, and you might also want to see further documentation in the light of the material you first obtain. Time is of the essence in this, and it's sensible to try to get the whole process proceeding as quickly as possible. You should notify the authority in advance of when you intend to arrive or fix an appointment, ideally making contact even before the inspection period itself is open in order to confirm the arrangement. You should also tell them what records you will wish to see, so that they can be retrieved ahead of time.

If you don't get to see what you want within the 30 working days, your chance has gone until next year.

17. Scotland

The legal situation governing freedom of information in Scotland is different to the rest of the UK. There is still a great deal in common between the two systems, including the broad structure of absolute and qualified exemptions, the role of the public interest test, a separate regime for environmental information, an internal review process, and an independent commissioner to receive appeals. The general advice I've given about how best to approach FOI in principle also applies in Scotland. However there are some significant variations which do affect the process for requesting information and challenging refusals.

Scotland has its own freedom of information law, the Freedom of Information (Scotland) Act 2002, usually called FOISA. This regulates access to information from the Scottish Government, its agencies, the Scottish Parliament and many Scottish public authorities, including local councils, Police Scotland, the NHS, universities and colleges, and a range of other public bodies, including the Scottish Information Commissioner (SIC), which is a separate office from the UK Information Commissioner (ICO). It is also available for use by people who live outside Scotland who are seeking material from one of these organisations.

The UK law - the Freedom of Information Act 2000 or FOIA - is still directly relevant to people in Scotland who want to get information from the UK-wide institutions it covers, such as UK government departments like the Foreign, Commonwealth and Development Office, the armed forces or the BBC. Requests to such bodies are dealt with under the UK legislation, wherever the requester resides.

In the particular situation of any information supplied by a UK government department 'in confidence' to the Scottish Government, that can only be requested from the UK department under FOIA, not from the Scottish Government under FOISA.[367]

While the Scottish Act is similar to the UK Act, several divergences of substance should be noted. There are also various points of process that are mainly relevant to public authorities, and some minor nuances with little practical impact, which I won't discuss here. For requesters the crucial differences are as follows.

Coverage

The list of bodies covered by the Scottish law is comparable to those under FOIA, while naturally reflecting the distinctive institutional arrangements of Scotland.[368]

However, unlike elsewhere in the UK, in Scotland FOI has been extended to certain private bodies performing important public functions or services, notably private prisons and registered social landlords (housing associations).[369] This is a significant step in the right direction. Nevertheless, there are many other private providers of public services who are still not covered by FOISA.

The Scottish Information Commissioner's website usefully publishes a list of major Scottish public authorities, which includes their email details for FOI requests.[370]

Requests

Under FOISA a request does not necessarily have to be in writing, as long as it is in some other form 'capable of being used for subsequent reference', such as an audio or video recording.[371]

You do have to state your name, and Scottish public authorities (and indeed the SIC) tend to adopt a stricter insistence on full and real names than often happens in practice elsewhere in the UK. If the person sending the request is actually doing so on behalf of someone else, then that other person must also be named in the request. This was made clear by the Court of Session in a case where a solicitor had sought information on behalf of a client.[372]

There was a period when some of the more obstructive public authorities in Scotland simply rejected requests phrased as asking for documents rather than explicitly for information. In one case appealed to the SIC, the Scottish Government bizarrely insisted that a request seeking 'notes of meetings' only indicated 'where they may find the information being sought without telling them what that information actually was'.[373] This practice followed the same Court of Session decision, which occurred in 2009 and caused some confusion for a time over what counted as a valid request.[374]

However the SIC indicates clearly and explicitly that requesters can define the information being sought in terms of a document or documents, stating: 'Where a requester has asked for a copy of a document and it is reasonably clear that it is the information recorded in the document which the requester wants, the public authority should respond to the request as a request properly made under FOISA.'[375] This is now accepted by the Scottish Government in its FOI code of practice.[376]

Exemptions

The exemptions in FOISA are numbered differently to those in FOIA but their subject-matter and division into absolute ones and qualified ones (whose use is dependent on a public interest test) is very similar.[377]

Some variations include the following: Scotland does not have the same concept of Parliamentary privilege; information intended for future publication can only be withheld where publication will be within 12 weeks; the exemption for communications with the sovereign and those next in line to the throne is qualified, not absolute; and legal professional privilege is replaced by the somewhat wider notion of 'confidentiality of communications in legal proceedings'.[378]

Also, the application of 'prejudice-based' or 'harm-based' exemptions - those which are engaged by a request if it may cause some harm - has to meet a higher bar in Scotland. The harm or prejudice has to be 'substantial'. However the difference this makes is limited, in that if it wasn't substantial then a public interest test would almost certainly favour disclosure anyway.

Generally other disparities are unlikely to affect how a requester should ask for material, although more often they will influence how an authority works through the process of handling a request.

If you want information to do with public sector procurement or contracts, and it might be caught by the exemption for protecting commercial interests, it's worth noting the relevant principles stipulated in the Scottish Government's FOI code of practice. This sets out a list of categories of information which the government says the public should be able to access in order to help ensure transparency and value for money.[379]

Costs

The Scottish law gives public authorities more scope theoretically to charge requesters for the provision of information, but in practice apart from a very small number of authorities or except in some rare cases requests are usually answered without a fee.[380]

The rules on charging specify three tiers: (i) requests costing under £100 must be free; (ii) for requests that cost between £100 and £600, the authority can charge the requester 10% of the cost above £100; (iii) requests costing over £600 can be rejected and indeed normally will be.[381]

So the most an authority would charge is for a request in the middle of these tiers and is £50 (10% of the difference between £600 and £100). Since it probably costs something like this sum or more to issue a fees notice and process a payment, there is little financial purpose in the authority doing so. Generally most authorities don't bother, and some have an explicit policy of not doing so.

But the £600 threshold for the third tier does have substantial practical effect, since it frequently leads to requests being turned down as too expensive. You then face the choice between challenging this via internal review or narrowing your request. The costings can reflect locating, retrieving and providing the information (this may include redaction), treating staff time at a maximum rate of £15 per hour.[382] Thus in Scotland the £600 limit represents 40 hours' work.

However FOISA does not contain a provision allowing authorities to aggregate similar or connected requests for the purpose of assessing if the cost limit is exceeded. Therefore requesters may split a broad request up into a group of several narrower ones (eg, on different aspects or with shorter time periods, and perhaps made by different people), to try to ensure they each come in under the £600 threshold. But this might not succeed. Authorities sometimes just amalgamate them anyway, then estimate the total cost. The SIC has upheld refusals from authorities who have argued that certain requests are so 'interconnected' that it is 'artificial' to consider them separately,[383] and in some extreme cases could dismiss such requests as vexatious.[384]

Advice and assistance

The Scottish Government's code of practice for FOI states that the guidance to the public issued by authorities should include 'the telephone number of someone who can provide advice and assistance'.[385] This option to talk to someone directly may be very useful, depending on how well-informed and helpful they turn out to be (although it is then wise to confirm the outcome of any discussion in writing).

Internal reviews

If you are not happy with the outcome of your request the next stage is to ask the public authority for an internal review. The extensive statistics collated on the SIC website show that approximately one in four reviews lead to the original decision being overturned.[386] This suggests that initial responses are quite often flawed and if your case is reasonable it is well worth the effort of asking for a review. If you are not satisfied with the result of a review, then you can complain to the SIC - see below.

Time limits

The legal time limits in Scotland are stricter than in the rest of the UK, which helps to prevent the worst delays.

Under FOISA there is no time extension allowed for the task of assessing the public interest. Requests have to be answered properly within 20 working days, even if a public interest test is needed for a qualified exemption (or 30 working days in the case of historical material which has already been transferred to the archives of the National Records of Scotland).[387]

If there is no substantive reply within this period, the SIC website advises requesters to treat this as if it is a refusal.[388] You should then move on to ask for an internal review from the public authority (rather than complaining to the SIC about the lack of a response).

Internal reviews also have to be conducted within a legal deadline of 20 working days (again, 30 working days for the National Records of Scotland).[389] This applies to all reviews, whether they are about an outright failure to reply or challenging a refusal. Requesters have time constraints too: you have to ask for a review within 40 working days of receiving a response or (if none received) of the passing of the 20-day deadline.[390]

The Commissioner

You have six months to appeal to the Scottish Information Commissioner after you have received, or should have received, the outcome of an internal review.[391] There is a form to do this on the SIC website.[392] You are not obliged to use this, but even if you don't, it's still a good idea to download and read it, so that you are aware of all the points the SIC wants to be addressed in an appeal and you can make sure you cover them.

The SIC is substantially better resourced for FOI work (compared to population size) than the ICO. This means it tends to process complaints with less delay and a smaller backlog than the ICO has. Nevertheless, delay can still be significant, with most substantive cases taking between four and 12 months.[393]

In contrast to the ICO, which frequently receives and investigates complaints about itself, the SIC is prohibited from doing this. You can put FOI requests to the SIC, and if unhappy with the outcome you can ask for an internal review in the normal way. But you can't then appeal further to the Commissioner as you could if dissatisfied with an internal review from another public body.[394] You also can't complain to the SIC about refusals to disclose issued by a procurator fiscal or the Lord Advocate in relation to a criminal prosecution.[395]

Appeals

Any appeal against a decision by the SIC has to be made within 42 days to the Court of Session. There is no procedure for taking cases to a lower ranking and less formal court like the First-tier Tribunal, which hears the appeals against ICO decisions and where an individual can easily represent themselves. Furthermore any appeal to the Court of Session has to be on a 'point of law', in other words an argument that the SIC got the law wrong or misapplied it. This is in contrast to the First-tier Tribunal which can reconsider and reach a new assessment on the facts of a case.

This makes it harder and more expensive for both authorities and requesters to challenge SIC decisions, and cases are comparatively infrequent. One result is that there is little Scottish judicial decision-making on how to interpret parts of FOISA that may be a source of contention. Given this absence, if you are composing your arguments in a complaint to the SIC, it could well be worth citing and making full use of any favourable similar precedents from tribunals or courts elsewhere in the UK, even though they don't have the same direct legal force in Scotland. The SIC's guidance for Scottish authorities often quotes such cases.

Environmental information

Scotland also has its own equivalent to the EIR, the Environmental Information (Scotland) Regulations or EISR, which govern access to environmental information. These are very similar indeed to the EIR, which is not surprising as both sets of regulations were introduced to implement the same international convention and European Union directive. This particularly applies to the exceptions and the time limits, which are the same. So for example, for environmental requests Scottish authorities can take 40 working days in complex and voluminous cases. This is just as laid down in the EIR, but unlike the 20-working-day maximum stipulated by FOISA for other kinds of information.[396] The advice in chapter 15 on the EIR is therefore almost all equally valid in Scotland.

Nevertheless there are some process differences between the EISR and the EIR. These largely stem from disparities between the broader Scottish FOISA and UK FOIA systems in both law and practice, particularly as follows: Since in Scotland registered social landlords come under FOISA, they are also covered by the EISR, unlike their equivalents elsewhere in the UK; given charging for information is legally allowed within the FOISA system at lower cost levels than with FOIA, the SIC does not object to the 'reasonableness' of fees and so prevent charges for certain environmental requests in the way the ICO tends to do;[397] and appeals against the SIC's decisions under EISR would have to be made on a point of law to the Court of Session, not to a tribunal.

Local audit records

The law on local government audits gives a right of access to many financial records which is far-reaching but can only be used for a short period each year.[398] The Scottish legislation on this is similar to that for elsewhere in the UK (see chapter 16), but some details differ. The annual inspection period when the records can be seen is only 15 working days in Scotland compared to 30 in England, so it is even more important to act promptly when exercising this right.

Data protection

Data protection policy is a 'reserved matter' which has not been devolved to Scotland. So unlike FOI, data protection law is UK-wide legislation that applies in Scotland just as it does elsewhere in the United Kingdom. This means that subject access requests to Scottish organisations are governed by the same rules and procedures as in the rest of the UK, and complaints about how they have been handled have to be made to the ICO, not to the Scottish Information Commissioner. See chapter 16.

18. International FOI requests

If you are interested in information in another country, then it might be possible to obtain it via that country's FOI process. Most nations have some kind of freedom of information law, although the extent to which it is useful or actually used ranges enormously. The policy may be called 'right to information' or 'access to information' rather than 'freedom of information'. In some places it is based on providing access to specific documents rather than responding to questions.

As with the UK, many states allow anyone in the world to submit a request, but there are some exceptions where you have to be a local resident or citizen. In these circumstances you would have to find someone suitable to make the request for you. The website of the Global Investigative Journalism Network has featured a guide to whether foreigners can use national FOI laws in over 100 countries, although it has not been kept up to date.[399]

In the case of the UK's Crown Dependencies, you have to be a resident of the Isle of Man or Guernsey to use their FOI procedures, but anyone can make an FOI request to the public authorities in Jersey.[400]

There are equivalents to the whatdotheyknow.com website in about 30 countries, based on the same software platform.[401] This includes asktheeu.org for the European Union. Using one of these sites will make it easier to submit a request somewhere where you are less familiar with the law and the institutional framework of the public sector. Some of them incorporate the 'Pro' version which allows you to keep your request hidden from public view until you are ready to make it open.

The information you can get from different countries depends not only on their laws, but also on record-keeping practices, administrative efficiency, and cultural attitudes to openness, privacy and responsiveness to citizens. All of these vary substantially across the globe. I have successfully used the FOI processes in the United States, Sweden and Norway, sometimes obtaining documents relating to the UK which I could not get here. These are some of the countries with more effective and wide-ranging FOI systems and comparatively open cultures where you are most likely to be able to make productive requests, although nowhere is completely free of obstructiveness and delay. The principle of 'ask both sides' applies to international exchanges of communications between two countries, just as it does when dealing with correspondence between two public authorities in the UK.

United States

In regard to the United States, which may be the most likely place for you to make a request to, bear in mind that there is a federal FOI law which relates to US government departments and federal agencies such as the FBI and the Environmental Protection Agency,[402] while each state has its own FOI legislation which applies to state authorities. The state laws vary, and some do not allow those from outside the state to make requests. The National Freedom of Information Coalition has a collection of resources on the FOI process in each US state,[403] as does the Reporters Committee for Freedom of the Press.[404] There is an extensive and detailed guide to using the federal FOI system at foia.wiki.[405]

At the simplest level of comparison, you may get larger volumes of material from the US than the UK, often with fewer exclusions or redactions (eg due to less concern over the privacy of personal information), but the process can be even slower. It also tends to be more bureaucratic and legalistic. There is no national equivalent of the Information Commissioner to complain to.

One important tip for journalists is that you should ask for a 'fee waiver', which if granted means you don't have to pay charges, on the basis that you will be reporting and disseminating the material received in a way which promotes public understanding.[406] This applies at the federal level and in some states. Requesters to federal authorities can also ask for 'expedited processing' of a request where there is a 'compelling need', which can include urgency in informing the public.

PART F: Disclosures

19. Using the information

If you have received information you wanted, you now have to decide how you are going to use it. There are some potential complications and pitfalls to bear in mind.

Note however that when the law entitles you to the information, the public authority itself can't impose any conditions on you as a requirement before giving you the material.

Getting it right

Sometimes the nature, status and meaning of the documents or data you've obtained is completely clear. However sometimes it isn't. This is particularly true where you've received a motley and disorganised collection of material, or isolated documents without any explanation of who wrote them or what they represent, or documents with significant passages or details redacted, or just a list of brief extracts, or material that contains unfamiliar terminology and abbreviations. But even simple individual facts presented out of context can be badly misinterpreted.

In particular, lengthy email chains involving multiple interspersed conversations full of jargon and informality and possibly numerous attachments, but from which identities of individuals have been redacted, can be tricky to make sense of.

Don't jump to conclusions. Before you form a view about any especially interesting elements in the disclosure, ask yourself if the following are really completely clear and beyond doubt:

Who actually wrote the passage or compiled the document? What was their status? When was it written? Is it a draft or the final version? Was it later amended? Who was the intended recipient? Was it approved by anyone? What was its purpose? How does it fit in to the context of action or decision-making? Is it ambiguous in what it's referring to? Could it contain terminology with a specialist meaning that outsiders (such as you) might not grasp? Is it reliable? And how does it compare to what is already public?

As in other spheres of life, it's worth taking a moment to think about how the situation appears to people on the other side - those staff of the public authority whose activity has just been partly revealed to you. To them it often feels like an FOI request has grabbed a small and fairly random component of the records of their working life, a bit like a plunge in a bran tub at a fair. (To extend the metaphor, if you've read this book carefully, you should now be good at retrieving the biggest prizes submerged in the lucky dip). This is an inevitable consequence of how the system works, the cost limit, the fact that requesters generally don't have full knowledge of how an authority's records are organised, and indeed the fact that the recipients of a request are often not aware what the requester's purpose is. Nevertheless it means that it's easy as a requester to misunderstand the significance or representativeness of something or misinterpret the context. So take care and check.

Furthermore, don't forget that authorities sometimes provide incorrect answers or wrong information. This could be because they have made a mistake somehow while processing the request, or maybe the information they actually hold is inaccurate or misleading. If some of the material supplied appears inconsistent or surprising, double-check it as soon as possible, to give time for it to be corrected if necessary. If one authority says it has a level of whatever you're asking about which is ten times as much as any other's, don't assume that must be right, as it probably isn't - go back to it to see if it might have made an error or misinterpreted the question.

Context

Sometimes authorities will add extra context or explanation on top of providing the raw information. This probably happens most often in the case of media requests, when the authority wants to include its spin or viewpoint. Some requesters find it irritating, but I'm perfectly happy about it. It can be useful and aid understanding, may sometimes stop a serious misinterpretation of the information supplied, and what you do with the additional material is up to you.

Data surveys and breadth of coverage

If you have sent a round robin request, asking all authorities of the same kind (eg police forces, universities, district councils) for the same data, then a tricky practical dilemma frequently arises: How many answers should you wait for before you publish your analysis of the responses?

Ideally of course you should collect all of them. In practice, if you try to follow everyone up and wait for the last one, you can wait for ever, or at least long enough that the prompt replies are getting out of date. There comes a point where you just have to go with what you've got. This is a difficult judgment call, not least because sometimes authorities who realise they have a bad track record on the topic in question won't reply until they are chased up and it is forced out of them.

I was often asked for advice on this at the BBC. I don't think you can set one arbitrary threshold for the level of responses, but there are a number of factors to take into account.

In terms of the proportion of replies, I'd be reluctant to publish with less than around 70-75%, if you're making any claim that it's representative of the national picture. But you also need to look at where the answers are from: Do they cover a wide range of the authorities involved - big and small, rural and urban, north and south, etc? Or are they concentrated in a particular subset? Do the replies include the particularly large and important authorities which may be crucial to the national picture (eg the Metropolitan Police and other large forces in the case of the police)? And does the data collected so far show limited or extensive variation between places? If there is a lot of variation, then a few authorities with the highest extent of whatever you're examining are making a big difference to the national total, and it's then more likely that the missing authorities will contain further outliers that could be an important aspect of what's happening.

Of course you will sometimes come across media reports where campaign groups, political parties, charities, companies or PR agencies have issued 'FOI surveys' which on closer examination have extrapolated from very low response rates, perhaps down to 20% or so. Obviously the instigators of these only want the useful publicity and don't much care how accurate or representative their results truly are. That's what they are paid to do to promote their cause, but bear in mind this sort of response level does not provide a reliable overall impression.

It's worthwhile whenever you can to publish the full table with data from all the authorities who provided it, and not just focus on the extreme results at either end, good and bad. It's more informative and makes proper use of the material you've bothered to collect and the authorities have complied to supply.

Volume of material

An FOI request can elicit a very large assortment of documents, and the thought of working through it all may be rather daunting. But remember that sometimes there can be a golden nugget of interest hidden somewhere in the extensive collection of tedium. At the BBC we once found a significant current news story within a pile of 1500 pages of guidance and instructions to staff that we had been sent by the Department for Work and Pensions. The more you know about the topic, the more likely you are to spot the nugget. There is also a skill to scanning through similarly formatted documents in a way which enables you to spot the unusual, the inconsistent or the newsworthy. It involves focus, concentration and the right kind of attention to detail.

On the other hand, sometimes there aren't any nuggets of interest hidden in the pile!

Exclusivity - or not

Once you're received the information, you might wonder if you can assume that disclosure is exclusively limited to you. In fact, it's possible that you might not have it to yourself for very long, for a variety of reasons. Release to you under FOI means that the material is fit for release to anyone.

Firstly, somebody else might have asked for the same information at the same time. You might reckon you're the only person smart enough to have thought of asking for a particular document, but as the saying goes, great minds think alike. Or if someone put in a request for the same information but some time later than you did, they'll still get it when you get it. Or if you're already received it, they'll then get it very quickly (doubtless much more quickly than it was for you). Given the material has been compiled for your request, it's a very simple matter to send it off promptly to another requester.

Secondly, some authorities publish disclosure logs where they automatically make public a selection or even all of their FOI responses. This might be more or less straight away, or maybe after a period of delay, perhaps a few days. One example is the Information Commissioner's Office itself.[407] If this is relevant in your case, you need to check the authority's website for the disclosure log and keep an eye on updates to it.

Disclosure logs are entirely voluntary for public authorities, and they come and go. Some authorities that maintained one regularly and for several years have stopped doing so; some start one which then falls into disuse after perhaps just a few months; others keep going. Many authorities are simply not keen on devoting resources to the extra work that is needed. FOI officers report that these logs tend to receive very limited web traffic and do little if anything to prevent the submission of requests more or less identical to ones already answered, negating one of the motives behind them.[408]

Journalists have often been anxious about disclosure logs in case authorities deliberately use them to frustrate a scoop. This can occur, although in practice authorities sometimes don't want to make available to the world an embarrassing response which they may hope the requester involved is too busy or careless or ignorant to grasp the significance of.

Of course, if there's an authority you are particularly interested in which does have a disclosure log, then the corollary is that by keeping across it you might beat someone else to their scoop.

Thirdly, and this again applies particularly to journalists, you may find that the press office of the authority tips off another journalist about the request and provides them with a copy of the response, with the intention that they do the story before you do. This could be in the hope of getting more favourable coverage, or simply to help build a relationship, or possibly even just to spite you. It has happened.

The consequence of all this is that you never know for sure how long you will have the material to yourself. On the other hand in many cases the FOI response is only one piece in an information jigsaw, and it would be of little use to anyone else who doesn't have the other pieces that you may already possess from your work on the subject.

Redaction

It can sometimes be tricky to make proper sense of significantly redacted documents. This is particularly true of intertwined email chains where the identities of recipients and senders have been blanked out. It can be hard to fathom which email is a reply to which. Take care over working this out.

Don't make assumptions about what you surmise redacted material to contain and let that influence you. While it might constitute 'the smoking gun', experience in cases when such information is released at a later stage shows that it may well be surprisingly boring and the point of redacting it is completely unclear.

Authorities sometimes fail to do redaction properly, whether on electronic information or hard copies. Such errors are rarer than they used to be, as officials are better acquainted with redaction software, but they still occasionally occur. For example, redacted passages may sometimes become readable when text is copied-and-pasted into another programme or printed out; or documents may still contain tracked changes; or spreadsheets may have hidden data which can be found by expanding items in pivot tables; or items physically blacked out by marker pen can sometimes be read when held up to the light.

If you come across an instance of this, you then have to assess the legitimacy in making public use of the redacted information, taking into account why the authority wanted to exempt it and what you believe is in the public interest. Think about it carefully, particularly any personal information or material relevant to someone's health and safety.

When I was at the BBC there were occasions when I used and reported information whose redaction had failed, because on looking at the material I and my colleagues felt that there was no valid justification for keeping it secret. On the other hand there was one instance when I simply notified an authority that it had failed to correctly redact a passage about its contact with an individual, which I had thus read. I did this because the public release of that information, if it received attention in the wrong places, could well have made that person into a target for people who wanted to cause him serious harm and had the capacity to do so. It should clearly have been properly redacted to protect his personal safety.

Copyright

Material obtained via FOI may be the copyright of the public authority or some other organisation or person. Requesters are sometimes puzzled or concerned by legalistic standard text about copyright and conditions of reuse which often accompanies information disclosed under FOI. In some cases the wording more or less appears to imply that it is forbidden to do anything very much with the information you've just been given. In most circumstances however there is nothing to worry about and no need to be dissuaded from reasonable use of the information received. As the ICO guidance states, copyright law provides 'ample scope for the contents of information disclosed under FOIA to be debated publicly'.[409]

As is sometimes noted in the copyright statements issued by authorities, but sometimes not, there is an exception from copyright restrictions for 'fair dealing' for various purposes, including non-commercial research and the reporting of current events.[410] This should constitute general protection for journalistic usage. 'Fair dealing' is not precisely defined in law but should cover quoting extracts from and summarising the material, while acknowledging the source.

In any case it is generally unlikely that a public authority will initiate legal action for copyright over reproduction of a limited amount of its own material which it would have to freely give to anyone else who asks, especially when the use is not commercial. This is particularly true because many public authorities are covered by regulations which mean that on request they would have to permit the reuse of many forms of information, in practice probably without charging.[411] Very few FOI/EIR requesters go through the formal process of using these regulations. Many disclosures are also already made in line with the Open Government Licence, which allows free reuse under certain simple and reasonable conditions, such as acknowledging the source.[412]

There are however some circumstances where it is sensible to be more cautious about copyright and take care to avoid infringement. One particular instance is where a third party's intellectual property is involved. This could be, for example, if the authority holds and has to release to you certain kinds of material originating from someone else who might well be unhappy about its reproduction, such as photographs taken by a freelance photographer or a deck of slides from a training course by an external commercial organisation. There can also be complex and somewhat fraught issues over intellectual property between universities and their academic staff. The public authority itself would be protected from breach of copyright when disclosing information in accordance with the law, but that does not safeguard any subsequent reuse by the requester.

Defamation

Occasionally it is possible that information you obtain under FOI could be defamatory about someone. If this seems like it could be the case, then be careful what you do with it. The FOI Act has no exemption relating to defamation, so a public authority may have to give material to a requester even if it is libellous. If this happens then the authority itself is protected against being sued for libel for passing on the defamatory material.[413] But if you then publish it, you have no such safeguard. The fact that you received it initially in an FOI response will be no defence to a libel action.

APPENDICES

Appendix 1: Request templates

FOI request

I am sending this request under the Freedom of Information Act to ask for the following information:
....

If you need any further information from me in order to deal with my request, please call me on ....

If you are encountering practical difficulties with complying with this request, please contact me as soon as possible (in line with your duty under section 16 to advise and assist requesters), so that we can discuss the matter and if necessary I can modify the request.

I would like the information to be emailed to me at ....

If you are able to supply some of this information more quickly than other items, please supply each item when you can rather than delay everything until it is all available.

If it is necessary for any reason to redact any information, please redact the minimum necessary and send me the rest of the material, explaining the legal grounds for each redaction.

Please can you acknowledge receipt of this request.

Many thanks for your assistance.

Note:

When appropriate, include:

Please send me the data requested in the form of an Excel spreadsheet or as a csv file.

EIR request

I am sending this request under the Environmental Information Regulations to ask for the following information:

....

If you need any further information from me in order to deal with my request, please call me on ....

If you are encountering practical difficulties with complying with this request, please contact me as soon as possible (in line with your duty under regulation 9 to advise and assist requesters), so that we can discuss the matter and if necessary I can modify the request.

I would like the information to be emailed to me at ....

If you are able to supply some of this information more quickly than other items, please supply each item when you can rather than delay everything until it is all available.

If it is necessary for any reason to redact any information, please redact the minimum necessary and send me the rest of the material, explaining the legal grounds for each redaction.

Please can you acknowledge receipt of this request.

Many thanks for your assistance.

Note:

When appropriate, include:

Please send me the data requested in the form of an Excel spreadsheet or as a csv file.

Subject access request

I am sending this request under the Data Protection Act and the UK GDPR to ask for a copy of the information you hold about me.

You are most likely to hold information about me in connection with ....

Please focus your searches in this area and ensure that all the material connected to this is included in your response.

I attach copies of documents to confirm my name and address.

If you need any further information from me in order to deal with my request, please call me on ....

I would like the information to be emailed to me at ....

Please can you acknowledge receipt of this request.

Many thanks for your assistance.

Combined SAR and FOI

This is a subject access request under the Data Protection Act and UK GDPR, and also a request under the Freedom of Information Act.

Please send me the following:
1. A copy of the personal data you hold about me.
2. Where any of this personal data consists of an extract from a longer document, the full text of that document.

You are most likely to hold information about me in connection with ....

Please focus your searches in this area and ensure that all the material connected to this is included in your response.

I attach copies of documents to confirm my name and address.

If you need any further information from me in order to deal with my request, please call me on ....

I would like the information to be emailed to me at ....

If you are able to supply some of this information more quickly than other items, please supply each item when you can rather than delay everything until it is all available.

If it is necessary for any reason to redact any information, please redact the minimum necessary and send me the rest of the material, explaining the legal grounds for each redaction.

Please can you acknowledge receipt of this request.

Many thanks for your assistance.

Appendix 2: Useful sources

The following are useful reference documents or sources of further information.

Legislation

The important items of legislation are:

FOI and EIR

Freedom of Information Act 2000
Freedom of Information and Data Protection (Appropriate Limit and Fees) Regulations 2004
Environmental Information Regulations 2004

FOI and EIR in Scotland

Freedom of Information (Scotland) Act 2002
Freedom of Information (Fees for Required Disclosure) (Scotland) Regulations 2004
Environmental Information (Scotland) Regulations 2004

Personal information

Data Protection Act 2018
United Kingdom General Data Protection Regulation
Access to Health Records Act 1990

All can be found on the legislation.gov.uk website. The UK GDPR, which may be the least easy to locate, is at https://www.legislation.gov.uk/eur/2016/679.

When consulting the text of legislation on this site, always make sure you are looking at the latest available version incorporating amendments, rather than the original version (whose url will end with either 'enacted' or 'made').

Codes of practice

These are issued by government as a guide to recommended best practice. They are advisory and do not have the force of law. However public authorities generally have regard to them, and the ICO or SIC will certainly expect authorities to comply with their contents.

Freedom of information code of practice (Cabinet Office):
https://assets.publishing.service.gov.uk/government/uploads/syst em/uploads/attachment_data/file/744071/CoP_FOI_Code_of_P ractice_-_Minor_Amendments_20180926_.pdf

Code of practice on the management of records issued under section 46 of the Freedom of Information Act 2000 (Department for Digital, Culture, Media and Sport):
https://assets.publishing.service.gov.uk/government/uploads/syst em/uploads/attachment_data/file/1010395/Freedom_Informatio n_Code_Practice_Web_Accessible.pdf

Code of practice on the discharge of the obligations of public authorities under the Environmental Information Regulations 2004 (Department for Environment, Food and Rural Affairs):
https://webarchive.nationalarchives.gov.uk/ukgwa/200907311443 34mp_/http://www.defra.gov.uk/corporate/opengov/eir/pdf/co p-eir.pdf

Scottish Ministers' code of practice on the discharge of functions by Scottish public authorities:
https://www.gov.scot/publications/foi-eir-section-60-code-of-practice

Information Commissioner's Office

Guidance

The ICO has issued a wide range of detailed guidance about

FOI/EIR and interpreting the law. While this is aimed at public authorities and is written from their perspective, it is also very helpful for requesters. If you are in dispute with an authority then it is worthwhile consulting the relevant pages. It is particularly useful for identifying earlier related decisions by the ICO or tribunals and courts. However, although the contents are often updated, they might not yet reflect the latest cases.

ICO guidance does not have legal force, but is very influential on the behaviour of public authorities. It is occasionally knowingly defied by some authorities, and can be disregarded by tribunals and courts who will reach their own view on the topic at issue. However FOI officers tend to take it very seriously and authorities normally seek to abide by it. It is also usually the starting point of legal argument on a contested matter, even if it doesn't always survive the discussion process to be the finishing point too.

There is an index to the guidance here: https://ico.org.uk/for-organisations/guidance-index/freedom-of-information-and-environmental-information-regulations

A list of what's been recently updated is here: https://ico.org.uk/for-organisations/guide-to-freedom-of-information/whats-new

A clear and detailed overall summary in one place is here: https://ico.org.uk/media/for-organisations/guide-to-freedom-of-information-4-9.pdf

Decision notices

Previous ICO decisions can be found here: https://icosearch.ico.org.uk/s/search.html?collection=ico-meta&profile=decisions&query

One point to be aware of if you apply the filter 'by authority' is that many public authorities are listed in a very unhelpful way, with names beginning with 'The', 'Office of', 'Governing Body of', etc, and what's even worse is that sometimes the naming is inconsistent. So, for example, decisions relating to the University of Oxford are listed partly under 'University of Oxford' and partly under 'The Governing Body of the University of Oxford'. Unfortunately you may need to scan the entire list rather than rely on its alphabetical order.

Scottish Information Commissioner

The SIC guidance is here:
https://www.itspublicknowledge.info/briefings-and-guidance

Previous decisions are here:
https://www.itspublicknowledge.info/decisions

A simple guide aimed at requesters is here:
https://www.itspublicknowledge.info/sites/default/files/2022-03/Your_Right_to_Know_-_Online_Version-compressed.pdf

First-tier Tribunal

A list of the FTT's current information rights cases is here (although it is sometimes not up to date):
https://www.gov.uk/government/publications/information-rights-appeals-register-of-tribunal-cases

FTT judgments are here:
https://informationrights.decisions.tribunals.gov.uk/Public/search.aspx

However it can be easier to locate FTT judgments (as well as those for higher courts) by using the more powerful and flexible search options on the BAILII website at:
https://www.bailii.org/form/search_cases.html

Websites

Other useful websites for more background on FOI and following the latest developments include:

My own at www.rosenbaum.org.uk

The Campaign for Freedom of Information, with thoroughly-researched briefing documents, news updates and details of how to support their hugely important campaigning work: https://www.cfoi.org.uk

The Campaign for Freedom of Information in Scotland, the partner organisation in Scotland: https://www.cfois.scot

To see what others have asked, how they asked for it, and what they got, plus informed discussion of FOI issues on the blog: https://www.whatdotheyknow.com

International equivalents of this can be located via: http://alaveteli.org/deployments

Access Info Europe, Europe-wide campaign group for greater rights of access to information: https://www.access-info.org

The campaigning news site openDemocracy has produced much determined and effective reporting on FOI and transparency in public life:
https://www.opendemocracy.net/en/freedom-of-information

The website of the data journalist Claire Miller has a rich supply of FOI content, including excellent examples of FOI news stories and good advice:
https://clairemiller.net/blog/category/freedom-of-information

Well-informed and astute commentary on information rights and law (FOI/EIR and data protection) can be found via the following:

Jon Baines, experienced specialist in information rights: https://informationrightsandwrongs.com

Tim Turner, trainer at 2040Training who sends out a useful and informative newsletter:
https://2040training.co.uk/update

Panopticon blog, written by specialist barristers from 11KBW chambers:
https://panopticonblog.com

ActNow Training, experienced practitioners in information law:
https://www.actnow.org.uk/news

Two sites which are no longer regularly updated but still feature a lot of valuable information and helpful resources:
FOI Directory (aimed at requesters): https://www.foi.directory
FOIMan (aimed at practitioners, but still useful for requesters): https://www.foiman.com

Books and reports

To understand the full legal implications and technicalities of an issue:
Damien Welfare, *Cornerstone on Information Law*, Bloomsbury Professional, 2019 - a detailed reference work aimed at lawyers and practitioners, with clear and logical exposition of information law and its intricacies

To appreciate the responsibilities and perspectives of FOI officers:
Paul Gibbons, *The Freedom of Information Officer's Handbook*, Facet Publishing, 2019 - a practically grounded and insightful guide to the law and its implementation from the viewpoint of public authorities

The following three books all contain a good range of helpful tips and information for FOI requesters, although they are no longer up to date:
Matt Burgess, *Freedom of Information*, Routledge, 2015
Brendan Montague and Lucas Amin, *FOIA Without the Lawyer*, Centre for Investigative Journalism, 2012
Heather Brooke, *Your Right to Know*, Pluto Press, 2007

For political background and context:
Ben Worthy, *The Politics of Freedom of Information*, Manchester

University Press, 2017 - a perceptive, highly informative and balanced account of the development of FOI, the political ramifications and international comparisons

For analysis of the workings of FOI in practice:

Lucas Amin, *Art of Darkness*, openDemocracy, 2020 - a well-researched and valuable investigation into failings in the operation and enforcement of the FOI system

Appendix 3: ICO priority criteria

The criteria to be used by the Information Commissioner's Office for deciding whether to prioritise complaints are as follows:[414]

• Is there a high public interest in the information requested? Does it raise a new, unique or clearly high-profile issue that should be looked at quickly?

Indicators of this may include whether:

the case is subject to significant media interest - eg there are existing news reports related to the subject matter in the public domain;

the case concerns an issue that is likely to involve a large amount of public money in the context of the size of the public body involved - eg a local council contract for provision of services across its whole area or a nationwide central government spend; or

the requester needs the information to respond to a live and significant public consultation and the time for achieving resolution is reasonable to inform the decision-making process.

• Are any groups or individuals likely to be significantly affected by the information requested? This may include information:

which covers policies, events or other matters that potentially have a significant impact on vulnerable people or groups;

that has a high potential impact or harm on a proportionately substantial number of people in relation to the information requested; or

that may directly affect the health or another personal issue of the requester or others, that means they need a swift resolution - eg it may impact on treatment or is about a live court case.

• Would prioritisation have significant operational benefits, or support those regulated? For example, is the request:

novel, or could provide the basis for guidance or support for other regulated bodies;

part of a round robin request or otherwise linked to other requests or appeals.

• Does the requester have the ability and desire to use the information for the benefit of the public? This may include where the requester has:

a clear aim of raising awareness around a topic of significant public interest and the means or contacts to do so;

access to a suitable platform to allow the public at large to use the requested information to scrutinise the decisions made in the public sector.

NOTES

1. 'Official failings in vetting of businessman for OBE revealed',
https://www.bbc.co.uk/news/uk-politics-55834106
2. 'Prince Charles warned Tony Blair against GM foods',
https://www.bbc.co.uk/news/uk-politics-46844454; 'MOT failure rates
released', https://web.archive.org/web/20100305075758/https://www.bbc.
co.uk/blogs/opensecrets/2010/01/mot_failure_rates_released.html; 'Large
employers fail to spend apprenticeship money', https://www.bbc.co.uk/news/
uk-politics-51505625; 'Month of birth affects chance of attending Oxbridge',
https://www.bbc.co.uk/news/uk-politics-21579484
3. https://www.mysociety.org/2022/11/17/how-many-people-use-freedom-of-
information-the-numbers-blog-post/
4. *Freedom of Information statistics: annual 2021 bulletin*,
https://www.gov.uk/government/statistics/freedom-of-information-statistics-
annual-2021/freedom-of-information-statistics-annual-2021-bulletin
5. My calculations from data at https://www.itspublicknowledge.info/statistics
6. Alex Parsons and Rebecca Rumbul, *Freedom of Information in Local Government*,
mySociety, 2019, https://research.mysociety.org/html/local-gov-foi/#foi-
statistics; Ben Worthy, Some are More Open than Others: Comparing the
Impact of the Freedom of Information Act 2000 on Local and Central
Government in the UK, *Journal of Comparative Policy Analysis: Research and Practice*,
2013, volume 15, issue 5, pages 395-414,
https://www.tandfonline.com/doi/abs/10.1080/13876988.2013.836300
7. https://www.whatdotheyknow.com
8. Tony Blair, *A Journey: My Political Life*, 2010, pages 516-7
9. Interview with Jenni Russell, *The Times* magazine, 28 March 2015, page 33
10. https://ico.org.uk/for-organisations/guidance-index/freedom-of-
information-and-environmental-information-regulations/
11. https://icosearch.ico.org.uk/s/search.html?collection=ico-meta&profile=
decisions&query
12. Brendan Montague and Lucas Amin, *FOIA Without the Lawyer*, Centre for
Investigative Journalism, 2012
13. FOIA section 16(1)
14. https://assets.publishing.service.gov.uk/government/uploads/system/
uploads/attachment_data/file/408848/zoo2-inspection-report-form.pdf
15. For a detailed analysis, see Lucas Amin, *Art of Darkness*, openDemocracy,
2020, https://www.documentcloud.org/documents/20415987-art-of-darkness-
opendemocracy
16. https://www.bbc.co.uk/blogs/opensecrets/2010/10/westland_cabinet_
minutes_relea.html
17. Chris Stokel-Walker, '£40k spent hiding how rarely northern powerhouse
minister visited north', *The Guardian*, 27 September 2018,

https://www.theguardian.com/politics/2018/sep/27/government-hid-details-of-northern-powerhouse-minister-james-wharton-visits-to-the-north

18. https://www.bbc.co.uk/news/uk-politics-46844454

19. This is documented in evidence I submitted to the House of Commons Public Administration and Constitutional Affairs Committee for its inquiry into the Cabinet Office and FOI, at https://committees.parliament.uk/writtenevidence/38235/pdf/

20. ICO, *Section 16 – Advice and Assistance*, https://ico.org.uk/for-organisations/guidance-index/freedom-of-information-and-environmental-information-regulations/section-16-advice-and-assistance/

21. Paul Gibbons, *The Freedom of Information Officer's Handbook*, Facet Publishing, 2019, pages 151, 172

22. FOIA section 8(1)

23. *Ghafoor v Information Commissioner*, EA/2015/0140, paragraphs 25-27, https://informationrights.decisions.tribunals.gov.uk/DBFiles/Decision/i1670/Ghafoor,%20Bilal%20EA.2015.0140%20(10.11.15).pdf

24. https://twitter.com/rosenbaum6/status/1499700577395257348/photo/1

25. ICO, *Recognising a request made under the Freedom of Information Act (Section 8)*, paragraphs 17, 30, https://ico.org.uk/media/for-organisations/documents/1164/recognising-a-request-made-under-the-foia.pdf

26. ICO, *Recognising a request made under the Freedom of Information Act (Section 8)*, paragraph 19, https://ico.org.uk/media/for-organisations/documents/1164/recognising-a-request-made-under-the-foia.pdf

27. ICO, *Recognising a request made under the Freedom of Information Act (Section 8)*, paragraphs 40-42, https://ico.org.uk/media/for-organisations/documents/1164/recognising-a-request-made-under-the-foia.pdf

28. ICO, *Recognising a request made under the Freedom of Information Act (Section 8)*, paragraphs 35-39, https://ico.org.uk/media/for-organisations/documents/1164/recognising-a-request-made-under-the-foia.pdf

29. FOIA section 8(1)(b)

30. FOIA section 8(2)

31. www.foi.directory/foi-directory-foi-emails

32. https://www.whatdotheyknow.com/pro

33. *Maurizi and others v Information Commissioner and others*, [2021] UKFTT 85 (GRC), https://www.bailii.org/uk/cases/UKFTT/GRC/2021/85.html

34. As laid down in this early and influential tribunal decision from 2006: *S v Information Commissioner and General Register Office*, EA/2006/0030, paragraph 80, https://informationrights.decisions.tribunals.gov.uk/DBFiles/Decision/i147/S.pdf; the term goes back to the parliamentary debates on the FOI legislation, eg https://hansard.parliament.uk/Lords/2000-10-17/debates/0ec990f0-a137-4a90-b814-e491c83101a7/PurposesOfThisAct#contribution-678eeea2-069f-43d0-8317-92e733c48c13

35. See the ICO guidance, *Consideration of the applicant's identity or motives*, https://ico.org.uk/for-organisations/guidance-index/freedom-of-information-and-environmental-information-regulations/consideration-of-the-applicant-s-

identity-or-motives/

36. https://www.legislation.gov.uk/ukpga/2000/36/schedule/1

37. FOIA section 5

38. FOIA schedule 1, part VI

39. See https://www.bbc.co.uk/news/uk-politics-36914926

40. https://www.whatdotheyknow.com/body/list/foi_no

41. *Independent Parliamentary Standards Authority v Information Commissioner and Leapman*, [2015] EWCA Civ 388, https://www.bailii.org/ew/cases/EWCA/Civ/2015/388.html; see also the earlier Upper Tribunal decision in the same case, [2014] UKUT 0033 (AAC), https://administrativeappeals.decisions.tribunals.gov.uk/Aspx/view.aspx?id=4089

42. ICO, *The right to recorded information and requests for documents*, https://ico.org.uk/for-organisations/guidance-index/freedom-of-information-and-environmental-information-regulations/the-right-to-recorded-information-and-requests-for-documents

43. ICO, *The right to recorded information and requests for documents*, https://ico.org.uk/for-organisations/guidance-index/freedom-of-information-and-environmental-information-regulations/the-right-to-recorded-information-and-requests-for-documents

44. ICO, *Determining whether we hold information*, https://ico.org.uk/for-organisations/guidance-index/freedom-of-information-and-environmental-information-regulations/determining-whether-we-hold-information

45. ICO, *Recognising a request made under the Freedom of Information Act (Section 8)*, paragraphs 82-83, https://ico.org.uk/media/for-organisations/documents/1164/recognising-a-request-made-under-the-foia.pdf

46. FOIA section 84

47. *Tintagel Parish Council v Information Commissioner and Jordan*, EA/2021/0036, https://informationrights.decisions.tribunals.gov.uk/DBFiles/Decision/i2901/017a%20050821%20Final%20Decision.pdf, paragraph 92

48. *Johnson v Information Commissioner and Ministry of Justice*, EA 2006/0085, paragraphs 45-49, https://informationrights.decisions.tribunals.gov.uk/DBFiles/Decision/i90/Johnson.pdf

49. ICO, *Determining whether we hold information*, https://ico.org.uk/for-organisations/guidance-index/freedom-of-information-and-environmental-information-regulations/determining-whether-we-hold-information

50. *Home Office v Information Commissioner*, EA/2008/0027, paragraph 15, https://informationrights.decisions.tribunals.gov.uk/DBFiles/Decision/i203/homeOffice_webDecision_15Aug08.pdf

51. ICO, *The Guide to Freedom of Information*, page 31, https://ico.org.uk/media/for-organisations/guide-to-freedom-of-information-4-9.pdf

52. ICO, *Requests about previous information requests (meta requests)*, https://ico.org.uk/for-organisations/guidance-index/freedom-of-information-and-environmental-information-regulations/requests-about-previous-information-requests-meta-requests

53. *Home Office and Ministry of Justice v Information Commissioner*, [2009] EWHC 1611

(Admin), paragraph 4, https://www.bailii.org/ew/cases/EWHC/Admin/2009/1611.html

54. ICO, *Requests about previous information requests (meta requests)*, https://ico.org.uk/for-organisations/guidance-index/freedom-of-information-and-environmental-information-regulations/requests-about-previous-information-requests-meta-requests

55. FOIA section 3(2)

56. For example, see this case where the ICO overruled the Department for Education: ICO Decision Notice FS50422276, https://ico.org.uk/media/action-weve-taken/decision-notices/2012/712854/fs_50422276.pdf

57. See this First-tier Tribunal case: *Lownie v Information Commissioner, Cabinet Office and University of Southampton*, EA/2020/0021, EA/2020/0026, EA/2020/0058, EA/2020/0059 and EA/2021/0125, https://www.bailii.org/uk/cases/UKFTT/GRC/2022/2020_0026.pdf

58. ICO, *Outsourcing - FOIA and EIR obligations*, https://ico.org.uk/for-organisations/guidance-index/freedom-of-information-and-environmental-information-regulations/outsourcing-foia-and-eir-obligations/

59. ICO, *Official information held in non-corporate communications channels*, https://ico.org.uk/for-organisations/guidance-index/freedom-of-information-and-environmental-information-regulations/official-information-held-in-non-corporate-communications-channels

60. *The Cabinet Office Freedom of Information Clearing House: Government Response to the Committee's Ninth Report of Session 2021–22*, page 5, https://committees.parliament.uk/publications/22985/documents/168393/default (the Cabinet Office's existing guidance to departments on the use of personal email - at https://assets.publishing.service.gov.uk/government/uploads/system/uploads/attachment_data/file/207131/Private_Email_guidance.pdf - was issued in 2013, has been thoroughly out of date for some time, and is in the process of being revised)

61. For example: https://www.theguardian.com/politics/2021/jun/27/hancock-faces-scrutiny-for-using-private-email-for-official-business - 'After weeks of delays and a complaint by the Guardian to the information commissioner, the Department of Health and Social Care (DHSC) wrote to the Guardian to apologise for "unintentionally misunderstanding" that the December request for emails was for exchanges between Hancock and Bourne rather than just the official correspondence which goes through his private office.'

62. Elizabeth Denham, 'Transparency – more key than ever in the WhatsApp era', *Municipal Journal*, 2 November 2021, https://www.themj.co.uk/Transparency--more-key-than-ever-in-the-WhatsApp-era/221861

63. ICO, *Official information held in non-corporate communications channels*, https://ico.org.uk/for-organisations/guidance-index/freedom-of-information-and-environmental-information-regulations/official-information-held-in-non-corporate-communications-channels

64. ICO, *Behind the screens – maintaining government transparency and data security in the*

age of messaging apps, pages 46-47, https://ico.org.uk/media/about-the-ico/documents/4020886/behind-the-screens.pdf

65. See ICO Decision Notice IC-40467-C7K2, paragraphs 62-64, https://ico.org.uk/media/action-weve-taken/decision-notices/2022/4020076/ic-40467-c7k2.pdf

66. ICO, *Official information held in non-corporate communications channels*, https://ico.org.uk/for-organisations/guidance-index/freedom-of-information-and-environmental-information-regulations/official-information-held-in-non-corporate-communications-channels

67. Tim Durrant, Alice Lilly and Paeony Tingay, *WhatsApp in Government*, Institute for Government, 2022, p22, https://www.instituteforgovernment.org.uk/sites/default/files/publications/whatsapp-in-government.pdf

68. Whitehead v Information Commissioner, EA/2013/0262, paragraph 16, https://informationrights.decisions.tribunals.gov.uk/DBFiles/Decision/i1334/EA-2013-0262_29-04-2014.pdf

69. ICO, *Determining whether we hold information*, https://ico.org.uk/for-organisations/guidance-index/freedom-of-information-and-environmental-information-regulations/determining-whether-we-hold-information

70. Cabinet Office, *Freedom of Information Code of Practice*, paragraph 1.11, https://assets.publishing.service.gov.uk/government/uploads/system/uploads/attachment_data/file/744071/CoP_FOI_Code_of_Practice_-_Minor_Amendments_20180926_.pdf

71. Cabinet Office, *Information and Records Retention & Destruction Policy*, paragraph 2.5, https://www.whatdotheyknow.com/request/804271/response/1914691/attach/4/CO%20Information%20Records%20Retention%20Destruction%20Policy%20v1.1%20Feb%202021%20Redacted.pdf

72. FOIA section 11(1)

73. *Innes v Information Commissioner and Buckinghamshire County Council*, [2014] EWCA Civ 1086, paragraphs 48-49, https://www.bailii.org/ew/cases/EWCA/Civ/2014/1086.html

74. ICO Decision Notice IC-90942-K0X5, https://ico.org.uk/media/action-weve-taken/decision-notices/2021/4017930/ic-90942-k0x5.pdf

75. *Innes v Information Commissioner and Buckinghamshire County Council*, [2014] EWCA Civ 1086, https://www.bailii.org/ew/cases/EWCA/Civ/2014/1086.html

76. FOIA section 11(1A)

77. FOIA section 11(5)

78. Cabinet Office, *Open Data White Paper - Unleashing the Potential*, https://assets.publishing.service.gov.uk/government/uploads/system/uploads/attachment_data/file/78946/CM8353_acc.pdf

79. Cabinet Office, *Freedom of Information Code of Practice*, paragraph 11.18, https://assets.publishing.service.gov.uk/government/uploads/system/uploads/attachment_data/file/744071/CoP_FOI_Code_of_Practice_-_Minor_Amendments_20180926_.pdf

80. ICO, *Means of communicating information (section 11)*, https://ico.org.uk/for-

organisations/guidance-index/freedom-of-information-and-environmental-information-regulations/means-of-communicating-information-section-11

81. FOIA section 10(1)

82. ICO, *Time limits for compliance under the Freedom of Information Act (Section 10)*, paragraph 24, https://ico.org.uk/media/for-organisations/documents/1165/time-for-compliance-foia-guidance.pdf

83. Freedom of Information (Time for Compliance with Request) Regulations 2004 , regulations 3-6

84. FOIA section 10(3)

85. ICO, *Time limits for compliance under the Freedom of Information Act (Section 10)*, paragraph 62, https://ico.org.uk/media/for-organisations/documents/1165/time-for-compliance-foia-guidance.pdf

86. ICO, *The Guide to Freedom of Information*, page 56, https://ico.org.uk/media/for-organisations/guide-to-freedom-of-information-4-9.pdf

87. FOIA sections 17(1), 17(2)

88. FOIA section 10(6)

89. Lucas Amin, *Art of Darkness*, openDemocracy, 2020, page 26, https://s3.documentcloud.org/documents/20415987/art-of-darkness-opendemocracy.pdf

90. Freedom of Information and Data Protection (Appropriate Limit and Fees) Regulations 2004, regulations 6(3), 6(4)

91. https://assets.publishing.service.gov.uk/government/uploads/system/uploads/attachment_data/file/744071/CoP_FOI_Code_of_Practice_-_Minor_Amendments_20180926_.pdf

92. FOIA section 16

93. Paragraph 2.10

94. Paragraph 2.12

95. ICO, *Section 16 – Advice and Assistance*, https://ico.org.uk/for-organisations/guidance-index/freedom-of-information-and-environmental-information-regulations/section-16-advice-and-assistance

96. FOIA section 16(1)

97. ICO Decision Notice IC-47340-Y0M6, https://ico.org.uk/media/action-weve-taken/decision-notices/2021/2619879/ic-47340-y0m6.pdf

98. https://www.bbc.co.uk/news/uk-politics-18708512

99. Cabinet Office, *Freedom of Information Code of Practice*, paragraph 1.11, https://assets.publishing.service.gov.uk/government/uploads/system/uploads/attachment_data/file/744071/CoP_FOI_Code_of_Practice_-_Minor_Amendments_20180926_.pdf

100. For example, 'Sheffield Council members attempted to block emails about controversial tree felling plans from being released', 5 March 2020, https://www.thestar.co.uk/news/politics/sheffield-council-members-attempted-block-emails-about-controversial-tree-felling-plans-being-released-2092120

101. FOIA section 17

102. ICO, *The right to recorded information and requests for documents*,

https://ico.org.uk/for-organisations/guidance-index/freedom-of-information-and-environmental-information-regulations/the-right-to-recorded-information-and-requests-for-documents

103. ICO, *The Guide to Freedom of Information*, page 58, https://ico.org.uk/media/for-organisations/guide-to-freedom-of-information-4-9.pdf

104. ICO Decision Notice IC-47382-L6C8, paragraphs 99-101, https://ico.org.uk/media/action-weve-taken/decision-notices/2021/4019322/ic-47382-l6c8.pdf

105. A couple of examples: https://www.whatdotheyknow.com/request/873715/response/2088989/attach/4/CO%20Information%20Records%20Retention%20Destruction%20Policy%20v1%20redacted.1%20Feb%202021.pdf and https://ico.org.uk/media/about-the-ico/disclosure-log/4020909/ic-175050-q0c2-disclosure.pdf

106. Philip Shaw, 'Kasimir Malevich's Black Square', in Nigel Llewellyn and Christine Riding (eds), *The Art of the Sublime*, Tate Research Publication, 2013, https://www.tate.org.uk/art/research-publications/the-sublime/philip-shaw-kasimir-malevichs-black-square-r1141459

107. Freedom of Information and Data Protection (Appropriate Limit and Fees) Regulations 2004, regulation 3; FOIA schedule 1, part I

108. Freedom of Information and Data Protection (Appropriate Limit and Fees) Regulations 2004, regulation 4(4)

109. Freedom of Information and Data Protection (Appropriate Limit and Fees) Regulations 2004, regulation 4(3)

110. *Chief Constable of South Yorkshire Police v Information Commissioner*, [2011] EWHC 44 (Admin), paragraph 32, https://www.bailii.org/ew/cases/EWHC/Admin/2011/44.html

111. Cabinet Office, *Freedom of Information Code of Practice*, paragraphs 6.7, 6.8, https://assets.publishing.service.gov.uk/government/uploads/system/uploads/attachment_data/file/744071/CoP_FOI_Code_of_Practice_-_Minor_Amendments_20180926_.pdf

112. ICO, *Requests where the cost of compliance exceeds the appropriate limit*, paragraphs 21-38, https://ico.org.uk/media/for-organisations/documents/1199/costs_of_compliance_exceeds_appropriate_limit.pdf

113. ICO, *Refusing a request: writing a refusal notice*, paragraph 31, https://ico.org.uk/media/for-organisations/documents/1628/refusing_a_request_writing_a_refusal_notice_foi.pdf

114. FOIA section 13

115. Freedom of Information and Data Protection (Appropriate Limit and Fees) Regulations 2004, regulation 7

116. See https://assets.publishing.service.gov.uk/government/uploads/system/uploads/attachment_data/file/544991/Digest_for_FOI_0351-16.pdf

117. ICO Decision Notice IC-72459-C8L5, paragraph 29, https://ico.org.uk/media/action-weve-taken/decision-notices/2022/4020196/ic-72459-c8l5.pdf

118. Cabinet Office, *Freedom of Information Code of Practice*, paragraph 2.10, https://assets.publishing.service.gov.uk/government/uploads/system/uploads/attachment_data/file/744071/CoP_FOI_Code_of_Practice_-_Minor_Amendments_20180926_.pdf

119. ICO Decision Notice FS50512601, paragraphs 29-33, https://ico.org.uk/media/action-weve-taken/decision-notices/2014/967468/fs_50512601.pdf

120. *Slater v Information Commissioner and Department for Work and Pensions*, EA/2019/0118, paragraph 69, https://informationrights.decisions.tribunals.gov.uk/DBFiles/Decision/i2656/Slater,%20John%20EA-2019-0118%20Part%20Allowed%20%20.pdf

121. ICO, *Recognising a request made under the Freedom of Information Act (Section 8)*, paragraph 68, https://ico.org.uk/media/for-organisations/documents/1164/recognising-a-request-made-under-the-foia.pdf

122. Freedom of Information and Data Protection (Appropriate Limit and Fees) Regulations 2004, regulation 5(2)

123. Freedom of Information and Data Protection (Appropriate Limit and Fees) Regulations 2004, regulation 5(1)

124. ICO, *Determining whether we hold information*, https://ico.org.uk/for-organisations/guidance-index/freedom-of-information-and-environmental-information-regulations/determining-whether-we-hold-information

125. Cabinet Office, *Freedom of Information Code of Practice*, paragraph 1.12, https://assets.publishing.service.gov.uk/government/uploads/system/uploads/attachment_data/file/744071/CoP_FOI_Code_of_Practice_-_Minor_Amendments_20180926_.pdf

126. Department for Digital, Culture, Media and Sport, *Code of Practice on the management of records issued under section 46 of the Freedom of Information Act 2000*, paragraphs 2.2.2, 2.3.1, 2.7.4, 2.7.6, https://assets.publishing.service.gov.uk/government/uploads/system/uploads/attachment_data/file/1010395/Freedom_Information_Code_Practice_Web_Accessible.pdf

127. FOIA section 1(4)

128. ICO, *Retention and destruction of information*, https://ico.org.uk/for-organisations/guidance-index/freedom-of-information-and-environmental-information-regulations/retention-and-destruction-of-information/

129. FOIA section 77

130. FOIA section 14(2)

131. ICO, *Dealing with repeat requests*, https://ico.org.uk/for-organisations/guidance-index/freedom-of-information-and-environmental-information-regulations/dealing-with-repeat-requests/

132. FOIA section 14(1)

133. ICO, *What does vexatious mean?*, https://ico.org.uk/for-organisations/guidance-index/freedom-of-information-and-environmental-information-regulations/dealing-with-vexatious-requests-section-14/what-does-vexatious-mean; see also section 7 of the Cabinet Office's *Freedom of Information Code of*

Practice at https://assets.publishing.service.gov.uk/government/uploads/
system/uploads/attachment_data/file/744071/CoP_FOI_Code_of_Practice_-
_Minor_Amendments_20180926_.pdf

134. https://blog.olliesemporium.co.uk/

135. *Information Commissioner v Dransfield*, [2012] UKUT 440 (AAC), paragraph 48,
https://www.bailii.org/uk/cases/UKUT/AAC/2013/440.html

136. *Information Commissioner v Dransfield*, [2012] UKUT 440 (AAC), paragraphs
26, 29-39, 61, https://www.bailii.org/uk/cases/UKUT/AAC/2013/440.html

137. *Dransfield v Information Commissioner and Devon County Council*, [2015] EWCA
Civ 454, paragraph 68,
https://www.bailii.org/ew/cases/EWCA/Civ/2015/454.html

138. ICO, *How do we deal with a single burdensome request?*, https://ico.org.uk/for-
organisations/guidance-index/freedom-of-information-and-environmental-
information-regulations/dealing-with-vexatious-requests-section-14/how-do-
we-deal-with-a-single-burdensome-request; see also the Cabinet Office's *Freedom
of Information Code of Practice*, paragraphs 7.12-7.15, https://assets.publishing.
service.gov.uk/government/uploads/system/uploads/attachment_data/file/74
4071/CoP_FOI_Code_of_Practice_-_Minor_Amendments_20180926_.pdf

139. *Office of the Gas & Electricity Markets v Information Commissioner*, [2021]
UKFTT 2020_0036 (GRC), https://www.bailii.org/uk/cases/UKFTT/GRC/
2021/2020_0036.html

140. FOIA section 2

141. FOIA section 2

142. It was introduced by the Intellectual Property Act 2014, section 20

143. *Baker v Information Commissioner and Cabinet Office*, EA/2006/0045, paragraph
26, https://informationrights.decisions.tribunals.gov.uk/DBFiles/Decision/
i24/Baker.pdf

144. ICO, *How sections 23 and 24 interact*, https://ico.org.uk/for-organisations/
guidance-index/freedom-of-information-and-environmental-information-
regulations/how-sections-23-and-24-interact

145. ICO, *Section 27 - International relations*, https://ico.org.uk/for-organisations/
guidance-index/freedom-of-information-and-environmental-information-
regulations/section-27-international-relations

146. FOIA sections 35(5), 35(1), and 84 (for definition of 'government
department')

147. FOIA section 35(1)

148. See definitions and links at https://www.gov.uk/guidance/public-bodies-
reform

149. ICO, *Government policy (section 35)*, paragraphs 43-61,
https://ico.org.uk/media/for-organisations/documents/1200/government-
policy-foi-section-35-guidance.pdf

150. ICO, *Government policy (section 35)*, paragraphs 30, 42,
https://ico.org.uk/media/for-organisations/documents/1200/government-
policy-foi-section-35-guidance.pdf

151. FOIA section 35(4)

152. ICO, *Government policy (section 35)*, paragraphs 88, 89, 192, 193, 199, 202, 206, 207, 224, 226, 227, https://ico.org.uk/media/for-organisations/documents/1200/government-policy-foi-section-35-guidance.pdf

153. ICO Decision Notice IC-144871-H3T3, paragraph 47, https://ico.org.uk/media/action-weve-taken/decision-notices/2022/4020290/ic-144871-h3t3.pdf

154. ICO Decision Notice IC-117190-V1F3, https://ico.org.uk/media/action-weve-taken/decision-notices/2022/4020648/ic-117190-v1f3.pdf

155. *The Civil Service Code*, https://www.gov.uk/government/publications/civil-service-code/the-civil-service-code

156. ICO, *Material in the course of completion, unfinished documents and incomplete data (regulation 12(4)(d))*, paragraph 17, https://ico.org.uk/media/for-organisations/documents/1637/eir_material_in_the_course_of_completion.pdf

157. FOIA section 35(5); ICO, *Government policy (section 35)*, paragraphs 100, 106, https://ico.org.uk/media/for-organisations/documents/1200/government-policy-foi-section-35-guidance.pdf

158. ICO, *Government policy (section 35)*, paragraph 213, https://ico.org.uk/media/for-organisations/documents/1200/government-policy-foi-section-35-guidance.pdf

159. *Cabinet Office v Information Commissioner*, EA/2010/0031, https://informationrights.decisions.tribunals.gov.uk/DBFiles/Decision/i436/Cabinet%20Office%20v%20IC%20EA.2010.0031%20Decision%2013.09.10%20(w).pdf

160. https://www.bbc.co.uk/blogs/opensecrets/2010/10/westland_cabinet_minutes_relea.html

161. FOIA section 35(2)

162. ICO, *Prejudice to the effective conduct of public affairs (section 36)*, paragraph 46, https://ico.org.uk/media/for-organisations/documents/2260075/prejudice-to-the-effective-conduct-of-public-affairs-section-36-v31.pdf

163. FOIA sections 36(2), 36(4)

164. FOIA section 35

165. Archived at https://webarchive.nationalarchives.gov.uk/ukgwa/20090608182148/http://www.foi.gov.uk/guidance/exguide/sec36/annex-d.htm

166. FOIA section 36(7)

167. ICO, *Prejudice to the effective conduct of public affairs (section 36)*, paragraphs 16, 75, https://ico.org.uk/media/for-organisations/documents/2260075/prejudice-to-the-effective-conduct-of-public-affairs-section-36-v31.pdf

168. *Cabinet Office v Information Commissioner and Corderoy*, EA/2020/0240, https://informationrights.decisions.tribunals.gov.uk/DBFiles/Decision/i2848/Cabinet%20Office%20%20EA.2020.0240%20Open%20Decision.pdf

169. ICO, *Prejudice to the effective conduct of public affairs (section 36)*, paragraphs 16, 75, https://ico.org.uk/media/for-organisations/documents/2260075/prejudice-to-the-effective-conduct-of-public-affairs-section-36-v31.pdf

170. FOIA section 36(1)(a)

171. See also the ICO's section 36 guidance, *Prejudice to the effective conduct of public*

affairs (section 36), paragraphs 48-49, 61, 63, https://ico.org.uk/media/for-organisations/documents/2260075/prejudice-to-the-effective-conduct-of-public-affairs-section-36-v31.pdf

172. ICO, *Section 38 – Health and safety*, https://ico.org.uk/for-organisations/guidance-index/freedom-of-information-and-environmental-information-regulations/section-38-health-and-safety/

173. *Rosenbaum v Information Commissioner and House of Lords Appointments Commission*, EA/2008/0035, https://informationrights.decisions.tribunals.gov.uk/DBFiles/Decision/i263/Rosenbaum%20v%20ICO%20&%20House%20of%20Lords%20(EA-2008-0035)%20Decision%2004-11-08.pdf

174. *Mersey Tunnel Users Association v Information Commissioner and Merseytravel*, EA/2007/0052, paragraph 51, https://informationrights.decisions.tribunals.gov.uk/DBFiles/Decision/i46/MerseyTunnelDecision_website.pdf

175. See ICO, *Legal professional privilege (section 42)*, paragraphs 42-48, https://ico.org.uk/media/for-organisations/documents/1208/legal_professional_privilege_exemption_s42.pdf

176. As encountered by Arthur Dent in Douglas Adams' *The Hitchhiker's Guide to the Galaxy*

177. FOIA sections 21(2), 21(3)

178. ICO, *Information reasonably accessible to the applicant by other means (section 21)*, paragraph 20, https://ico.org.uk/media/for-organisations/documents/1203/information-reasonably-accessible-to-the-applicant-by-other-means-sec21.pdf

179. *Ames v Information Commissioner and Cabinet Office*, EA/2007/0110, paragraph 19, https://informationrights.decisions.tribunals.gov.uk/DBFiles/Decision/i122/Ames.pdf,

180. *Benson v Information Commissioner and University of Bristol*, EA/2011/0120, https://informationrights.decisions.tribunals.gov.uk/DBFiles/Decision/i628/%5b2011%5d_UKFTT_GRC_EA-2011-0120_2011-11-10.pdf, paragraph 15

181. See ICO Decision Notice FS50849464, paragraphs 73-86, https://ico.org.uk/media/action-weve-taken/decision-notices/2020/2617398/fs50849464.pdf

182. *Corderoy and Ahmed v Information Commissioner, Attorney General and Cabinet Office*, [2018] AACR 19, https://www.bailii.org/uk/cases/UKUT/AAC/2017/495.html

183. See the following reports from the Joint Committee on Parliamentary Privilege: Report of Session 2013-14, https://publications.parliament.uk/pa/jt201314/jtselect/jtprivi/30/30.pdf; and First Report 1999, especially paragraphs 3-16, https://publications.parliament.uk/pa/jt199899/jtselect/jtpriv/43/4305.htm

184. FOIA sections 34(3), 34(4)

185. Constitutional Reform and Governance Act 2010, schedule 7

186. *R (Evans) and another v Attorney General*, [2015] UKSC 21, https://www.supremecourt.uk/cases/docs/uksc-2014-0137-judgment.pdf

187. 'Prince Charles's "black spider memos" show lobbying at highest political level', *The Guardian*, 13 May 2015, https://www.theguardian.com/uk-

news/2015/may/13/prince-charles-black-spider-memos-lobbying-ministers-tony-blair

188. See for example *Freedom of Information statistics: annual 2021 tables*, table 12, https://www.gov.uk/government/statistics/freedom-of-information-statistics-annual-2021

189. FOIA sections 2(3)(fa), 40(3A), 40(3B), 40(4A)

190. FOIA section 40(1)

191. FOIA sections 40(2), 40(3A); the principles are laid down in the UK General Data Protection Regulation, article 5(1)

192. UK GDPR article 6(1)(f)

193. ICO, *Requests for personal data about public authority employees*, https://ico.org.uk/media/for-organisations/documents/1187/section_40_requests_for_personal_data_about_employees.pdf

194. UK GDPR article 6(1)(a)

195. UK GDPR article 5(1)(a)

196. ICO, *Personal information (section 40 and regulation 13)*, page 31, https://ico.org.uk/media/for-organisations/documents/2619056/s40-personal-information-section-40-regulation-13.pdf

197. UK GDPR article 9(1)

198. UK GDPR article 10(1); Data Protection Act 2018 section 10(5)

199. ICO, *Personal information (section 40 and regulation 13)*, page 15, https://ico.org.uk/media/for-organisations/documents/2619056/s40-personal-information-section-40-regulation-13.pdf

200. ICO, *FOIA/EIR Foundation Training Module 3: s40/r13 – the personal data provisions*, notes to slide 9, downloaded July 2022

201. UK GDPR article 4(1)

202. *Information Commissioner v Miller*, [2018] UKUT 229 (AAC), https://assets.publishing.service.gov.uk/media/5b59ab68e5274a3ff594d141/GIA_2444_2017-00.pdf

203. *NHS Business Services Authority v Information Commissioner and Spivack*, [2021] UKUT 192 (AAC), https://assets.publishing.service.gov.uk/media/6135fb748fa8f503c7dfb8a3/GIA_0136_2021-00.pdf

204. ICO Decision Notice, IC-166259-J8V3, https://ico.org.uk/media/action-weve-taken/decision-notices/2022/4022696/ic-166259-j8v3.pdf

205. FOIA sections 40(3B), 40(4A)

206. FOIA section 2

207. ICO, *Information provided in confidence (section 41)*, paragraphs 22-100, https://ico.org.uk/media/for-organisations/documents/1432163/information-provided-in-confidence-section-41.pdf

208. ICO, *Information provided in confidence (section 41)*, paragraphs 17-21, https://ico.org.uk/media/for-organisations/documents/1432163/information-provided-in-confidence-section-41.pdf

209. ICO, *The public interest test*, https://ico.org.uk/for-organisations/guidance-index/freedom-of-information-and-environmental-information-regulations/the-public-interest-test

210. SIC, *FOISA Guidance: The public interest test in FOISA*, paragraph 11, https://www.itspublicknowledge.info/sites/default/files/2022-03/PublicInterestTestFOISA.pdf

211. FOIA section 2(2)(b)

212. ICO, *The public interest test*, https://ico.org.uk/for-organisations/guidance-index/freedom-of-information-and-environmental-information-regulations/the-public-interest-test

213. *Rosenbaum v Information Commissioner and House of Lords Appointments Commission*, EA/2008/0035, paragraph 51, https://informationrights.decisions.tribunals.gov.uk/DBFiles/Decision/i263/Rosenbaum%20v%20ICO%20&%20House%20of%20Lords%20(EA-2008-0035)%20Decision%2004-11-08.pdf

214. ICO, *The public interest test*, https://ico.org.uk/for-organisations/guidance-index/freedom-of-information-and-environmental-information-regulations/the-public-interest-test

215. FOIA section 62

216. Constitutional Reform and Governance Act 2010 schedule 7, paragraph 4

217. FOIA section 63

218. FOIA section 64

219. FOIA section 63

220. *Baker v Information Commissioner and Cabinet Office*, EA/2006/0045, paragraph 45, https://informationrights.decisions.tribunals.gov.uk/DBFiles/Decision/i24/Baker.pdf

221. https://www.bbc.co.uk/blogs/opensecrets/2009/05/give_me_your_answer_fill_in_a.html

222. ICO Decision Notice FS50154349, https://ico.org.uk/media/action-weve-taken/decision-notices/2009/466018/FS_50154349.pdf

223. FOIA section 53

224. *R (Evans) and another v Attorney General*, [2015] UKSC 21, https://www.supremecourt.uk/cases/docs/uksc-2014-0137-judgment.pdf

225. https://www.gov.uk/government/speeches/open-and-transparent-government

226. *Information Commissioner v Home Office*, [2011] UKUT 17 (AAC), https://www.bailii.org/uk/cases/UKUT/AAC/2011/17.html; *Birkett v Defra*, [2011] EWCA Civ 1606, https://www.bailii.org/ew/cases/EWCA/Civ/2011/1606.html

227. ICO, *Retention and destruction of information*, https://ico.org.uk/for-organisations/guidance-index/freedom-of-information-and-environmental-information-regulations/retention-and-destruction-of-information

228. ICO, *The right to recorded information and requests for documents*, https://ico.org.uk/for-organisations/guidance-index/freedom-of-information-and-environmental-information-regulations/the-right-to-recorded-information-and-requests-for-documents

229. https://www.gov.uk/government/statistics/freedom-of-information-statistics-annual-2021

230. Alex Parsons and Rebecca Rumbul, *Freedom of Information in Local Government*, mySociety, 2019, page 15, https://research.mysociety.org/media/outputs/mysociety-local-government-foi.pdf

231. Cabinet Office, *Freedom of Information Code of Practice*, paragraph 5.9, https://assets.publishing.service.gov.uk/government/uploads/system/uploads/attachment_data/file/744071/CoP_FOI_Code_of_Practice_-_Minor_Amendments_20180926_.pdf

232. ICO, *Request handling, Freedom of Information – Frequently Asked Questions*, https://ico.org.uk/for-organisations/guidance-index/freedom-of-information-and-environmental-information-regulations/request-handling-freedom-of-information/#internal

233. Cabinet Office, *Freedom of Information Code of Practice*, paragraph 5.1, https://assets.publishing.service.gov.uk/government/uploads/system/uploads/attachment_data/file/744071/CoP_FOI_Code_of_Practice_-_Minor_Amendments_20180926_.pdf

234. Cabinet Office, *Freedom of Information Code of Practice*, paragraph 5.3, https://assets.publishing.service.gov.uk/government/uploads/system/uploads/attachment_data/file/744071/CoP_FOI_Code_of_Practice_-_Minor_Amendments_20180926_.pdf

235. ICO, *Request handling, Freedom of Information – Frequently Asked Questions*, https://ico.org.uk/for-organisations/guidance-index/freedom-of-information-and-environmental-information-regulations/request-handling-freedom-of-information/#internal

236. Cabinet Office, *Freedom of Information Code of Practice*, paragraph 5.4, https://assets.publishing.service.gov.uk/government/uploads/system/uploads/attachment_data/file/744071/CoP_FOI_Code_of_Practice_-_Minor_Amendments_20180926_.pdf

237. ICO, *When can we refuse a request for information?*, https://ico.org.uk/for-organisations/guide-to-freedom-of-information/refusing-a-request/

238. Lucas Amin, *Art of Darkness*, openDemocracy, 2020, page 14, https://s3.documentcloud.org/documents/20415987/art-of-darkness-opendemocracy.pdf

239. ICO, *Request handling, Freedom of Information – Frequently Asked Questions*, https://ico.org.uk/for-organisations/guidance-index/freedom-of-information-and-environmental-information-regulations/request-handling-freedom-of-information/#internal

240. *Information Commissioner's Annual Report and Financial Statements 2021-22*, page 48, https://ico.org.uk/media/about-the-ico/documents/4021039/ico-annual-report-2021-22.pdf

241. https://ico.org.uk/for-organisations/guidance-index/freedom-of-information-and-environmental-information-regulations/

242. https://icosearch.ico.org.uk/s/search.html?collection=ico-meta&profile=decisions&query

243. See https://ico.org.uk/action-weve-taken/information-notices/

#information-notices

244. *Information Commissioner's Annual Report and Financial Statements 2021-22*, page 50, https://ico.org.uk/media/about-the-ico/documents/4021039/ico-annual-report-2021-22.pdf

245. A searchable database is here: https://informationrights.decisions.tribunals.gov.uk/Public/search.aspx

246. The Tribunal Procedure (First-tier Tribunal) (General Regulatory Chamber) Rules 2009, https://assets.publishing.service.gov.uk/government/uploads/system/uploads/attachment_data/file/1006547/consolidated-ftt-grc-rules-21072021.pdf

247. The Tribunal Procedure (First-tier Tribunal) (General Regulatory Chamber) Rules 2009, rule 22(1)(b), https://assets.publishing.service.gov.uk/government/uploads/system/uploads/attachment_data/file/1006547/consolidated-ftt-grc-rules-21072021.pdf

248. https://www.gov.uk/government/publications/form-t98-notice-of-appeal-general-regulatory-chamber-grc

249. The Tribunal Procedure (First-tier Tribunal) (General Regulatory Chamber) Rules 2009, rules 23-24, https://assets.publishing.service.gov.uk/government/uploads/system/uploads/attachment_data/file/1006547/consolidated-ftt-grc-rules-21072021.pdf

250. https://www.bbc.co.uk/news/uk-politics-29825258

251. See *DVLA v Information Commissioner and Williams (Rule 14 Order)*, [2020] UKUT 310 (AAC), https://assets.publishing.service.gov.uk/media/5fb4e60a8fa8f54ab280c7dc/GIA_779_2019_rule_14_Order.pdf

252. The Tribunal Procedure (First-tier Tribunal) (General Regulatory Chamber) Rules 2009, rule 11, https://assets.publishing.service.gov.uk/government/uploads/system/uploads/attachment_data/file/1006547/consolidated-ftt-grc-rules-21072021.pdf

253. The Tribunal Procedure (First-tier Tribunal) (General Regulatory Chamber) Rules 2009, rule 10(1), https://assets.publishing.service.gov.uk/government/uploads/system/uploads/attachment_data/file/1006547/consolidated-ftt-grc-rules-21072021.pdf

254. https://www.gov.uk/government/publications/information-rights-register-of-tribunal-cases

255. *First-tier Tribunal Practice Note: Closed Material in Information Rights Cases*, paragraphs 12-13, https://www.judiciary.uk/wp-content/uploads/2014/07/practicenote-closed-material.pdf

256. https://www.gov.uk/government/publications/form-t96-application-for-permission-to-appeal-to-the-upper-tribunal-first-tier-tribunal-general-regulatory-chamber

257. *Appealing to the Administrative Appeals Chamber of the Upper Tribunal*, https://assets.publishing.service.gov.uk/government/uploads/system/uploads/attachment_data/file/713002/ut13-leaflet-eng.pdf

258. https://www.bbc.co.uk/news/uk-politics-46844454

259. UNECE Convention on Access to Information, Public Participation in

Decision-making and Access to Justice in Environmental Matters, especially article 4, https://unece.org/environment-policy/public-participation/aarhus-convention/text

260. Article 1

261. Directive 2003/4/EC, 28 January 2003, on public access to environmental information, https://eur-lex.europa.eu/legal-content/EN/TXT/PDF/?uri=CELEX:32003L0004&from=EN

262. EIR regulation 2(1)

263. EIR regulation 9(1)

264. Defra, *Code of Practice on the discharge of the obligations of public authorities under the Environmental Information Regulations 2004*, paragraphs 8-21, https://webarchive.nationalarchives.gov.uk/ukgwa/20090731144334mp_/http://www.defra.gov.uk/corporate/opengov/eir/pdf/cop-eir.pdf

265. EIR regulation 6

266. EIR regulation 18

267. EIR regulation 2(1)

268. EIR regulation 5(5)

269. ICO, *Regulation 2(1) - What is environmental information?*, https://ico.org.uk/for-organisations/guidance-index/freedom-of-information-and-environmental-information-regulations/regulation-2-1-what-is-environmental-information

270. *Department for Business, Energy And Industrial Strategy v Information Commissioner & Henney*, [2017] EWCA Civ 844, especially paragraphs 43-54, https://www.bailii.org/ew/cases/EWCA/Civ/2017/844.html

271. Paragraph 48

272. *Omagh District Council v Information Commissioner*, EA/2010/0163, https://informationrights.decisions.tribunals.gov.uk/DBFiles/Decision/i521/20110520%20Decision%20EA20100163.pdf

273. *London Borough of Haringey v Information Commissioner*, EA/2016/ 0170, https://informationrights.decisions.tribunals.gov.uk/DBFiles/Decision/i1946/Mayor%20and%20Burgesses%20of%20the%20London%20Borough%20of%20Haringey%20(EA-2016-0170)%2028.1.17.pdf

274. *Ofcom v Information Commissioner*, EA/2006/0078, paragraph 31, https://informationrights.decisions.tribunals.gov.uk/DBFiles/Decision/i104/Ofcom.pdf

275. *Mersey Tunnel Users Association v Information Commissioner and Halton Council*, EA/2009/0001, https://informationrights.decisions.tribunals.gov.uk/DBFiles/Decision/i319/MTUA%20v%20IC%20&%20HBC%20(0001)%20Decision%202023-06-09%20(w).pdf

276. *Department for Transport, DVSA and Porsche Cars GB v Information Commissioner and Cieslik*, [2018] UKUT 127 (AAC), https://assets.publishing.service.gov.uk/media/5ae970eeed915d42f42b60bb/GIA_0224_2016-00.pdf

277. ICO, *Regulation 2(1) - What is environmental information?*, https://ico.org.uk/for-organisations/guidance-index/freedom-of-information-and-environmental-information-regulations/regulation-2-1-what-is-

environmental-information/

278. FOIA schedule 1

279. EIR regulation 2(2)(b)(i)

280. EIR regulations 3(3), 3(4)

281. EIR regulation 2, paragraphs 2(c) and 2(d)

282. *Fish Legal v Information Commissioner and others*, [2015] UKUT 52 (AAC), https://www.bailii.org/uk/cases/UKUT/AAC/2015/52.html

283. https://www.gov.uk/make-a-freedom-of-information-request/ organisations-you-can-ask-for-information

284. ICO Decision Notice FER0678164, especially paragraphs 40-48, https://ico.org.uk/media/action-weve-taken/decision-notices/2020/2617169/ fer0678164.pdf

285. ICO Decision Notice FER0809814, https://ico.org.uk/media/action-weve-taken/decision-notices/2019/2615371/fer0809814.pdf; ICO Decision Notice FER0621831, https://ico.org.uk/media/action-weve-taken/decision-notices/2016/1624468/fer_0621831.pdf

286. *Port of London Authority v Information Commissioner and Hibbert*, EA/2006/0083, https://informationrights.decisions.tribunals.gov.uk/ DBFiles/Decision/i160/PLA.pdf

287. ICO Decision Notice FER0534921, https://ico.org.uk/media/action-weve-taken/decision-notices/2015/1432175/fer_0534921.pdf

288. *Information Commissioner v Poplar Housing Association and Regeneration Community Association*, [2020] UKUT 182 (AAC), https://assets.publishing.service.gov.uk/ media/5fad2483e90e0703a20ac825/GIA_1078_2019-00.pdf

289. *Heathrow Airport Limited v Information Commissioner*, EA/2020/0101, https://informationrights.decisions.tribunals.gov.uk/DBFiles/Decision/i2861/ Heathrow%20Airport%20Ltd%20(EA-2020-0101)%20Allowed.pdf

290. *Cross v Information Commissioner and Cabinet Office*, [2016] UKUT 153 (AAC), https://assets.publishing.service.gov.uk/media/58a3416ded915d7f3700002f/_2 016__AACR_39ws.pdf

291. SIC Decision Notice 044/2021, https://www.itspublicknowledge.info/sites/default/files/Decision044-2021.pdf

292. See the ICO letter at https://files.whatdotheyknow.com/request/ food_wastage/20081004-ico-number10-letter.pdf

293. EIR regulation 9(2)

294. https://www.bbc.co.uk/blogs/opensecrets/2010/02/what_spooks_waste_ or_recycle.html

295. EIR regulation 14(3)

296. UNECE Convention on Access to Information, Public Participation in Decision-making and Access to Justice in Environmental Matters, the recitals and article 4(4), https://unece.org/DAM/env/pp/documents/cep43e.pdf

297. EIR regulation 12, paragraphs 4(a)-4(c)

298. *Bright v Information Commissioner*, EA/2015/0107, paragraph 14, https://informationrights.decisions.tribunals.gov.uk/DBFiles/Decision/i1711/ Bright,%20Timothy%20EA.2015.0107%20(16.11.15).pdf; ICO, *Regulation 9 –*

Advice and Assistance, https://ico.org.uk/for-organisations/guidance-index/ freedom-of-information-and-environmental-information-regulations/regulation-9-advice-and-assistance

299. See for example the section headed 'What are the differences between 12(5)(b) and related provisions in FOIA?' in the ICO guidance *Regulation 12(5)(b) – The course of justice and inquiries exception*, https://ico.org.uk/for-organisations/ guidance-index/freedom-of-information-and-environmental-information-regulations/regulation-12-5-b-the-course-of-justice-and-inquiries-exception

300. EIR regulation 15

301. ICO, *Intellectual property rights (regulation 12(5)(c))*, paragraphs 13-15, https://ico.org.uk/media/for-organisations/documents/1632/eir_intellectual_property_rights.pdf

302. EIR regulation 12, paragraph 6

303. EIR regulation 12, paragraph 9

304. EIR regulation 12, paragraphs (5)(e)-5(g)

305. EIR regulation 12, paragraph 4(d)

306. See *Secretary of State v Information Commissioner*, EA/2008/0052, paragraphs 80-83, https://informationrights.decisions.tribunals.gov.uk/DBFiles/ Decision/i307/Sec%20of%20State%20for%20Transport%20v%20IC%20(EA-2008-0052)%20-%20Decision%2005-05-09.pdf

307. ICO Decision Notice FER0321779, paragraph 51, https://ico.org.uk/ media/action-weve-taken/decision-notices/2011/584598/fer_0321779.pdf

308. EIR regulation 14(4)

309. EIR regulation 12(4)(e)

310. EIR regulation 12(8)

311. ICO, *What are internal communications?*, https://ico.org.uk/for-organisations/guidance-index/freedom-of-information-and-environmental-information-regulations/regulation-12-4-e-internal-communications/what-are-internal-communications/

312. EIR regulation 5(6)

313. EIR regulation 5(3)

314. EIR regulations 12(3), 13

315. EIR regulations 13(1)(b), 13(2B), 13(3A)

316. EIR regulation 12(2)

317. See especially the recitals to the UNECE Convention on Access to Information, Public Participation in Decision-making and Access to Justice in Environmental Matters (Aarhus Convention), https://unece.org/DAM/env/pp/documents/cep43e.pdf

318. ICO, *How exceptions and the public interest test work in the Environmental Information Regulations*, https://ico.org.uk/for-organisations/guidance-index/ freedom-of-information-and-environmental-information-regulations/how-exceptions-and-the-public-interest-test-work-in-the-environmental-information-regulations

319. *Office of Communications v Information Commissioner*, [2011] ECJ C-71/10, paragraph 32, https://eur-lex.europa.eu/legal-content/EN/TXT/HTML/

?uri=CELEX:62010CJ0071&from=en

320. ICO, *How exceptions and the public interest test work in the Environmental Information Regulations*, https://ico.org.uk/for-organisations/guidance-index/freedom-of-information-and-environmental-information-regulations/how-exceptions-and-the-public-interest-test-work-in-the-environmental-information-regulations

321. EIR regulations 5(2), 14(2)

322. ICO Decision Notice FER0355639, https://ico.org.uk/media/action-weve-taken/decision-notices/2011/593614/fer_0355639.pdf

323. Defra, *Code of Practice on the discharge of the obligations of public authorities under the Environmental Information Regulations 2004*, paragraph 25, https://webarchive.nationalarchives.gov.uk/ukgwa/20090731144334mp_/http://www.defra.gov.uk/corporate/opengov/eir/pdf/cop-eir.pdf

324. EIR regulation 7

325. EIR regulation 11

326. EIR regulation 8(8), 8(3)

327. ICO, *Charging for information under the Environmental Information Regulations*, https://ico.org.uk/for-organisations/guidance-index/freedom-of-information-and-environmental-information-regulations/charging-for-information-under-the-eir

328. No longer on the ICO website, but a copy is available at https://web.archive.org/web/20201212110037/https://ico.org.uk/about-the-ico/news-and-events/news-and-blogs/2019/06/blog-counting-the-cost-of-accessing-environmental-information

329. ICO Decision Notice FER0763266, https://ico.org.uk/media/action-weve-taken/decision-notices/2019/2615045/fer0763266.pdf; ICO Decision Notice IC-70949-R6S7, https://ico.org.uk/media/action-weve-taken/decision-notices/2021/2619717/ic-70949-r6s7.pdf

330. ICO Decision Notice IC-46917-Z1Y4, https://ico.org.uk/media/action-weve-taken/decision-notices/2021/2620366/ic-46917-z1y4.pdf

331. ICO, *Manifestly unreasonable requests - regulation 12(4)(b)*, paragraphs 21, 23, https://ico.org.uk/media/for-organisations/documents/1615/manifestly-unreasonable-requests.pdf

332. ICO Decision Notice IC-102828-G5M1, https://ico.org.uk/media/action-weve-taken/decision-notices/2022/4020005/ic-102828-g5m1.pdf

333. ICO, *Charging for information under the Environmental Information Regulations*, https://ico.org.uk/for-organisations/guidance-index/freedom-of-information-and-environmental-information-regulations/charging-for-information-under-the-eir

334. EIR regulation 5(4)

335. ICO Decision Notice IC-57021-V4C4, paragraphs 23-24, https://ico.org.uk/media/action-weve-taken/decision-notices/2021/2619938/ic-57021-v4c4.pdf

336. ICO Decision Notice IC-57021-V4C4, https://ico.org.uk/media/action-weve-taken/decision-notices/2021/2619938/ic-57021-v4c4.pdf

337. *R (Evans) and another v Attorney General*, [2015] UKSC 21, paragraphs 99-108, 147-149, https://www.supremecourt.uk/cases/docs/uksc-2014-0137-judgment.pdf

338. EIR regulation 18(6), as amended by the Environment, Food and Rural Affairs (Miscellaneous Amendments and Revocations) Regulations 2018, regulation 10, and the Environment, Planning and Rural Affairs (Miscellaneous Amendments) (Wales) Regulations 2018, regulation 5

339. FOIA section 40(1), and also EIR regulation 5(3), and similarly in Scotland under FOISA section 38(1)(a) and EISR regulation 11(1)

340. UK General Data Protection Regulation article 15(1)

341. UK GDPR articles 12(5), 15(3)

342. UK GDPR article 12(3)

343. UK GDPR article 12(1)

344. Article 4(1)

345. ICO, *How do we find and retrieve the relevant information?*, https://ico.org.uk/for-organisations/guide-to-data-protection/guide-to-the-general-data-protection-regulation-gdpr/right-of-access/how-do-we-find-and-retrieve-the-relevant-information

346. Data Protection Act 2018, schedules 2, 3, 4

347. This is probably the best place to start: ICO, *Guide to the GDPR - Exemptions*, https://ico.org.uk/for-organisations/guide-to-data-protection/guide-to-the-general-data-protection-regulation-gdpr/exemptions

348. ICO, *What to do if the organisation does not respond or you are dissatisfied with the outcome*, https://ico.org.uk/your-data-matters/your-right-to-get-copies-of-your-data/what-to-do-if-the-organisation-does-not-respond-or-you-are-dissatisfied-with-the-outcome

349. ICO, *The Guide to Freedom of Information*, p51, https://ico.org.uk/media/for-organisations/guide-to-freedom-of-information-4-9.pdf

350. UK GDPR recital 27

351. Section 3(1)(f)

352. Access to Health Records (Northern Ireland) Order 1993

353. AHRA section 3(1)(f)

354. *Bluck v Information Commissioner and Epsom & St Helier University Hospitals NHS Trust*, EA/2006/0090, https://informationrights.decisions.tribunals.gov.uk/DBFiles/Decision/i25/mrspbluckvinformationcommissioner17sept07.pdf

355. ICO, *Information about the deceased*, https://ico.org.uk/media/for-organisations/documents/1202/information-about-the-deceased-foi-eir.pdf

356. Department of Health, *Guidance for Access to Health Records Requests*, paragraphs 33-52 (especially paragraph 43), https://www.nhs.uk/chq/documents/guidance%20for%20access%20to%20health%20records%20requests.pdf

357. AHRA section 1(1)

358. Section 26

359. Local Government (Scotland) Act 1973, section 101, and Local Authority Accounts (Scotland) Regulations 2014, regulation 9; Public Audit (Wales) Act

2004, section 30, and Accounts and Audit (Wales) Regulations 2005, regulations 12-15; Local Government (Northern Ireland) Order 2005, article 17, and Local Government (Accounts and Audit) Regulations (Northern Ireland) 2015, regulations 11-14

360. LAAA schedule 2 and section 26(1)

361. Local Audit (Public Access to Documents) Act 2017

362. Local Audit and Accountability Act 2014, section 26(1)(a)

363. *Moss v Royal Borough of Kingston Upon Thames*, [2021] EWHC 1032 (Admin), especially paragraph 70, https://www.bailii.org/ew/cases/EWHC/Admin/2021/1032.html

364. Accounts and Audit Regulations 2015, regulations 14(1), 15(1)

365. Accounts and Audit Regulations 2015, regulation 14(3)

366. Accounts and Audit (Amendment) Regulations 2021

367. FOISA section 3(2)(a)(ii)

368. FOISA schedule 1

369. Freedom of Information (Scotland) Act 2002 (Designation of Persons as Scottish Public Authorities) Order 2016; Freedom of Information (Scotland) Act 2002 (Designation of Persons as Scottish Public Authorities) Order 2019

370. https://www.itspublicknowledge.info/sites/default/files/2022-03/List%20of%20Scottish%20Public%20Authorities.pdf

371. FOISA section 8(1)

372. *Glasgow City Council v Scottish Information Commissioner*, [2009] CSIH 73, https://www.scotcourts.gov.uk/search-judgments/judgment?id=cc8f86a6-8980-69d2-b500-ff0000d74aa7

373. SIC Decision 096/2010, paragraph 15, https://www.itspublicknowledge.info/decision-0962010

374. *Glasgow City Council v Scottish Information Commissioner*, [2009] CSIH 73, https://www.scotcourts.gov.uk/search-judgments/judgment?id=cc8f86a6-8980-69d2-b500-ff0000d74aa7

375. SIC, *FOISA/EIRs Guidance: Does FOI law give a right to information or to copies of documents?*, paragraphs 13-18, https://www.itspublicknowledge.info/sites/default/files/2022-03/RighttoInformationorCopies%20%281%29.pdf

376. *Code of Practice on the Discharge of Functions by Scottish Public Authorities*, paragraph 5.2.1, https://www.gov.scot/publications/foi-eir-section-60-code-of-practice

377. FOISA part 2

378. FOISA sections 27(1)(a), 41, 2(2), 36

379. *Code of Practice on the Discharge of Functions by Scottish Public Authorities*, section 8, https://www.gov.scot/publications/foi-eir-section-60-code-of-practice

380. This is confirmed in the statistical data on the SIC website at https://www.itspublicknowledge.info/statistics

381. Freedom of Information (Fees for Required Disclosure) (Scotland) Regulations 2004, regulations 4, 5

382. Freedom of Information (Fees for Required Disclosure) (Scotland) Regulations 2004, regulation 3

383. For example, SIC Decision 108/2012, paragraphs 18-19, https://www.itspublicknowledge.info/sites/default/files/Decision108-2012.pdf
384. SIC, *FOISA Guidance: Charging a fee or refusing to comply with a request on excessive cost grounds*, paragraphs 38-39, https://www.itspublicknowledge.info/sites/default/files/2022-03/FeesandExcessiveCostofComplianceBriefing.pdf
385. *Code of Practice on the Discharge of Functions by Scottish Public Authorities*, paragraph 4.1.2, https://www.gov.scot/publications/foi-eir-section-60-code-of-practice
386. My calculations from the statistical spreadsheets downloadable at the SIC website, https://www.itspublicknowledge.info/statistics
387. FOISA sections 10(1), 10(2)
388. SIC, *Asking the authority for a review*, https://www.itspublicknowledge.info/asking-for-a-review
389. FOISA sections 21(1), 21(2)
390. FOISA section 20(5)
391. FOISA section 47(4)
392. https://www.itspublicknowledge.info/appeal
393. SIC, *2021-22 Report on Investigations Performance*, https://www.itspublicknowledge.info/sites/default/files/2022-05/DashboardKPIs2021-22. pdf
394. FOISA section 48(a)
395. FOISA section 48(b), 48(c)
396. EISR regulation 7
397. For example, SIC Decision 097/2021, paragraph 45, https://www.itspublicknowledge.info/decision-0972021
398. Local Government (Scotland) Act 1973, section 101, and Local Authority Accounts (Scotland) Regulations 2014, regulation 9
399. https://gijn.org/gijns-global-guide-to-freedom-of-information-resources
400. https://www.gov.im/about-the-government/freedom-of-information/how-to-make-a-freedom-of-information-request/#accordion; https://www.gov.gg/CHttpHandler.ashx?id=149645&p=0, paragraph 1.4; https://jerseyoic.org/resource-room/guide-to-freedom-of-information
401. https://alaveteli.org/deployments
402. https://www.foia.gov
403. https://www.nfoic.org/state-foi-resources
404. https://www.rcfp.org/open-government-guide
405. https://foia.wiki/wiki/Main_Page
406. https://www.justice.gov/oip/blog/foia-update-new-fee-waiver-policy-guidance
407. https://icosearch.ico.org.uk/s/search.html?collection=ico-meta&profile=disclosurelog&&query=
408. Alex Parsons and Rebecca Rumbul, *Freedom of Information in Local Government*, mySociety, 2019, https://research.mysociety.org/html/local-gov-foi/#foi-administration-disclosure-log
409. ICO, *Intellectual property rights and disclosures under the Freedom of Information Act*,

paragraph 18, https://ico.org.uk/media/for-organisations/documents/2021/2619017/intellectual-property-rights-disclosures-under-foi.pdf

410. Copyright, Designs and Patents Act 1988, sections 29(1), 30(2)

411. Re-use of Public Sector Information Regulations 2015

412. https://www.nationalarchives.gov.uk/doc/open-government-licence/version/3/

413. FOIA section 79

414. ICO, Delivering a better FOI service, pages 15-16, https://ico.org.uk/media/about-the-ico/consultations/4024648/responses-to-the-consultation-on-a-prioritisation-framework.pdf

INDEX

HS2, 122

identifiability, 107-108, 109
'in writing', 22, 24-25, 163
inaccurate information, 33-34,
  116, 173-174, 197
Information Commissioner's
  Office, 27-28, 37, 48, 72, 80,
  90, 91, 98, 102, 107, 108, 114,
  115-116, 121, 122, 123, 130,
  142, 143-144, 146-147, 149, 162,
  163, 174, 180, 200, 211-213;
    complaints, 4, 6, 11, 15-16,
  17, 18, 45, 64, 70, 126, 127, 128,
  133, 137-141, 156, 157, 178,
  217-218;
    guidance, 12, 19, 23-24, 31,
  33, 34, 36, 37, 38-39, 40, 43, 46,
  65, 69, 70, 77, 78, 90, 91-93, 96,
  98, 101, 106, 107, 112, 115, 131,
  132, 133, 135, 159, 169, 170,
  171, 172-173, 174, 211-212
information 'not held', 34-36, 46,
  77-78, 128, 164
inspection in person, 39, 41, 173
Institute for Government, 38
intellectual property rights, 165,
  201-202
'intended for future publication'
  (exemption), 85-86, 116, 119,
  186
internal communications (EIR),
  166
internal reviews, 11, 17, 34, 64,
  85, 121, 126, 127, 128, 131, 132-
  136, 188-189
international relations, 87, 120,
  165
international requests, 56, 192-
  193
investigations and proceedings,
  88, 89, 119

Iraq war, 122
Isle of Man, 192

Jersey, 192
journalists' requests, 4, 6, 16, 19,
  24, 25, 181, 200

keyword searches, 31-32, 75
Kinnock, Neil, 147

Lambeth Council, 173, 174
late claiming of exemptions, 129
law enforcement, 13, 88-89, 120
Law Society, 30
'league tables', 16
legal advice, 89, 94, 98-99, 119,
  122, 167, 177, 186
Lennon, John, 122
leopards, 100
libel, 203
LloydsPharmacy, 28
Local Audit and Accountability
  Act, 181-183

Malevich, Kazimir, 65
'manifestly unreasonable' (EIR),
  164-165, 172, 173
Merseytravel, 99
metadata, 31, 41
meta-requests, 34
Metropolitan Police, 122, 198
MI5, 29, 101, 164
MI6, 29, 101
Miggins, Mrs (crime boss), 121
Miller, Claire, 108, 214
'mining', 13
ministerial communications, 93
ministerial veto, 122-123, 174
Montague, Brendan, 13, 215
MOTs, 4
MPs, 29, 30
museums, 27

Milton Keynes UK
Ingram Content Group UK Ltd.
UKHW020005131023
430453UK00004B/46